Boys at Home

Boys at Home

Discipline, Masculinity, and "The Boy–Problem" in Nineteenth-Century American Literature

Ken Parille

The University of Tennessee Press • Knoxville

Copyright © 2009 by The University of Tennessee Press / Knoxville.
All Rights Reserved. Manufactured in the United States of America.
Cloth: first printing, 2009.
Paper: first printing, 2011.

Frontispiece: From Jacob Abbott's *Rollo at Play,* 1841.

Library of Congress Cataloging-in-Publication Data

Parille, Ken.

Boys at home: discipline, masculinity, and "the boy-problem" in nineteenth-century American literature / Ken Parille.—1st ed.
    p. cm.

Includes bibliographical references and index.

ISBN-13: 978-1-57233-787-9
ISBN-10: 1-57233-787-7

    1. Children's stories, American—History and criticism.
    2. Boys in literature.
    3. Childhood in literature.
    4. Masculinity in literature.
    5. American fiction—19th century—History and criticism.
    6. Boys—Education—United States—History—19th century.
    7. Boys—Books and reading—United States.
    I. Title.

PS374.B69P37 2009
813'.409352341—dc22   2009010595

*This book is dedicated to my parents,
for all of their encouragement and support.*

Contents

Acknowledgments	ix
Introduction: Literary Critics and "The Boy"	xi
Chapter 1. Work and Play, Pleasure and Pedagogy in Nineteenth-Century Boys' Novels	1
Chapter 2. "Desirable and Necessary" in "Families and Schools": Boy-Nature and Physical Discipline	17
Chapter 3. "The Medicine of Sympathy": Mothers, Sons, and Affective Pedagogy in Antebellum America	43
Chapter 4. "Wake Up, and Be a Man": *Little Women*, Shame, and the Ethic of Submission	61
Chapter 5. "What Our Boys Are Reading": Lydia Sigourney, Francis Forrester, and Boyhood Literacy	79
Coda: "Real Boys" of the Twentieth and Twenty-first Centuries: Educators, Academics, and Sociologists on Boyhood	97
Notes	103
Works Cited	121
Index	139

Illustrations

From Jacob Abbott's *Rollo at Work*, 1850	xxviii
From Jacob Abbott's *Rollo at Work*, 1850	16
From Jacob Abbott's *Rollo's Philosophy: Water*, 1842	42
From Louisa May Alcott's *Little Women, Part Two*, 1869	60
From Francis Forrester's *Dick Duncan*, 1860	78

Acknowledgments

At the University of Virginia: Steven Railton, the director of my dissertation, whose belief in my work, and the strength and clarity of his own teaching and scholarship, were inspirational. Marion Rust, the second reader, whose commentary on my work was invaluable. Jennifer Wicke, Eric Lott, Steve Arata, Elizabeth Fowler, Gordon Braden, John Sullivan, Laura Smolkin, the English Department staff, Lou Bloomfield and the Hereford Fellows Program, and the Edgar F. Shannon Postdoctoral Fellowship Committee.

At East Carolina University: The Harriot College Research Award Committee, for the funding that allowed me to finish this book. All of my friends in the English Department.

At Central Connecticut State University: Mary Anne Nunn and Gil Gigliotti, as well as Bob Dunne, Tom Hazuka, Dorothy Cook, and Jack Heitner.

At the University of Tennessee Press: Scot Danforth and the editorial board. Kenneth Kidd and the anonymous reader, both of whom provided extensive commentary on the manuscript.

Elsewhere: Ann Baldoni, Tony Bleach, Jules Boykoff, Kim Brooks, Alvin Buenaventura, John Charles, Howie Cohen, John D'earth, Max Deutsch, Mike Engle, Karen Evatt, Brian Griffin, Jim Kim, Anne Mallory, Ana Mitric, the staff at Nostalgia Newsstand, Neil Parille, John Picker, Kaia Sand, Scott Saul, Danny Siegel, Bridget Todd, Matt Wyatt, friends and members of *Ponded*, and all of the musicians I played with in Charlottesville, Virginia.

Places: Charlottesville, Virginia: Runk Dining Hall, Newcomb Dining Hall, Alderman Library (fourth floor stacks), Clemons Library (fourth floor and Robertson Media Center), Albert Small Building, Café Royal, and the Downtown Mall. Greenville, North Carolina: University Starbucks, and Tenth Street McDonalds.

Journal editors and publishers: Elizabeth Keyser and Julie Pfeiffer at *Children's Literature:* a version of chapter 4 appeared in volume 29 (2001) and appears here by permission of the journal and Johns Hopkins University Press, which holds the copyright. Holly Laird and Laura M. Stevens at *Tulsa Studies in Women's Literature:* a version of chapter 3 appeared in volume 25, number 1 (2006), and appears here courtesy of the journal. Richard Flynn at *Children's Literature Association Quarterly:* a version of chapter 5 appeared in volume 33, number 1 (2008), and appears here courtesy of the journal and Johns Hopkins University Press, which holds the copyright. And thanks to the scholars who commented on my essays as readers for these journals.

Introduction

Literary Critics and "The Boy"

The Boy is a dreadful animal, under whatever aspect we regard him.
—"Against Boys," 1863

The good conduct of our boys has at all times cheered and comforted us, and spread around our home the invaluable blessings of peace, content, and love.
—*Boys at Home*, 1854

The boy problem is confessedly one of the most perplexing with which . . . society has to deal.
—*The Advocate of Peace*, 1845

In many ways, the figure of "the boy" has been at the center of our understanding of nineteenth-century literature and culture in the United States. Boy characters like Tom Sawyer and the "good bad-boys" that followed in his wake have been seen as crucial metaphors for numerous kinds of male-centered literary, political, social, economic, and moral value systems. As the visionary young American Adam, the boy is a sign of American exceptionalism, Thoreauvian individualism, and Emersonian self-reliance. He often serves as an occasion for reveries about the country's "innocent" past because, like the early nation, he is adventurous and rough around the edges, with a heart that is always in the right place. In the form of Horatio Alger's Ragged Dick and other upwardly mobile boy heroes, he represents the future of the capitalist patriarchy. He can even be seen, as Huck Finn is, as a figure for the writer who resists an emasculating culture; in this formulation, Twain's protagonist embodies an American consciousness articulated in an authentic dialect that expresses universal—which is to say American and male—truths.

The boy is thus inscribed as all that is traditionally not feminine. Even more so than the adult male, he has come to be a kind of critical shorthand for the physical and ideological spaces outside of the home, spaces often defined in opposition to formations of sentimentalism. We can understand sentiment, domesticity, women, and girls in literature and history, the argument goes, by conjuring Tom Sawyer, Huck Finn, or their many quintessentially American antecedents and descendants, like James Fenimore Cooper's Natty Bumppo or any number of Ernest Hemingway protagonists, characters who seem to personify the masculinist critique of home values and the suffocating bonds of domesticity. Given that children were perhaps the great obsession of nineteenth-century domestic theorists, it is surprising that boys have not been studied as the carefully produced offspring of domestic ideology, rather than the antithesis of it. Many recent critical discussions of the domestic, such as Amy Kaplan's "Manifest Domesticity," are largely interested in the political and national implications of domestic theory. My interest, however, is closer to home. I employ the term "domestic ideology" to refer to writings about the family environment and relationships within it (such as parent-child, mother-daughter, brother-sister), and I include under this heading writings addressed to adults and children about boys, their nature, and how they should be treated by family members. In addition, I examine writings about children and school that are closely related to domestic discourse and often express similar beliefs about boys and management.[1] A fundamental conflation—confusing "the boy" and "boys"—has plagued literary and historical studies. "The boy" has been so useful as a way into broader social and historical concerns that we have ignored what writings about boyhood have to say about boys and their relationship to the culture in which they lived.

Educators and authors from Horace Mann and Jacob Abbott to Louisa May Alcott and Lydia Sigourney certainly talked about "the boy," yet they were not interested in making abstract claims about, say, "the boy as figure for the nation," but in furthering a literary and pedagogical dialogue about the meanings and functions of boys in public and private spaces. Sigourney, for example, wrote a history of Roman emperor Marcus Aurelius that she believed would serve as a "domestic education" for her boy readers (iii). She meant that not only could the book be used in home instruction, but that it would be an education in home values. Boys would learn of Aurelius's achievements in public life and, far more importantly, of the domestic virtues of familial affection and social obligation that made his narrative exemplary.

These authors were especially anxious about the difficulties that boys posed for the culture at large; those who were not well managed when young presented numerous problems when older, becoming neglectful fathers, abusive husbands, dishonest merchants, or even slave-owners. To avoid such outcomes, domestic theorists wrote at length about numerous forms of discipline and how each was suited to shape a boy's nature. Some strongly endorsed corporal punishment, for example, because it was adapted to boys' corporeal temperament, while others counseled mothers on controlling sons through the affective, nonphysical form of discipline called "moral suasion." Writers like Alcott and Sigourney spoke to children and adults in stories that looked carefully at gender and its connection to forms of maturation that endorsed the use of shame as a way to bring about the transition from child to adult. Both writers viewed themselves as advocates for boys, criticizing what they saw as a widespread and often unacknowledged animus toward boys that informed theories of management and were counterproductive to successful discipline, an orderly domestic environment, and even to a boy's happiness. Writings about boyhood discipline offer us an important way to complicate current critical narratives of gender, childhood, and literary history, which have not always been sufficiently attuned to beliefs about boyhood pedagogy, for such beliefs are not always visible when we look only at the metaphorical "boy." Thus, exploring issues that circulate around boyhood can help us to expand and revise our notions about the diverse goals and practices of domestic ideologies, and to dissolve the binary that situates boyhood in opposition to the home.

This book is not a historical or literary overview of writings about boyhood education, but a series of arguments about five forms of pedagogy: play-adventure, corporal punishment, sympathy, shame, and reading. I have selected these five because they illuminate a host of relationships that exist within, and help to express the expansive and overlapping contours of, domestic and other cultural spaces in which boys were discussed and disciplined. My reading of theories of childhood gender and corporal punishment, for example, examines the adult-child relationship in the form of parents and sons, as well as teachers and students. In a chapter on affective discipline I look at mother-daughter and mother-son bonds to argue that the latter were seen as perhaps the greatest challenge for mothers due to the special difficulties that "boy-nature" presented to a woman. A chapter on shame, Louisa May Alcott's *Little Women* (1868), and boys' conduct literature investigates familial relationships and Alcott's fictional representations of the ways that a shame-centered discipline could be directed at boys and young men by family members, love interests, and pervasive cultural narratives about what it meant to "be a man." The chapter on Francis Forrester, Lydia Sigourney, and literacy develops this question by exploring the central role that the solitary domestic act of reading played in the relationship between a boy's subjectivity and his culture's ideas about him. Boys' fictional play, which seems to offer an alternative to or escape from many of these relationships, often replicated the values of boyhood masculinity as enforced by the relationships discussed in my other chapters. When boys were away from parents, teachers, or domestic spaces, the pedagogical imperatives of authorities went with them, educators argued, guiding a boy's activities and articulating their moral purpose. The picture of boyhood created by this nexus of relationships offers us a detailed portrait of the pedagogical environment in which New England boyhood was constructed, and it gives us a multitude of perspectives ranging far beyond those of the few nineteenth-century literary figures who have monopolized critical discourses on "the boy."

Just as looking at the metaphor of "the boy" has led criticism away from boys, so too has an emphasis on the genderless "child" obscured crucial questions of similarities and differences between girls and boys. I am not arguing that we should ignore writings that do not specify a gender of the childhood subject; indeed, I talk about the significance of these texts for our understanding of both boyhood and girlhood. I am only saying that we should not always accept an author's word that the generic "child" is his or her real subject. Such an assumption repeatedly appears in criticism on the transcendental philosopher and educator Bronson Alcott, for example, who always claimed that he was solely interested in the education of the child, whose nature he described in the gender-neutral and celebratory way that transcendentalists often talked about children: the "child," Alcott said, is "a Type of Divinity" (cited in Mintz 76). But when we look at Alcott's ideas about boys in the context of his educational practice, we see a notion of childhood that is something less than divine. In *Record of a School* (1835), he articulates both a theory of boy-nature and one of the period's more condemnatory approaches to boyhood discipline. Critics often argue that Alcott's forward-looking beliefs about childhood education were in conflict with the views of middle-class culture and the educational establishment, but his attitudes toward boys and their management are often fully in line with mainstream values.

Boys at Home explores debates about boys and their management as developed in fiction and educational material written by New England authors from 1830 to 1885. While almost all of the important scholarship on nineteenth-century boyhood focuses on post–Civil War texts, exploring the antebellum period is crucial if we are to gain a fuller understanding of boyhood because, as historian of childhood Steven Mintz notes, the decades before the war witnessed the "inventi[on] of the middle-class child," a creation developed and expanded in "the nation's first extensive body of advice literature on childrearing," a group of texts that devote considerable attention to what writers called "the boy-problem" (80). Critics often begin in 1870 because it is the year in which Mark Twain's friend Thomas Bailey Aldrich published *The Story of a Bad Boy*, the first novel in the genre that would become known as the "boy-book," a group of post–Civil War novels by Aldrich, Twain, Charles Dudley Warner, William Dean Howells, and a few others.[2] Though written after the Civil War, boy-books are often set decades before it and thus appear to capture a historical sense of boyhood that spans around four decades, from the 1840s to the 1880s.

Critics often use these texts as representative of literary production for and about boys throughout the century, even though antebellum texts (and many from the postwar period) about boys often look very different from the boy-book. Marcia Jacobson's *Being a Boy Again* examines boy-books and their authors, exploring the way "a particular crisis in male adulthood" is "the motive and shaping force" behind each novel, a force that overshadows the authors' desire to represent boyhood as it was (24). Jacobson's study reveals that, while these texts have much to say about their authors, they often tell us little about boyhood's histories. Historian E. Anthony Rotundo's work on nineteenth-century boy culture examines the same period and novelists as *Being a Boy Again* and anticipates aspects of Kenneth Kidd's impressive *Making American Boys: Boyology and the Feral Tale*, which is also largely concerned with postwar writing about boys. The literary imaginings of the "bad boy" authors inspired the movement Kidd has called "boyology," a term borrowed from Henry William Gibson's 1916 *Boyology; or, Boy Analysis*. Kidd describes this movement as "a cluster of ideas about boyhood and the national character" that advanced the theory of "recapitulation," the belief that boyhood "was analogous to earlier stages of civilization and to contemporaneous primitive societies" (49). The subject of the boyologist, then, is often not boys. Instead, "the boy" is used as a vehicle for arguments about national or racial identity, or as the ground upon which numerous attacks were launched against the "feminizing" of men and male institutions by women. For this reason, the work of the boyologists, though it might appear to tell us about boys and their education, often does not.

Kidd rightly notes that the boyology of the late nineteenth century was "the legacy of at least half a century of meditation on boyhood," yet in seeing the study of boys in the mid-nineteenth century as separate from the "domestic ideology [that] has shaped the lives of girls" he reiterates two familiar binaries—boyhood-domesticity and boy-girl—that my study seeks to complicate (68). Writings about boys, I argue, are a part of domestic ideology. These texts are often written by the same educators and authors who write about girls, appear in the same print venues, frequently talk about both genders together, and often are addressed to mothers, who as the central domestic figures were responsible for much of their children's moral education and discipline. Kidd recognizes that we need to change the ways that scholarship on boys has been approached and framed, and I begin in the 1830s because during the century's middle decades many authors theorized boyhood within the confines of writings about home, even if the study of it became a highly organized endeavor only toward the end of the nineteenth century.

The celebration of "the boy" found in works of fiction and boyology often contrasts with the criticism that boys received in post– and pre–Civil War novels and educational writings. Critics who often talk about the popular "boy as savage" trope, for instance, tend to cite examples of its use in the century's last three decades, claiming that this represents its use throughout the century. Writers like Howells, Warner, and the boyologists employ it to celebrate "the boy" as instinctual and uncivilized: "Every boy who is good for anything is a natural savage," Warner proclaims in an often-cited line from his 1877 boybook *Being a Boy* (198). But this trope often carried with it a sense of a moral deficiency rather than inherent nobility, and the notion of boyhood depravity was in wide circulation in all kinds of texts and played a central role in aspects of pedagogical philosophy.

Though this idea about boys had always been present to some degree in American writings about childhood, critics have not noted that, as the belief in infant depravity was fading from the 1780s through the 1820s, boys were being repeatedly characterized in the same language, as "depraved" and "immoral." Girls, on the other hand, were often described as having a "morally refined" nature, and this gender contrast would be replayed in debates throughout pedagogical culture, especially those about children, sentiment, and corporal punishment. The binary of depravity-refinement reflects sentimental ideology's tendency to talk about gender in dualistic terms. As I claim, though, what I call the "pragmatic" versions of domestic theory found in educational materials and maternal advice literature were often critical of the claims of sentimental ideology. While "the mother" was celebrated as an icon of embodied sympathy, pragmatic discourses argued that mothers had plenty of sympathy for daughters but little or none for sons. Arguments about maternal sympathy speak to larger questions of sentimentality, affect, and discipline, and to the intimate relationship between boyhood and maternal domesticity.

My study presents a New England culture deeply invested in the management of boys, but conflicted about the particulars, which often changed based upon the author's theory of what was frequently called "boy-nature." Many writers characterized boys in harsh terms, calling them "corrupt" or "dissolute," descriptions found throughout literature about male children. Others stopped short of this kind of condemnation but still argued that boys lacked the natural ethical faculties that defined girls—even if boys were not depraved, they exhibited a pronounced tendency toward immorality or mischievous behavior and showed a lack of concern for others, the fundamental sign of their immorality. Some writers believed that boys were less refined than girls but did not define this gap negatively or in ethical terms; they simply felt that parents, especially mothers, would have to work harder to manage boys by appeals to the emotional bonds that existed—or should exist—among all member of the "family circle."

Each chapter explicitly or implicitly examines the theories of boy-nature held by the authors I examine. Chapter 2, for example, looks at the intimate connection between condemnatory notions of this nature and the widespread endorsement of corporal punishment for male children but not for girls. Chapter 3 studies the relationships among a range of ideas about boys and their ability to respond to affective discipline as employed by mothers. Interestingly, some of the authors discussed in both of these chapters have similar ideas about boy-nature, but they derive from these ideas strikingly dissimilar management approaches. Many of the writers I talk about in chapter 3 express a sympathy toward boys that is completely absent from those explored in chapter 2, suggesting that some authors bear an animus toward boys that may be partially accounted for by their antagonistic attitudes about boy-nature. Louisa May Alcott and her father, Bronson Alcott, sometimes expressed similar general beliefs about differences between boys and girls, but while Bronson expressed negative attitudes about boys in his schoolroom practice and applied the ferule only to them, Louisa May asked readers to recognize the ways that boys were mistreated by a culture that misunderstood them, and her children's novels in what her publisher would eventually call the "Little Women Series" can be seen as one of the culture's most detailed and sympathetic portrayals of boys and the space of boyhood.[3]

Although all of the authors I examine are concerned with problems they believed parents faced when managing their children, my study emphasizes literary and pedagogical writings. I look at a wide variety of genres of writing about boys, but I explore diaries, journals, or letters in only a limited way. By centering on literary and non-literary discourses and not on arguments about the metaphorical "boy," my approach follows Frances Cogan's examination of "real womanhood." Cogan distinguishes between two important nineteenth-century discourses about women, one that describes the "ideal woman," and the other that examines the "real" nature of women and the problems they faced, the kinds of issues explored in the discourses I refer to as "pragmatic" (4). My interest lies with authors' and educators' beliefs about the pedagogy boys needed, and how this management compared to that applied to girls. Because my approach centers on pedagogical theory, I avoid judgments about the actual effects that theories of management had, and I do not make claims about whether boys or girls suffered the most repressive pedagogy.

Yet I do talk about the effects that educators hoped such strategies would have on children and their reasons for endorsing them. I see myself as trying to reconstruct and reinterpret the pedagogical culture surrounding boys, and I believe that this requires discussing nineteenth-century beliefs about girls as well as current scholarship on girlhood. I would argue that, in a broad sense at least, the evidence I have found suggests that boyhood was likely just as much a rule-governed space as girlhood. Yet it is important to note that I see my project not as a reaction against feminist studies of girlhood and gender, but as an outgrowth of them. When I am critical of such studies it is only to the extent that they have not yet fulfilled their promise to expose fully the workings of gender ideology in the nineteenth century. Indeed, my approach is indebted to the feminists who sparked my interest in gender and popular literature, the first literary critics I read as an undergraduate: Jane Tompkins and Nina Baym. My work continues their exploration of the ways that popular ideology as represented in literary and educational writings creates and affects readers' subjectivity; like these writers, I recover neglected texts and revise our understanding of canonical ones in order to enrich our knowledge of the history of writing for and about boys and girls.

The boyhood that this study covers is chronologically imprecise, a stage that started around age five or six, when boys began to be differentiated from girls in ways such as the clothes they wore, the toys they played with, and the kinds of work that was expected of them. When Jacob Abbott's popular boy character Rollo is almost six, his father begins the lengthy process of training his son to work, suggesting that a boy of seven is able to earn his own living, a claim that shows how intimately boyhood was connected to adulthood and work.[4] Boyhood's end was even less defined; it sometimes occurred in the late teens or at twenty-one, but males well into their twenties were sometimes called "boys," especially if they did not live up their culture's standards of manhood.[5] And the division between boyhood and manhood, when it existed, was always more ideological than chronological. In Alcott's *Little Women,* for example, Laurie becomes a man not when he reaches a certain age but when he gives up "boyish" dreams of "living for what [he] like[s]" (29). Throughout the novel, as in many others by Alcott, boyhood is characterized as a dream from which he, and indeed all boys, must awake. In *Nuts for Boys to Crack* (1866), the reverend John Todd speaks of the vague parameters of boyhood and excludes from it "young men," a term often used for males around ages seventeen to twenty: boys "are not young men, nor . . . children. They are boys" (57). Harvey Newcomb says that his *How To Be a Man: A Book for Boys* (1846) "is intended for boys,—or, if you please, for young gentlemen,—in early youth, from eight or ten to fifteen or sixteen years of age" (4). At the age of seven, Lydia Sigourney's son wrote in his journal, "This is my birthday. Now, I am a boy," perhaps emphasizing even at his young age that boyhood was a stage of development with its own expectations and pressures (*Faded Hope* 47).

While many writers disagreed about the precise chronological definition of boyhood, all agreed it was a disciplinary space in which male children became a special kind of problem. Some even argued that boys' intellectual and moral faculties were distinct from what they had been as young children and would later become as men, a distinction for which they rarely offered a biological or social explanation. The author of "Against Boys," suggests some tentative explanations of how "savage" boys become "respectable" men:

> How is it, if boys are so bad as you represent, that they become, as men, respectable members of society? I confess I can make no reply. Perhaps their savage nature is mollified, when they begin to appreciate the softening influences of the fair sex. Perhaps they are suddenly impressed on their emergence from Barbarism by being brought face to face with Civilization. Certain it is that their worst characteristics disappear, or find some legitimate channel in the world of men. (86)

But most writers never addressed the issue. They simply believed that boys were a problem that could be solved by the correct disciplinary practices.

☞ ☞ ☞

In a pioneering book on communities of girls and women in British and American fiction, Nina Auerbach said that "the nineteenth century claimed to know exactly what it meant by 'boyhood,'" calling it a "universal known" for those who wrote about it, implying that there was little need for scholarship that addressed it in detail (31, 32). Since Auerbach's study, many scholars have defined girlhood by comparing it to boyhood, treating the latter as a static and transparent category around which there has always been a consensus. These critics often discuss boyhood only briefly, employing it as a foil for what they see as the more multifaceted and "difficult" versions of girlhood found throughout nineteenth-century writing (Brown 92). Others have made sweeping claims about girlhood without any reference to boyhood, a move that might seem strange to nineteenth-century theorists of childhood, who constantly talked about the relationship between the two. Boyhood was repeatedly staged as a problem: important writers argued about the nature of boys, what books they should read, how they should be represented, the best methods of management and discipline, and how they and the space of boyhood they inhabited were similar to and different from their counterparts, girls and girlhood.

Since the mid-1970s many of our ideas about nineteenth-century boys and their literature have come from scholarship on girlhood. This work typically emphasizes the different designs that books had on their respective boy or girl readers, designs that reflected discrete cultural ideologies about each gender. Critics repeatedly argue, for example, that girls were required to submit to forms of repressive discipline that boys were immune from or allowed to rebel against, for such rebellion represented the individualism expected of and granted to males. To reframe this point in terms of the genres identified with each gender, girls' lives, these critics argue, can be accurately represented by the constraints of domestic novels and boys' lives by the autonomy of adventure novels. The categories of the "boys' adventure novel" and "girls' domestic novel" have been staples of children's literature scholarship, but as I argue in chapter 1, they are misleading for a number of reasons, the most important being that many boys' novels situate the protagonists in domestic environments and replicate some of the values of girls' novels. And this generic opposition recalls another familiar and misleading binary from studies of nineteenth-century men and women: female submission (the bonds of domesticity) and male independence (the unfettered adventure). The freedom valued by canonical male writers such as Melville, Emerson, Whitman, Thoreau, Twain, and the male critics who canonized them, I contend, has wrongly been seen as an essential feature of boys' fiction.

Critics such as Auerbach, Beverly Lyon Clark, Claudia Nelson, Lynne Vallone, Elaine Showalter, Ann Murphy, and Gillian Brown have been influential in drawing our attention to the ways that educational and disciplinary imperatives are openly or covertly enacted in girls' texts. Yet the belief that boys' books always endorse the virtues of freedom and self-reliance missing from girls' fiction has made it difficult for critics to recognize that, as Rita Felski has said, ideologies of gender need to "be understood as a complex formation of beliefs, structures, and representations which shapes and permeates the subjective sense of self of" males and females (*Beyond* 27). Catherine Driscoll rightly says that "girls are products and performances of the long history of Western discourses on gender, sex, age, and identity" (7), and I am simply suggesting that this holds true for boys as well. Writings for boys and girls (and the larger cultural notions they reflect) are different in important ways, yet we have not explored the pedagogical content of popular boys' novels, for example, with the belief that we might find important similarities with girls' fiction.[6]

In a widely cited study, Rotundo makes claims about boyhood that repeat those made by the scholars of girlhood I have just discussed. Arguing that boys' lives were "surprisingly free of adult supervision," he characterizes boys as "free" and "independent," creating the impression that their lives and the fictions that represented them were devoid of the kind of intrusive pedagogy directed at girls (32). Rotundo says that when adults tried to intervene in "boy culture"—which he sees as the opposite of domesticity—boys recognized and rejected such threats to their autonomy, as Tom often does in *The Adventures of Tom Sawyer* (1876). As historians of masculinity Mark Carnes and Clyde Griffen note, however, Rotundo defines "boy culture" using a familiar and limited set of materials (the fictions and personal writings of a few male authors who wrote after the Civil War about their antebellum boyhoods), certainly not enough texts, they argue, to support the kinds of generalizations he offers (10). And critics who talk about nineteenth-century girlhood by making brief comparisons to boys' novels almost always cite the same boy-books as Rotundo. In this version of boyhood, boys carefully create their own world. Yet many writings about boys present a very different picture of boyhood education and the disciplinary roles played by fathers, mothers, friends, school, reading, the fear of corporal punishment, and norms of masculinity. All of these forces were intended to supervise continually the construction of boyhood masculinity, even while boys were at play, suggesting that the notion of "free" play for girls or boys, then, is itself a fiction.

Although scholarship on girls and their literature has addressed boyhood in a limited way, scholarship on nineteenth-century American masculinity has centered mostly on men and male authors. Joe Dubbert's *A Man's Place: Masculinity in Transition*, Carnes and Griffen's *Meanings for Manhood*, David Leverenz's *Manhood and the American Renaissance*, Michael Kimmel's *Manhood in America*, Dana Nelson's *National Manhood*, Paul Gilmore's *The Genuine Article*, Jacobson's work on boy-books, and Glenn Hendler and Mary Chapman's collection *Sentimental Men* are all about crisis and adult masculinity. *Boys Don't Cry?* a collection on masculinity and emotion that builds upon *Sentimental Men*, is, like its predecessor (and despite its title), not actually interested in boys.[7] Judith Kegan Gardiner correctly notes that recent studies of masculinity have paid insufficient attention to "age categories," and it would be a mistake, therefore, to read them as necessarily telling us about the content of boyhood masculinity (91). In a recent essay on masculinity and domesticity, Sarah Wilson says that "[b]y masculinity, I mean the white, middle-class gender identity that is the focus of recent masculinity studies" (81). The gender identity she equates with masculinity, however, is not fully attuned to the ways that notions of masculinity differ based on age categories, a critical tendency visible throughout studies of masculinity in the nineteenth century, such as Adams and Savran's adult-focused *The Masculinity Studies Reader* or David Leverenz's study of Emerson, Melville, Hawthorne, Whitman, and Thoreau, which also explores how anxieties about "what it means to be a man," "male rivalry and fears of humiliation" (especially in the marketplace), and "fears of heterosexual intimacy" shaped their writing (41).

Hendler and Chapman draw our attention to the pervasiveness of these kinds of anxieties when they remind us that "American masculinity has always been in crisis," and the essays in their collection look at these problems in terms of debates about bachelorhood, racial politics, the marketplace, as well as numerous other cultural and literary formations (9). Building upon these seminal works, *Boys at Home* broadens the field to explore boyhood masculinity, especially in terms of the anxiety that managing boys produced in educators and authors and the ways that these concerns are informed by questions about the nature of boys and the efficacy of various forms of discipline. I do not argue that there was any particular crisis in boyhood during the period I study, only that "the boy-problem" was a constant source of concern.

Despite focusing on adults, recent writing on masculinity has been important in establishing the ground upon which my work is based, for much of this scholarship is invested in dissolving the binaries and generalizations that have sustained many discussions of gender. Hendler and Chapman's collection has been particularly important because it critiques an opposition that has structured many studies of nineteenth-century American culture: the gendering of sentiment as feminine and the exclusion of males as authors and subjects of sentimental discourses. My discussion of sympathy and pedagogy within the mother-son relationship expands upon this new understanding of the field, for it shows boys as the problematic subjects of a discipline based on sympathy and it explores a prominent discourse that describes women as inherently unsympathetic toward boys, a characterization in conflict with many popular representations of mothers. Perhaps most importantly, my project is indebted to the work of sociologist and masculinity scholar Michael Kimmel, who argues for understanding gender as a "relational construct" whose contours are always shifting (*Changing Men* 13). Scholarly works such as Monika Elbert's *Separate Spheres No More* and Laura McCall and Donald Yacovone's *A Shared Experience* have taken the relational approach suggested by Kimmel, exploring the operations of gender codes by studying the lives and writings of men and women together, often emphasizing the ways that social norms and practices affect both sexes. Christina Florin and Ulla Johansson's essay in *Discipline, Moral Regulation, and Schooling* applies this relational approach to an examination of schools in nineteenth-century Sweden, a study compelling in large part because it moves between examinations of disciplinary strategies for boys and girls, using the pedagogy directed at one gender to help understand the other. Although boys are at the center of my project, the chapters draw on scholarship about girls and use numerous nineteenth-century texts about girls to show how the educational issues I discuss were treated in writings for and about them. My chapter on discipline, work, and play, for instance, relies on critical examinations of girls' fiction, and my chapter on sympathy in the mother-son relationship employs numerous primary texts about girls as well as historical scholarship on affect and the mother-daughter bond.

The relational approach is particularly appropriate because nineteenth-century writers of pedagogical theory constantly compared the management of both genders without relying on a single notion of relation, either difference or similarity. Abbott suggests, for example, that boys and girls would probably not respond to the same motivational strategies, such as "emulation" (motivation by reward), so he recommends disparate strategies and explains the relational logic behind them.[8] But others emphasize similarities in the disciplinary approaches appropriate for both sexes, such as the use of shame as a tool for creating obedience. A detailed comparative study of advice books for each gender has yet to be done, but such a study would reveal some important parallels: authors repeatedly advocate self-denial and social responsibility for all children, and they share the same concerns for each gender about the positive effects of "proper" companions and the dangers of "licentious" or "sensational" reading.[9]

Many novels likewise endorse comparable narratives of development for boys and girls; Alcott's *Little Women,* for example, follows a boy's and the March girls' transitions into adulthood, dramatizing how the same pedagogical strategies could be used on both genders. Despite the presence of such correspondences, the long-running critical consensus about cultural limitations in *Little Women* (an often-cited text in discussions of girlhood pedagogy) has been that difference fully articulates the novel's attitude: girls submit, boys don't. The relationship between contemporaneous notions of girlhood, boyhood, and pedagogy is always complicated, and *Little Women* (and Alcott's work in general) illustrates important differences between the lives of her boy and girl characters. But critics often approach the novel with what seems like an a priori assumption that they will find in it only a theory of difference.[10] The fact that writers like Alcott believed that boys had a distinct nature did not always mean that they would recommend different management strategies. Newcomb notes that his *How To Be a Man: A Book for Boys* explores some of "the same ground occupied by a work for girls issued simultaneously with it [*How To Be a Lady: A Book for Girls*]; and some of the chapters are identical in the two books, while others are entirely different, and some partially so" (4). With each form of management that I study, I follow Newcomb's threefold approach and try to categorize accurately what sense of relation each writer employed: similarity, difference, or a combination of the two.

The critical valorization of difference—what Felski has called "the doxa of difference"—has often defined studies of writing about girls and boys and has been supported by the limited range of texts about boyhood to which critics constantly return ("Doxa" 1). Comparisons of play in canonical works such as *Little Women* and *The Adventures of Tom Sawyer* may give the impression that a criticism of difference is justified, for these texts theorize play for boys and for girls in distinct ways. But when we look, for example, at the less-studied boys' stories of Oliver Optic, we find that boyhood play and adventure are strongly informed by concerns that animate fictional representations of girlhood play.[11] And in Alcott's case, this should not be surprising; *Little Women* was written in response to her publisher's request that she create a female version of Optic's popular boys' stories. In an essay on Alcott and Optic (the pen name of William T. Adams), Sarah Wadsworth notes that

> literature for American children had its own cultural work to perform in preparing boys and girls for adulthood, and for girls this meant teaching them that a woman's most valuable contribution was in using her feminine influence for good and virtuous ends within the context of the domestic sphere. (27)

To suggest what this work might be in regard to boys, she cites well-known children's literature scholar Anne MacLeod, who says that boys' novels "revolved around . . . active, extroverted adventure," as if to say that plot equals pedagogy: boys' novels have no designs on boys other than encouraging them to be active, extroverted, and adventurous in a context apart from the domestic sphere (14).[12] As my reading in chapter 1 of the novels of Optic and other boys' writers shows, most of these authors were explicitly concerned with a boy's social responsibilities, advocating subordination to authority, the rejection of pleasure, and involvement in domestic and public life; the ideals of individualism and self-reliance associated with the canonical figures of the American renaissance are nowhere to be found. Optic repeatedly insists that a boy must learn "that he [is] one wheel in the vast machine" (*Sailor Boy* 199), and Francis Forrester reframes the notion of self-denial in the language of adventure: "it was heroic to submit" (183).

Although authors and educators frequently made broad generalizations about differences between boys and girls, I stop short of making any strict generalizations about the relationship between the gender of the educator and the belief about childhood pedagogy that she or he held. We cannot say, for instance, that as a group men endorsed narratives of "Great Men" as proper reading materials for boys, while women criticized them. Although this is true in many cases, I have found enough instances in which women endorsed such books and men warned about their dangers to negate any categorical claim. And the same holds true for theories of boy-nature or the endorsement of specific disciplinary practices, such as corporal punishment, which was widely advocated by both men and women. I try to avoid such generalizations about authors because I find them inaccurate or misleading, and because they recall and reinforce the kind of binaries that I critique.

Because the canon of nineteenth-century writings about boyhood has been constituted almost solely by male authors, comparisons between girlhood and boyhood tend to be between the former as depicted by women and the latter by men; when it comes to the relation between the gender of an author and the gender of the child they are writing for, we could call this the "doxa of similarity." But popular writers like Alcott, Sigourney, and Lydia Maria Child wrote at length about boys and the "boy problem." Sigourney authored numerous magazine articles and book-length readers for boys that included her own widely published fiction, prose, and poems, and she played a vocal role in debates about what books boys should read by criticizing genres—especially histories and biographies—that were often endorsed. All of these writers engaged in conversations about boyhood education, and some, like Sigourney and Alcott, saw themselves as advocates for boys, calling particular attention to their widespread mistreatment as a problem that needed to be solved. A tremendous amount of influential writing about boys was produced by women, a fact obscured by the critical emphasis on late-century novelists like Twain and Howells, and the male-authored sociological material about boys that began to emerge in the 1880s. In 1994 Judith Fetterley wondered "why there have been . . . no . . . studies focusing [on] Sigourney, Sedgwick . . . Stowe in relation . . . to their male contemporaries" (606). Indeed, such dual-gender studies—of which there still are relatively few—are essential if we are to claim to comprehend anything as complex as the nineteenth century's views on boyhood.

Though I focus on gender and age, the categories of race and class are essential to a full understanding of boyhood in the period. Any single study like mine, however, cannot offer such a comprehensive understanding. I center on boyhood masculinity in large part because the categories that help to define it—girlhood femininity and adult masculinity—continue to receive extensive critical treatment. Although I do not discuss whiteness, it would be accurate to say that my study is really about a kind of middle-class white boyhood masculinity as theorized by male and female New England writers. The authors I explore and the boys they wrote about were white; indeed, in the vast amount of texts I studied for this project authors seldom address race explicitly or at length, assuming a white subject. Because the pedagogical culture was obsessed with how to discipline middle-class white boys and the cultural importance of such an act, I have chosen the management of such boys as my subject.

By looking at writings on boyhood by neglected female and male authors, these chapters become acts of recovery. In my discussion of *Little Women*, perhaps the most studied text on nineteenth-century girlhood, I recover its least examined narrative—that of Laurie and the pedagogy applied to him. The chapter on maternal sympathy uses materials about child-rearing that appeared in popular mother's magazines and maternal advice books but have not been studied by scholars, who typically examine advice literature for what it can tell us about the lives of women and girls. The chapter on pedagogy and pleasure looks at popular works by Optic, Alger, and Francis Forrester, as well as Abbott's famous, but now often neglected Rollo books—such as *Rollo at Work* (1841) and *Rollo at Play* (1841)—all of which complicate our picture of the pedagogy advanced by boys' novels in the mid- and late-century. And I look at material from educational journals, teacher training manuals, and other texts about home and classroom pedagogy that have been left out of literary scholarship on childhood.

It is often expected that a literary-historical book like *Boys at Home* will make claims about the ways in which cultural narratives about its key terms changed during the period under examination. Given that near the chronological midpoint of this study lies the schism of the Civil War—a national trauma involving many young men and boys—we might expect this event to have dramatically affected how the country thought about boyhood. Yet, perhaps surprisingly, in regard to the New England writers I examine we do not see many significant changes in boyhood pedagogy. We might be tempted to imagine that as sentimental ideology about women and children permeated the culture from the republican era until the late antebellum period, by the time of the Civil War boys would somehow be sentimentalized too. But this also was not the case. The boyology of the late nineteenth century and early twentieth takes a more favorable view of boys than did many antebellum educators (though the views that inspired boyology were present prewar), but during the nineteenth century, positive views always coexisted with less favorable beliefs that were equally available throughout the culture.

One of the central points of my book is that numerous beliefs about boys and their education circulated simultaneously throughout literary and pedagogical writings from 1830 to 1885. And the presence of competing and often contradictory attitudes makes master narratives about change or development hard to establish and maintain. As chapter 2 explains, my argument about corporal punishment is in part a response to claims about a dramatic transformation in this practice near the mid-century, claims that are complicated by the materials that I discuss. Even if we thought, for instance, that we had found a pattern of change in children's novels that signaled a new understanding of boys, we must look at canonical and popular novels, poetry, magazine writing, children's and boys' readers, educational materials, and fiction for adults in order to be confident that we understand what the culture as a whole had to say about boys and their pedagogy.

To try to develop this kind of broader cultural understanding, I have taken the approach favored by the emerging field of childhood studies, which seeks to understand aspects of childhood by using texts and methods that cut across conventional disciplinary interests. I look to critical debates within the fields of children's literature, nineteenth-century American cultural and literary studies (which is tacitly adult-centered), and the histories of childhood and education, and I examine literary and nonliterary writings for adults and for children, without prioritizing any single kind of writing. In this way, I have tried to write a book that will be equally useful to those interested in a number of fields, and particularly to those whose work involves the intersection of these disciplines. But most important, I have taken this approach because I think it is the best and most accurate way to present a narrative about boyhood and discipline in the period.

Boyhood, then, was not a "universal known" in the United States during the nineteenth century, and it generated far less agreement than we might believe. The discipline of boys was given the same kinds of scrutiny that characterized the management of girls, and diverse forms of pedagogy certainly were ever-present in novels for boys and other writings about them. Thus the idea of nineteenth-century boys as always "free to rebel" or unencumbered by the discipline that informed girls' fiction and lives is a narrative largely created by a group of influential late-nineteenth-century fictions about boyhood (especially *Tom Sawyer*), endorsed by successive generations of writers, and repeated by twentieth- and twenty-first-century critics, who have concentrated largely on the postbellum period. *Boys at Home* proposes that we expand the conversation about childhood, gender, education, and the cultural work of literature in the nineteenth century by putting neglected popular male writers like Abbott, Forrester, and Optic into conversation with authors such as Twain, Aldrich, Sigourney, Susan Warner, Catherine Sedgwick, Harriet Beecher Stowe, and the many women who wrote for mothers' and children's magazines. We should also bring advice writing about boys and girls into dialogue with fictional representations of children in books for and about children; scholars of girlhood who discuss boys have overlooked boys' conduct literature, a large body of writing that has a lot to say about how boys should be managed. And we should be wary of a critical disposition that continues to privilege difference, because such a disposition precludes us from seeing correspondences in types of discipline or cultural pressures directed at all children. Plenty of evidence in and outside of literary fictions shows us that numerous cultural forces were everywhere directed at boys, and that antebellum and postbellum culture always had designs on them, as it did on girls. Ultimately, we need to do for nineteenth-century boys what the past few decades of scholarship have done for girls: show the complexities of the texts written about them, complexities that likely reflect the lives they lived.

From Jacob Abbott's *Rollo at Work*, 1850.

Chapter 1

Work and Play, Pleasure and Pedagogy in Nineteenth-Century Boys' Novels

> Boys should never rebel.
> —Francis Forrester to his readers in *Dick Duncan*

> [W]e must not rebel.
> —Mrs. Montgomery to her daughter, Ellen, the heroine of Susan Warner's *The Wide, Wide World*

> Boys and girls should always be obedient.
> —Georgiana Hall

I've had the following conversation numerous times. It begins when someone asks:

"What's your research about?"
"Well, I study boys and boyhood in nineteenth-century American culture and literature."
"So you probably look at Mark Twain and books like *Huck Finn* and *Tom Sawyer*?"
"Sure, but there were a lot of other people who wrote for and about boys: Jacob Abbott, Lydia Sigourney, Oliver Optic, Francis Forrester—"
"Hmm. I haven't heard of them."

Exchanges like this, which have occurred with family, friends, and fellow scholars, attest to the role that the works of Twain have had, and continue to have, in defining nineteenth-century American boyhood. Tom, Huck, and their respective novels represent to us a theory of boy-nature (mischievous, but good-hearted), an archetypal narrative of boyhood adventure, a new way to write for and about children (without the didacticism of Twain's predecessors), a national nostalgia for a "simpler past," and the personal nostalgia of adults who, like Twain, sought release from the pressures of adulthood by reliving their childhoods.

Even more than *Adventures of Huckleberry Finn* (1884), *The Adventures of Tom Sawyer* (1876) has come to be seen as "the quintessential boy's book of the nineteenth century" (Vallone 122), and a novel that occupies a "central place ... in our national literature" (See 251).[1] Indeed, the "hypercanonization" that Jonathan Arac ascribes to *Huckleberry Finn* is also applicable to Twain's earlier novel. Although *Tom Sawyer* does not hold the same status as *Huckleberry Finn* in national discussions of American identity, literature, and race, it has achieved hypercanonization in critical examinations of childhood by being one of "a very few individual works [that] monopolize ... critical attention" (Arac 113). Scholarship on boyhood, girlhood, and childhood repeatedly uses *Tom Sawyer* when generalizing about the disparate natures of boys' and girls' experiences and their literatures, often pointing to Twain's linkage of play with pleasure, freedom, and adventure as the standard account of boyhood play in the period, and indeed, as the terms that define boyhood itself; it is as if *Tom Sawyer* tells the history of boyhood. Even though *The Adventures of Tom Sawyer* is not representative of ideas about play in the boys' fiction published in the period, Tom Sawyer has become for literary critics, to adapt Emerson's phrase, a "representative boy."

These critics have created an uncomplicated opposition between ideologies of boyhood and girlhood, claiming that girls' play is always disciplinary, while boys' is not. Boys' texts, the argument goes, model for their readers the pleasure and autonomy that culture grants them. For example, prominent scholar of girlhood Lynne Vallone has argued for what she calls "the fundamental difference between the boys' adventure and the girls' learning experience" (123). For her, girls' play has a pedagogical content absent from the pleasure-oriented boys' adventure. Likewise, Gillian Brown has said that, while "nineteenth-century accounts of boyhood advance the values of pleasure and carelessness," writings about girlhood activities advocate the value of 'usefulness'" (25).

Vallone and Brown are certainly correct about the pedagogical content of girls' books, but boys' texts similarly redefine pleasure as a feeling generated by work that is useful and therefore pedagogical. And the type of pleasure that follows such work, these texts claim, is fundamentally superior to that generated by "careless amusements." Even when play and adventures take place away from home, the fictional boys take domestic values with them. In Oliver Optic's *Work and Win* (1866), for example, the hero Noddy Newman becomes the new man his name promises when he learns "that work," not play, is "a positive luxury," a phrase that completely redefines the conventional connotations of work (254). It is misleading to support the characterization of boys' play as devoid of pedagogical content by invoking only the late-nineteenth-century boy-books discussed in the introduction and ignoring writers like Optic.[2]

Though these novels play an important role in literary and cultural history—especially that of the twentieth century—they represent only a small segment of books for boys published in the nineteenth century, and they embody only one strand of boyhood pedagogy.

I do not want to erase the many significant differences between boys' and girls' fiction, such as the ways that girls' texts endorse a limited set of postchildhood opportunities available for girls. I believe, however, that these children's texts have some important similarities that we have missed, especially in regard to their disciplinary contents and narrative trajectories. Recognizing these connections, I argue, will fundamentally change our understanding of boys' and girls' fiction in nineteenth-century America and will lead to a more nuanced appreciation of the diverse ways in which fiction theorized both childhood and masculinity. Claims about a strict opposition between boys' and girls' fiction and their pedagogical content have remained popular and compelling because they have the polemical force and appeal of all "separate spheres" arguments, but as Cathy Davidson and Jessamyn Hatcher's collection *No More Separate Spheres!* has shown, such arguments have a cost: they erase the complex ways that social, political, gender, and literary formations operate. Although intent on dismantling all binaries, this collection leaves two intact. No mention is made of the boy-girl or boyhood-domesticity pairs, both of which have a history in studies of the nineteenth century as entrenched as any other binary.[3]

This chapter starts by examining the role that *The Adventures of Tom Sawyer* has played in narratives of literary and cultural history, and goes on to show the problems with difference-based criticism by looking at pedagogical imperatives dramatized in poetry, advice manuals, and, most importantly, popular boys' fiction. Focusing on play, I employ a broad definition of the term that reflects its use by the authors and literary critics I discuss: play refers to the games and adventures that children and child characters undertake, activities that seem to them or their readers to be about pleasure.[4] I use this definition because scholarship on girlhood often equates boys' play and adventures and then contrasts these activities with girls' play. Because my definition encompasses many kinds of activities, it allows me to enter ongoing critical conversations about boyhood, girlhood, and domesticity. Indeed, because discussions of play are ultimately discussions of childhood pedagogy, to look at play is to make visible some of the foundational assumptions of domestic ideology itself. In order to get a fuller understanding of what writings about boys have to say about these issues, I bring into the critical conversation neglected boys' texts, which help us to see that *Tom Sawyer* offers only one version of boyhood, one that is vigorously contested by authors who are not a part of the canon. And even when the boy's adventure takes place away from home, these books reveal themselves as advocates of the primary importance of home values. Thus, the adventure is never an escape from domestic ideology, but rather a journey into it.

⁓ ⁓ ⁓

In a discussion of play in children's books, Vallone relies on *The Adventures of Tom Sawyer* to divide issues along gender lines: "girls' play . . . as opposed to boys' play" (108); "the distinctions in subject matter between boys' and girls' books" (123); "[t]he fundamental difference between the boys' adventure and the girls' learning experience" (123). Brown acknowledges similarities, yet her interest lies with differences, as she contrasts "boyhood's purpose" with girlhood's, notes the "gendering of play," and argues that "boys embody the radical difference and distance of childhood, [while] girls embody the continuity between children and adults" (25). She says that a "romance of play circulated in nineteenth century literature about boys" and that these accounts of boyhood always advance the "values of pleasure and carelessness" (27, 25). As a "characteristic description of boys at play," she looks at a poem from the children's magazine *Merry's Museum* that portrays boyhood as a "life / Without its shades of cares and strife," a depiction that she says echoes the values of *The Adventures of Tom Sawyer* (24). Although this poem certainly advocates a rougher form of play than was endorsed for girls, its narratives about freedom and pleasure are characteristic of the period's poetry about girlhood and childhood, as well as boyhood. William Gilmore Simms writes about "girlhood," in which "thoughtless children bound and play . . . in one long holiday" ("Harbor by Moonlight" 6). In a poem to a young girl, Simms notes that her "buoyant, wild and free" childhood was a space in which she "can find no pleasure wanting" ("Six Years" 18, 19). Another poet similarly describes the "careless tone" and "free step" of "girlhood" activities (Lydia J. Peirson, "Life's Changes" 3, 4) and well-known poet Frances Osgood writes about her own childhood of "endless play" ("Hours of Yore" 5) and "careless play" ("My Mother's Sigh" 8). All of these poets argue against the notion that play must be useful; and the idea of childhood as a space of pleasure, one disconnected from the concerns of adulthood, is a common theme in poetry about boyhood and girlhood.[5]

Critics rightly claim that girls' play is disciplinary because it prepares girls for the lives they will live as adults, a preparation predicated on the self-sacrifice critics see as missing from boys' fiction. Writing about play, Melanie Dawson has recently argued that because boys were "unfettered" and "carefree," "boyhood is effectively severed from adult concerns" (63, 80, 69). And Gillian Brown similarly believes that "girls embody the continuity between children and adults," a continuity irrelevant to boys (25). While girls were constantly trained by mothers to reproduce the domestic environment and its ideologies, boyhood's activities are unrelated to the kind of adult life that, as critics have noted, Twain chooses not to narrate in *Tom Sawyer*. But many popular books for boys followed their protagonists where Twain feared to go—into manhood and to work—and argued that scenes of play and adventure were valuable ways to train boy readers for the transition into adulthood that would take place throughout their boyhood.

Antebellum advice manuals for boys and Gilded Age success manuals for young men repeatedly advocate the doctrine of utility and dramatize the continuity between childhood and adulthood that girls' fictions and advice writing endorse. As Daniel Eddy says in *The Young Man's Friend* (1855), activities and "amusements . . . must be blended with utility" (91). *Useful Lads* (1847) reminds its readers that real pleasure comes from work, and that while "innocent play" is not without value, "a livelihood is not to be earned by" it (61). And William Alcott's *The Boy's Guide to Usefulness* (1844) argues that domestic utility must infuse every activity a boy undertakes, be it playing, dressing, or even eating. In fact, the utility of play endorsed by these texts permeates boys' fiction, from the primers of the 1820s to the Rollo stories of the 1840s and through the works of Oliver Optic, first published in the mid-nineteenth century and reprinted into the twentieth.[6]

The universalizing of Tom Sawyer and the figure of the carefree boy whose activities are "useless" is both a cause and a symptom of arguments that acknowledge no overlap between the pedagogical lives of fictional boys and girls. Critics have argued that *Tom Sawyer* is valuable to us because it tells us a kind of generic history of boyhood, and although they have given us a detailed historical context for the analysis of girls' books by discussing girls' and women's domestic literature, we have not done the same for boys' books by looking in depth at a sufficient amount of material for or about boys or young men. Instead, the boy-book has come to represent writings about boys *and* the historical context in which such books were initially produced and read.

If play is often its own reward in *The Adventures of Tom Sawyer*, it serves a different purpose in the texts of Jacob Abbott, Optic, and Francis Forrester (the pen name of Daniel Wise), authors who combined to write hundreds of boys' novels. At times, these texts resemble *Tom Sawyer*—they have moments of carefree play unlike much of the activities in domestic texts like *Little Women*, for example. Play as pleasure, however, is not the focus of Abbott's *Rollo at Work* and *Rollo at Play*, Optic's *Work and Win* (1870), or Forrester's *Dick Duncan*. Some of these texts can be seen as a kind of "domestic-adventure novel," in which domestic ideology is dramatized in an adventure context (Optic), or the "boys' domestic novel" (Abbott), whose scenes are largely based around the home and its values.[7] Like hundreds of other such texts, these novels often degrade pleasure and sanction scenes of discipline closely connected to adventure.[8] Reading the ethos of adventure in authors like Optic and Forrester allows us to see that, outside of the postwar boy-book, boyhood was thought of as a space of intense pedagogy.

The authors I study are some of the most popular writers for boys of the mid- and late century. Jacob Abbott was one of the period's most important educators and authors, writing for numerous educational journals and publishing a respected teacher's manual as well as childrearing advice literature. He also authored more than forty-five texts for boys, and his numerous Rollo books were a reading staple from the 1840s through the 1890s and were often endorsed by other educators. Oliver Optic, celebrated by many as the successor to Peter Parley (the most popular children's writer during the first half of the century), wrote four or five popular boys' novels every year from 1860 to 1871 and a total of more than seventy-five boys' novels during his career. His 1855 book *The Boat Club* (which he turned into a successful series of the same name) was in print for more than forty years and went through sixty editions. Optic published children's magazines and wrote more than a hundred articles for children that appeared in his own periodicals and elsewhere, and when he died in 1897 many claimed he was the best-selling author of his time. Though less popular than Optic and Abbott, Forrester wrote around twenty books for boys and under his real name (Daniel Wise) authored well-received advice books. Accurate sales figures are difficult if not impossible to determine, but there can be little doubt that these authors were in wider circulation than Twain and his peers during the nineteenth century (indeed, *The Adventures of Tom Sawyer* was not a best seller until the twentieth). Much evidence suggests that by virtue of the quantity of titles produced, the number of printings, the length of time for which they were in print, the amount of reviews they generated, and the numerous endorsements received by educators, these writers represent a more active presence and influence throughout the century than did Twain and other boy-book authors.[9]

Abbott's *Rollo at Work* and *Rollo at Play* present a kind of model for theories of play and pedagogy found in many popular mid- and late-century domestic novels for boys. Like many girls' texts, both novels attempt to diminish the value of activities not connected with work and to show that true pleasure can come only from "useful" activities, what one writer calls "pleasurable employments" ("Training V" 182).[10] And so intent is Abbott on making this point that he offers dozens of repetitive scenes and speeches on the topic. The primary fault of "*boy work*," Rollo's father argues, "is confounding work with play. . . . There is great pleasure in doing work. . . . While you are doing [it], it requires *exertion* and *self-denial*" (*Rollo at Work* 124–25; emphasis in original).[11] Abbott acknowledges that children should engage in "amusements," activities exclusively about pleasure. "It is right for you to play sometimes," his father says, a dictate expressed so sternly as to make his idea of play seem far from pleasurable (103). Yet he is far more interested in valorizing productivity as a boy's fundamental obligation than in advocating pleasure, a philosophy that confuses Rollo:

> "Father . . . you told me there was pleasure in work, the other day. But how can there be any pleasure in it, if you choose such things that have no amusement in them at all?"
>
> "The pleasure of working," said his father, "is not the fun of doing amusing things, but the satisfaction and solid happiness of being faithful in duty, and accomplishing some useful work." (53)

In *Rollo at Play*—a text almost exclusively about work—Rollo's mother, like his father, tells him that he should often "give up pleasure altogether and turn to . . . duty," for this "will make it most useful to you" (87, 94). In both novels, enjoyment always disappears as it merges into utility and obligation, and proper boyhood masculinity is made visible as Rollo's desire for personal pleasure gives way to material productivity: "you would take a great deal of more solid and permanent satisfaction in such a thing, if you were to use it for doing some useful work" (44).

The "thing" is a wheelbarrow, a key object for Abbott because it literally and symbolically unites play and utility; and what it represents is so important to the narrative that four of the first five engravings in the book feature one.[12] Though Rollo wants his own wheelbarrow to "*play* with," his father says he will get one only when he has "learned to work" (43; emphasis in original). The narrator tells us that the boys are "playing very pleasantly" with wheelbarrows, yet the way this "play" redirects enjoyment into a kind of moral satisfaction and imitates adult activities—in particular, economic exchange and negotiation—is made readily apparent to boy readers (67). After destroying a miniature city made from sand, the boys take the remains to Rollo's mother with the expectation that she will buy it. Because the sand is impure, however, she refuses—an early lesson for the boys in the difficulties and disappointments of the marketplace. All of this "play" prepares the boys for what happens next in the narrative—and what will happen at the next stage in their development, adulthood—and the satisfaction it should produce: Rollo's father hires the boys "to do some useful work . . . with your wheelbarrows" (75). For Abbott, a space in which boys did nothing but engage in pure play, if it existed at all, certainly precedes boyhood and ends with its onset. Rollo's training as a worker begins when his boyhood starts; as his father says, "*I* have to do that . . . and you must learn to do it, or you will grow up indolent and useless" (53–54; emphasis in original). To reject the doctrine of utility would make a boy or man "useless," which is to say, morally worthless.

Play often exists in boys' texts as an explicitly coded form of work, and true pleasure is reimagined as an affect produced solely by a nexus of production and obedience: Rollo learns how satisfying it is to "please his father" (49). Thus, like the parental figures in most girls' fiction, Rollo's father sees no real distinction between childhood and adulthood, repeatedly lecturing Rollo about his life when he "become[s] a man": "Men will hold you to your agreements . . . and I want you to be accustomed to it when you are a boy" (128, 117). When Rollo complains that the tasks he is told to do are difficult and tedious, his father tells him that his work as a man will often be little different, hoping to shame Rollo (who constantly feels ashamed for failing to live up to his father's and the other adult males' ideals) by showing him that men reject the desire for pleasure (125). Abbott celebrates the stoic Jonas, an older boy who works for Rollo's father, as the model of the masculine qualities he wants boys to possess: an unyielding sense of duty and self-denial, and a firm opposition to pleasure.[13] And *Rollo at Work* documents Rollo's eventual embrace of the notion that meaningful pleasure is a by-product of labor:

> whenever he saw what he had done, it gave him pleasure. After he picked up the loose stones . . . for instance, he drove his hoop about there, with unusual satisfaction; enjoying the neat and tidy appearance of the road much more than he would have if Jonas had cleared it. In fact, Rollo became quite a faithful and efficient little workman. (58)

Here Rollo's play—driving his hoop—involves admiring his work. As one mother's advice writer says, "habits of industry, economy, and enterprise are inculcated, in the form of recreation and pastime, and labor becomes insensibly incorporated among his thoughts of pleasure" ("Training V" 182).

In Abbott's novels, then, boys will be workmen. The claim that boys' lives embody the distance between childhood and adulthood is destabilized by popular texts like Abbott's, which repudiate a familiar phrase about boys found in late-century writings: "Boys will be boys." Essentially a theory of pedagogy, it holds that the best way to manage boys is not to manage them at all, allowing them to develop naturally into adults through autonomous play and adventures. Boy-nature was biologically encoded with the pedagogical imperatives that would unfold naturally as boys play and age. Critics claim that nineteenth-century culture in general—and especially writers like Twain, Howells, Aldrich, and other boy-book authors—advocated this philosophy, yet many popular male and female educators and writers, such as Abbott, Bronson and Louisa May Alcott, Optic, Horace Mann, and Lydia Sigourney openly opposed it. As the author of "Two Ways of Being Manly" says, "don't believe the doctrine" of "boys will be boys," and as Rollo learned, one of the most powerful ways to perform manliness was to reject a self-centered, independent, and pleasure-seeking boyhood (48). In *Little Women,* Alcott writes "[S]ome Mrs. Grundy will [say] 'boys will be boys.' . . . I have a persuasion that [women] may raise the standard of manhood by refusing to echo such statements" (422–23).

And many men were intent on raising this standard, too. Optic's *Little by Little* (first published in 1860 and in print until the end of the century) confronts this pedagogy directly, taking the same stance as Alcott and Abbott. Explaining why a boy character behaves so poorly, Optic blames the father's ideas about education: "It was a favorite theory with him that a boy would do well enough if only let alone. It was of no use to cram his head or heart with notions. . . . the boy would find them out when he wanted" (18). The father's son, Thomas, repeatedly disproves the efficacy of this theory by constantly misbehaving, in ways both trivial and serious. Throughout Optic's novels, boys like Thomas who are "let alone" fail. His successful boy protagonists typically are educated by stern but loving parents, or by a surrogate parent, such as a successful business man or an experienced ship's mate, all of whom arrange activities that teach boys about the pleasure and moral value of labor. When Optic's boys appear to educate themselves, it is only by following the internalized dictates of an absent mother or deceased parent, whose maxims about work and discipline the protagonist dutifully recalls and repeats for the readers' benefit. In this way, Optic joins the many authors and educators who believed that "boys will be boys" pedagogy was incompatible with the real nature of boys, whom they believed needed to be managed as much as girls did.

Indeed, the freedom from authority inherent in this philosophy is sometimes completely banished from Optic's novels. Although *Little by Little*'s protagonist engages in acts of play and adventure similar to those in *The Adventures of Tom Sawyer,* in Optic's adventure novel *The Sailor Boy* (1863) the adventures of its hero, Jack Somers, are reminiscent of scenes in Richard Henry Dana's popular *Two Years before the Mast* (1840), a book about the harshness of naval life. *The Sailor Boy* features events that Optic hoped would satisfy the reader's desire for "stirring incidents"—the staple of the adventure novel—yet also would dramatize the difficulties that boys will face when they become men. In Optic's works, boys are told, as Captain Littleton tells Paul throughout *Little by Little,* that a boy could never be too disciplined or too prepared for future troubles—so Optic's fiction always depicts boys in literal and figurative battles, "fighting [their] way through the world" (83). Importantly, these kinds of adventures away from home are rarely found in girls' novels, and they certainly reflect some of the different behaviors encouraged for each gender; in particular they function as training for the competition that boys would face when they entered the market, an opportunity often denied women.[14] But boyhood, as Optic, Abbott, and many others understood it, is one long initiation into adulthood and into the kinds of duty and obedience expected of all members of "the family circle." Just as girls were "little women," boys were often considered "little men." As one author reminded his readers, "The boy is father to the man" (John Hall 45).

Optic's characters sometimes expect their lives to be a "romance of play," but their authors and narratives have other ideas. Like most of Optic's adventure novels, *The Sailor Boy* narrates a boy's initiation into manhood and his renunciation of all forms of autonomy; a veteran sailor tells Jack, "[Y]ou don't know no more about discipline nor a heathen do about Watt's hymns" (73). Learning about discipline means shedding boyish attitudes toward pleasure and play—"waking up" as Louisa May Alcott called it for both boys and girls—and learning how to function within a system, an attitude of self-denial endorsed throughout girls' and boys' conduct literature. As W. W. Everts tells his young male readers, reject autonomy and "associate yourselves . . . with the existing system of society" (39). As a teenager entering the navy, Jack represents a not too distant future for Optic's boy readers, many of whom will eventually enter occupations guided by rules that they may not want to follow.

A central focus of *The Sailor Boy* is the way that the navy, and especially each ship, represents a rigid system of discipline, surveillance, and control immediately applicable to boys' lives.[15] For Optic, each reader needs to learn that he is merely "one of the wheels in a complicated machine," an idea he often repeats: "every man knows his place" and that "he [is] one wheel in the vast machine" (79, 197, 199). Making sure that boys understand the transferable nature of these lessons of compliance—the move from reading about "exciting adventures" to living unadventurous middle-class lives—Optic says "a man finds his level board a man-o'-war just as he does everywhere else" (60). Although many parents allowed their sons to read adventure novels, they ultimately rejected, as Rotundo notes, a "code" for boys that valued adventure (43). Jack learns to negotiate a system that will "make a man of" a boy by showing him that all discipline—whether fair or not—plays a valuable role in conquering the self, the ethos of girls' fictions (72). Gillian Avery argues that British boys' novels "reminded [their readers] that they were part of a whole more important than themselves" (184), and the novels of Optic and Abbott, I argue, illustrate that many American writers fully shared this concern.

Like Optic and Abbott, Francis Forrester organizes scenes of play and adventure around an ideology of obedience, going so far as to say that any discipline enacted on a boy by an authority figure must be embraced, even if the boy has done nothing wrong or the punishment is excessive. In *Dick Duncan*, as in *The Adventures of Tom Sawyer*, the title character is the stimulus for the novel's play and adventures, and therefore is its disciplinary focus. Although Dick's Sawyer-esque "pardonable tricks" (104) are sometimes endorsed by the narrative, his playfulness is also seen as the quality that will deny him the purchase of middle-class respectability, and the violent discipline directed at Dick teaches him that he must learn to govern himself if he is to find his place within what Horatio Alger's Ragged Dick called "spectable" society. "By the grace of God I will conquer myself," Dick Duncan proclaims (179), sounding like a Susan Warner, Maria Cummins, or Louisa May Alcott heroine—or an Alger or Abbott hero. For Forrester, true heroism comes not by imitating the exploits of heroes, but by obeying the culture's demands. And advice writing repeatedly made the same point. In *Familiar Talks to Boys* (1876), for example, John Hall says that a boy must always be "willing to deny himself" and submit to the will of others (34).

Forrester's narrative uses the violent and incompetent schoolmaster Mr. Nailer to provide Dick with an opportunity for such self-mastery; here adventure and play lead not to pleasure, but to the pain of the whip. Not only do the parents approve the teacher's excessive punishment, they blame the boys: "[M]y father said if we hadn't tried to hustle him out the first day," one of the boys says, Nailer would have been fired (182). In an earlier scene, the parents' endorsement of physical punishment for boys is predicted by another of the novel's advocates of the practice. When the boys "hook" a few strawberries from a farmer, he and his farmhand ambush the boys and whip them: "suddenly fell the strokes of a raw hide upon the shoulders of the two boys.... 'I expect your fathers would thank me for this,'" an expectation that proves correct (54). The novel claims, as many proponents of moral suasion did, that "boys were better governed by love" than the whip, but Forrester's parent characters are happy to let surrogates do the whipping for them (159). Forrester's sanctioning of such violence makes it clear that for him, boyhood is not a time of "carelessness" or freedom. It is difficult to imagine any of the boy-book authors recommending that boys accept the dictates of authority, especially one so corrupt, yet many educators like Abbott and Optic stressed that boys should be obedient even when the authority enforces an unjustified discipline; *Useful Lads*, for example, councils its readers in no uncertain terms to "obey in all things masters" (37).

The play and pranks that lead to corporal punishment in *Dick Duncan* are the kinds of activities endorsed by Twain and other boy-book authors. Yet in Abbott, Optic, and Forrester, games and adventures, be they playing Robin Hood, boating to a picnic, or trying to outwit a schoolmaster, are always structured as scenes of pedagogy, occasions for boys like Dick Duncan to learn that "true" adventure means "to conquer [the] self" (179). As Forrester's novel ends, the narrator predicts Dick's future as a "merchant" (254, 256). Twain's abrupt ending of *Tom Sawyer* is starkly different: "it being strictly the history of a *boy*, it must stop here; the story could not go much farther without becoming the history of a *man*," a history that holds no interest for Twain (247; emphasis in original). Forrester, Abbott, and Optic, however, tell a story in which boyhood always functions as a disciplinary staging ground for manhood, and they often follow their protagonist into adulthood, or at least to a point in his development (usually his late teens) when the narrative describes him as "manly" or no longer "boyish," often because he has left play behind him and accepted a job—the prerequisites for manhood. As Optic's *Work and Win* ends, Noddy undergoes a transformation: he is "made over new," becoming Ogden Newman and attending a military school whose regime of discipline will complete the process of making "a man of" him (281, 283). Noddy, who eventually becomes a minister, represents the fate of many fictional boys who enter a decidedly tame profession, one that would likely be of little interest to boy readers.[16]

In her afterword to Susan Warner's best-selling *The Wide, Wide World* (1850), Jane Tompkins articulates a still widely held critical view about gender and endings of nineteenth-century novels: the success of the "female protagonist is the extinction of her personality, and thus the inversion of a" male's (600). In Warner's novel, the "extinction," Tompkins argues, results from the heroine, Ellen, being trained to be a dutiful wife, the kind of training that shapes *Little Women*'s Jo March and countless other girl protagonists. Tompkins argues that a male success story will include the preservation of personality, but this gendered binary breaks down when we look at the endings of popular boys' novels. Alger's *Ragged Dick*, like many fictions for girls, concludes in a marriage, albeit a metaphorical one. Dick echoes the promises made by countless sentimental heroines to their husbands as he recites the vows of submission to James Rockwell, wealthy businessman and surrogate for the mercantile patriarchy that Dick is now bound to: "I'll try to serve you so faithfully, sir, that you won't repent having taken me into your service" (131). Dick has achieved his goal of respectability and incorporation into society. He is wedded to the system, entering Rockwell's firm as a low-level clerk, and there is even the obligatory name change. Immediately prior to reciting the vows, Mr. Rockwell asks Dick to write his name on a piece of paper: "Dick wrote in a free, bold hand, the name Richard Hunter. He had very much improved in his penmanship . . . and now had no cause to be ashamed of it" (130). The raggedness that had made Dick such an appealing character has been drastically diminished to ensure his desirability as a subordinate partner. His penmanship, idiosyncratic pronunciation, humor, and name have changed. As Alger comments in the epilogue, "he is Ragged Dick no longer" (132), an extinction that represents a part of the narrative formula that Alger would use over a hundred times. Boy protagonists in his novels always arrive at what was for Alger and Optic the ultimate goal: staid middle-class respectability.

☞ ☞ ☞

Criticism on literature and girls' lives in the nineteenth century mines texts like *The Wide, Wide World,* Alcott's *Little Women,* Susan Coolidge's *What Katy Did*

(1872), and Elizabeth Stuart Phelps's *Gypsy Breynton* (1866) for examples of the "useful" play endorsed by popular novels, girls' books, and other cultural authorities. Critics typically argue for an intimate relationship between these fictions and life, believing that the close connection between the experiences of characters in girls' novels and the lives of nineteenth-century girls makes these texts a vital object of literary and historical inquiry. Biographical studies of Alcott by scholars such as Martha Saxton and Madeleine Stern, for example, have shown numerous important similarities among the lives of Alcott, *Little Women*'s Jo March, and other real and fictional New England girls.[17] *Little Women* has thus become a representative dramatization of girlhood pedagogy, a fiction as and historical account.[18] Similarly, a tradition of literary scholarship sees the contours of mid- and late-century boyhood as accurately portrayed by boy-books, a tradition that has neglected authors like Abbott, Optic, and Forrester. From the moment of its publication *The Adventures of Tom Sawyer*, for instance, was celebrated as a "record" of boyhood, a reading Twain's preface encouraged: "most of the adventures recorded in this book really occurred" (i). In a review, Howells celebrated Twain's novel for documenting of the "universality" of boy culture and boy-nature, a nature that, no matter how "human nature varies, is the same everywhere" (621).[19] Reviews often emphasized the connection between the text and the world, repeatedly praising the novel's "fidelity to circumstance" (622). Twain not only got boy-nature right, but he accurately depicted every boy's life; *Tom Sawyer* was "realistic in the highest degree," he noted, a "picture of life" (622).

These types of claims have continually been made for books whose vision of boyhood freedom critics have equated with boy-books. Joel Chandler Harris said of *Adventures of Huckleberry Finn* that "it is history . . . [and] it is life" (cited in Pattee 308), and early works of canon formation such as Fred Pattee's 1915 *American Literature since 1870* claimed that Twain was merely "dictating . . . autobiography" (45). Children's literature scholarship, too, has been a proponent of the fiction-life equation. Decades ago Alice Jordan said that *The Story of a Bad Boy* is "an historical photograph" of "boy life" in New England (33), and MacLeod associates *The Adventures of Tom Sawyer* with the "often autobiographical" nature of late-century fiction for children and claims that Twain's "concept of boyhood must have matched that of most Americans" (90, 69). Steven Mintz twice refers to Huck and Tom when characterizing the lives of real boys and girls (82, 85), and the title of his history of American childhood, *Huck's Raft*, attests to the powerful association between Twain's fiction and the lives of children in the nineteenth century.

The foregrounding of a few canonical texts and the neglect of novels by Abbott, Optic, and others is reminiscent of the treatment accorded girls' and women's fiction prior to the project of recovery that began in the 1980s. Dismissed as a body of second-rate fiction, these novels were seen as unworthy of serious critical attention. Because Twain held the literary and social values of the nineteenth- and twentieth-century male critics who formed the androcentric canon, his works were celebrated, while texts by women were denigrated as poorly written sentimental narratives that did not deserve a place of importance in literary history. In a famous essay on *Adventures of Huckleberry Finn,* Henry Nash Smith praised the book's "theme of freedom" and its celebration of "the autonomy of the individual" (344). What made the book so important for many influential mid-twentieth-century male critics such as Smith was that, like *Moby-Dick* and *Walden,* it celebrated masculine individualism and the quest to escape "stupid conformity"—the values of women and the home—and it encouraged the pursuit of autonomy and promoted an oppositional attitude to a culture that was trying to feminize men (344). To be Huck or Tom was to avoid this fate by being an eternal boy by escaping home. But to be Rollo, Jack Somers, or any number of Forrester or Alger heroes was to embrace the domestication and discipline of cultural authorities and reject the antisocial, individualist ethic of writers like Emerson, Melville, and Thoreau. In using Twain's novels as the "masculine text," recent criticism has tacitly accepted the claims of those like Nash who believe that these novels are the texts we must look to if we want to understand boys and masculinity in the period.

I am not arguing that we should substitute *Rollo at Work* for *The Adventures of Tom Sawyer* as the quintessential boys' novel or that Abbott offers the real picture of a boy's life. I do believe, though, that Abbott's pedagogy and his beliefs about pleasure and play are more representative than are Twain's of the disciplinary theory found throughout literary and educational writings during the century. Simply put, boys' novels depict many different kinds of play that have different degrees of pedagogical value. As in Twain and other late-century stories, it can be the kind that we have come to associate with a "carefree" childhood, the kind that Gillian Brown associates with boyhood, a play in which pleasure is the sole motivation and reward. It can also be the adventures in Forrester's or Optic's novels, which are always structured with specific pedagogical goals in mind, and sometimes become occasions for a physical pedagogy to be enacted on a character. It can also be, as in the Rollo books, a form of "play" so carefully managed by the father that it is almost impossible to imagine it having any pleasurable content; after all, if work "consists of what a body is obliged to do"—as Tom Sawyer has famously said—then Rollo's play is almost all work. These last two kinds of play, and not the type found in Twain's novels, I argue, are the versions of play most commonly found throughout both boys' and girls' novels of the mid- and late century.

Many of these lesser-known boys' novels have gone unread by scholars and untaught in their classes. An important part of hypercanonization, Arac notes, is the constant presence of a text on syllabi for literature courses, and students will likely assume that such a book must be historically important or a representative dramatization of some of the key issues that it explores. And *Adventures of Huckleberry Finn* and *The Adventures of Tom Sawyer* have been adapted so many times (into movies, plays, comic books, animated cartoons that it does not matter if a student has read either novel in its first form: nearly every American knows of their significance and of the kind of narrative of boyhood that they depict. Perhaps college literature anthologies could begin to excerpt chapters on the relationship between work, play, and boys from the fictions of Abbott or Optic, placing them alongside of the full text or sections from *Huckleberry Finn* or *Tom Sawyer*. If a student reads one of the sections of the Rollo books that were published as chapter books after reading Twain, she could begin to see that literary production about childhood and boyhood in the century does not privilege the "boys will be boys" kind of pedagogy that might appear as representative to those who are only aware of Twain's boy narratives.

It should come as no surprise that all of the major anthologies of American literature that cover the nineteenth century feature Twain but omit Abbott (or any boys' author like him); they typically have very little material, if any, written primarily for children. When anthologies do include the work of an author like Lydia Sigourney who wrote for adult and child readers, they do not incorporate any writing addressed to children or boys. Yet some collections have selections or excerpts by Louisa May Alcott that are often offered as representative of popular narratives for girls and domestic fiction, and which seem to many readers to form a "natural" pair with *Tom Sawyer*. And *The Norton Anthology of Children's Literature*, one of the most prominent collections of children's writing, reinforces ideas about gender and reading that anthologies have helped to create. In the "Domestic Fiction" and "Adventure Stories" sections (headings that echo an ever-present binary that this chapter complicates), all of the pre-twentieth-century material can be neatly divided by the gender of the author, and the vast majority of it by the gender of the child to whom it is primarily addressed. Most students would therefore likely assume that men wrote adventure stories for boys and women wrote domestic fiction for girls. The inclusion of a writer like Abbott would complicate this assumption, as would the inclusion of any of Sigourney's writing addressed to boys. Students would be able to see the diversity of approaches that writers took toward boyhood, adventure, pedagogy, and domesticity, and they would realize that children's books, just like adult fictions, are places in which a culture works through issues it believes to be of the greatest significance.

From Jacob Abbott's *Rollo at Play,* 1850.

Chapter 2

"Desirable and Necessary" in "Families and Schools"

Boy-Nature and Physical Discipline

> The committee . . . abolished [corporal punishment] . . . in all grammar schools for girls. I moved to amend by adding "boys' grammar," but was in that defeated.
> —Judge Richard Warner

> I said to the school these boys have violated the laws. . . . What shall be done with them? "WHIP THEM," was the answer. I said as many are in favor of having these two boys whipped, hold up the right hand. The vote was unanimous—EVERY HAND WAS RAISED.
> —Lyman Cobb

> He that spareth his rod, hateth his son.
> —Old Testament proverb repeatedly cited by New England educators

When Twain depicts corporal punishment in *The Adventures of Tom Sawyer*, he often exposes the sadism of the person who inflicts it, an approach in stark contrast to that taken by Forrester in *Dick Duncan*. And just as Twain's version of antebellum boyhood and his embrace of "boys will be boys" pedagogy should not be seen as the mainstream view during the period, neither should his opposition to corporal punishment be taken—as it has been—as representative of a larger cultural movement to abolish the practice. While it is true that some reformers opposed physical discipline under any circumstance, the majority did not. As Charles Northend says in his 1859 manual *The Teacher's Assistant*, "You ask, if you must ever resort to corporal punishment. In answer to this, I wish I might feel warranted in saying that it is never necessary. I hope the time may come when it is wholly unnecessary; but I do not believe that the time has yet arrived" (58).

The figure who best represents the most widely held belief, I argue, would be Horace Mann. Perhaps the most influential educator in nineteenth-century America, Mann wrote his famous "Lecture on School Punishments" in 1839 and delivered, revised, and reprinted it in the following decades. The lecture was not, as its title suggests, a broad examination of disciplinary practice, but rather a sustained look at corporal punishment and boys. According to Mann, the debate about the physical punishment of girls was largely over, at least in the North. He mentions girls in only a single footnote, in which he claims that "in ninetynine towns in every hundred, in the State, the flogging of girls, even where it exists at all, is an exceedingly rare event" (319). In his 1843 annual report to the Massachusetts Board of Education, he explains why girls do not need physical discipline: "the differences of organization and temperament which individualize the sexes" meant that girls "need kindness and not force. . . . They can feel a thing to be right or wrong . . . and hence, appeals should be addressed to their sentiments" (28). The elevated moral "feeling" of girls, a staple conceit of antebellum domestic and sentimental ideologies, meant that only boys should be corporally punished. Like other reformers, Mann opposed a ban for boys because he believed the practice, and equally important, the threat of it, promoted "manliness" ("Lecture" 27).[1] In fact, he could not imagine the creation of a healthy masculinity without it, for a prohibition would be dangerous, encouraging boys to think that physical pain should be avoided at all cost. And the nation's stability was at stake. Mann argues that as future "men of war," boys "need to be trained to a disregard, and even a contempt of bodily pain, so that they may not be unnerved and unmanned" and "will be able to march, with unfaltering step, to the post of duty, though their path is enfiladed by a hundred batteries" (313–14).

Many scholars have characterized Mann as an opponent of corporal punishment, claiming that he "had a horror of the rod" (Reynolds 62), yet the lecture shows otherwise: he endorsed it for boys, even specifying that it should be performed "with a rod . . . and below the loins or upon the legs" (324).[2] "Discipline—Moral and Mental," an essay in the inaugural issue of the *American Journal of Education* (1855), argued that the close connection between boys and physical punishment made by Mann reflects an association in wide circulation: "Ask what is meant by a good disciplinarian in school and the general reply will be, 'the teacher who knows how to . . . make boys learn . . . by a liberal use of the rod'" (Richards 108). While "the child" was often the subject of sentimental discourses on affective discipline, boys were sometimes characterized as being outside of the "circle of sentiment" that helped to create and define both the domestic and social relationships in which boys—as husbands, fathers, merchants, or politicians—would eventually play a key role.

Although they have not been seen in this way, fiction and educational writings about corporal punishment are, I argue, discussions of gender difference, and they are one of the most important sources for theories of boyhood masculinity. The two most influential critical examinations—Richard Brodhead's "'Sparing the Rod': Discipline and Fiction in Antebellum America" and Myra Glenn's *Campaigns Against Corporal Punishment*—make no mention of the role played by childhood gender.[3] In *Discipline and Punish* and *The History of Sexuality,* Foucault claims that modernity is a condition in which power, surveillance, and discipline become more diffuse and therefore more productive. Following Foucault, Brodhead argues that antebellum corporal punishment reformers endorsed a ban on physical discipline in order to create a management strategy that would be more coercive because it was less visible. Under the regime of moral suasion, the child learns to internalize authority, and thus the need for corporal punishment is eliminated. The child disciplines himself without recognizing "self-government" as discipline.

Foucault often speaks of power as if it affected all subjects equally, and feminists have rightly rejected this premise because it obscures the way that power has always had specific designs on female bodies. Foucault's attention to the production of "docile bodies" often obscures the fact that bodies are gendered, and Brodhead's Foucauldian reading of corporal punishment debates similarly overlooks how gender discourses work in the texts he examines. A Foucauldian approach creates the appearance that corporal punishment debates made no distinction between girls and boys, when such distinctions were in fact essential. "The rod gets laid aside," Brodhead says, "because it is no longer needed in the disciplinary arsenal" (*Cultures* 41).[4] But while most reformers wanted to shield girls from the practice, they were unwilling to lay the rod aside for boys. And although Glenn studies the role gender difference played in determining who applied physical punishment, she, like Brodhead, does not discuss its role in determining who would receive it.

Antebellum theorists of childhood discipline were acutely concerned with gender and they talked at length about why differences necessitated different disciplinary strategies. Even though Bronson Alcott often wrote about "childhood" discipline, Elizabeth Peabody's *Record of a School* (1835) shows Alcott applying the rod exclusively to boys and repeatedly explaining why their nature makes such punishment necessary. Jacob Abbott also argues that social and intellectual distinctions between girls and boys meant the strategies that will work for one might fail for the other. And Lyman Cobb, author of *The Evil Tendencies of Corporal Punishment as a Means of Moral Discipline in Families and Schools, Examined and Discussed* (1847), categorically claimed that because girls would respond to appeals to their reason and emotion, they should be exempt from bodily punishment. Examining these authors and debates about corporal punishment, then, can help us understand the ways in which questions of gender difference and boyhood masculinity were articulated in antebellum America. Texts that represent what historian of education David Hogan has called "New England pedagogy"—Cobb's treatise, Peabody's *Record*, and Sedgwick's *Home* (1835)—show that such beliefs, especially widely circulating negative ideas about boy-nature, were a crucial component of a domestic theory that informed and organized disciplinary practice in home and at school in many of the same ways (2). These texts complicate our ideas about sentimental ideology by showing that it was, at times, decidedly unsentimental in its beliefs about boys.

Corporal Punishment, Gender Difference, and the Historical Context of "Boyhood Depravity"

> Moral Suasion's my theory, but Lickin's my practice.
> —Teacher Lucia Downing

Reformers like Cobb, Alcott, and Sedgwick thought of themselves (as many historians have thought of them) as the vanguard of liberal innovation in childhood pedagogy. The works of these writers were published at a time when the northern middle class and New England educational establishment turned their gaze toward childhood with a drive previously unseen. As historian of education Barbara Finkelstein has noted, during this period a network of "tutelary complexes" were, for the first time, directed at influencing the subjectivity of children (111). Assisted by advances in the publishing industry, the 1820s and subsequent decades witnessed a rapid growth in childrearing literature.[5] The decades preceding the Civil War were a time of considerable interest in educational reform that saw the birth of the common school movement, a dramatic increase in the number of female teachers, and the publication of numerous educational journals and instructional materials for teachers. The 1830s and 1840s produced a number of important manuals, such as Abbott's *The Teacher* (1833) and David Page's *Theory and Practice of Teaching* (1847), which went through ninety printings before the end of the century.[6] This period also marks the emergence and growth of the American children's literature industry, which had a profound, and often disciplinary, influence on its young readers.[7] All of this pedagogical activity makes this a crucial historical moment for the creation and dissemination of ideas about masculinity and disciplinary practice.

In these teaching manuals and elsewhere, educational theorists articulated the appeals at work in the two most widely discussed disciplinary methods: corporal punishment and moral suasion. Moral suasion involved appeals to the child's reason and ethical sense. As an appeal to reason, or to the "understanding" as Lydia Maria Child, E. C. Wines, and others called it, suasion held that a child could be made to understand why its action was wrong and why the behavior endorsed by a parent or teacher was in the child's best interest. But most importantly, as an affective form of discipline, suasion was an appeal to the child's innate moral sense, or to its "affection" (Child 46, Wines 282). Following Francis Hutcheson and other Scottish Common Sense philosophers, many antebellum reformers believed that children would naturally respond to petitions that emphasized their emotional bond with a parent. The goal of moral suasion was to situate children within social and affective structures and to demonstrate to them how bonds with parents and teachers could be strengthened or withdrawn as a result of proper or improper action.

Corporal punishment, typically seen as the counterpart to suasion, was an appeal to the child's body, and many reformers, educators, and parents believed it should be used when rational and moral appeals were not likely to work or had already failed. As one educator said, "[W]hen mind *alone* fails to reach mind, then the rod must be used to inflict pain on the body" (Richards 111; emphasis in original). The more a child is a "creature of sense," Wines believed, the less "susceptible [he is to] that moral treatment which may be so efficacious as a means of discipline" (284–85). In his *Lectures on School-Keeping* (1829) Samuel Read Hall showed the relationship between the approaches: the instructor should rely on the "moral sensibilities and show the child the nature of its faults," but if the child be "devoid of sensibility" and cannot be "controlled by his reason," Hall argued that corporal punishment can then be used (71).

It is important to note that the rational and affective components of moral suasion were seen as more likely to work on girls, because of their intellectual and empathetic capacities. In fact, many writers maintained that suasion was almost universally effective for them. Just as Cobb claimed that girls "certainly *can* be *persuaded* to do what is right" (11), Morrill Wyman argued that "certainly . . . whips . . . can be dispensed with in the case of a reasoning girl"—but not in the case of boys (6). For most reformers, children who lacked rational and moral sensibilities needed physical correction—and that usually meant boys. A convention of nineteenth-century gender ideology associates males with reason and females with sentiment, yet as the comments of Cobb and Wyman show, this binary is complicated when it comes to ideas about children and learning. The fictional and pedagogical writings of Abbott, for example, repeatedly show girls as both more sensible and affectionate than boys; even though Rollo's father talks to his son about abstract concepts, the narrator says "it was not at all probable that . . . [he] could be *reasoned* into liking work" (55; emphasis in original).[8] And when authors argued that boys are "depraved" or act like savages (notions that appeared throughout educational and noneducational discourses), this was another way to say that boys lacked the rational and moral sensibilities of girls.[9]

By the time the books I have been discussing were published, the Calvinist notion of "infant depravity" had been largely abandoned, invalidated by educational theories based on Locke, the Scottish Common Sense school, Rousseau, Johann Pestalozzi, and others. Educators who rejected the Calvinist idea, as nearly all New England reformers did, instead understood the child in two distinct ways. Many, like Bronson Alcott, Elizabeth Peabody, and domestic-advice writer Lydia Maria Child, saw the child as born innocent, and they created an educational philosophy intended to foster children's natural intellectual and moral intelligence. Others viewed the child as neither inherently good nor depraved, but rather as a surface upon which character could be written. Yet for many of these educators, the notion of depravity had not totally disappeared. When children grew into girlhood and boyhood, the halo of innocence, or at least of the potential for goodness, hung much more over girls than boys.

Depravity had resurfaced, but with a difference: now it was "boyhood depravity." MacLeod says that "the nineteenth-century child was (generally) absolved of innate depravity" (102), a claim that reflects the widely accepted narrative of a steady movement away from the belief in infant depravity during the eighteenth century, a narrative perhaps best represented by Nancy Cott's influential 1978 article, "Notes toward an Interpretation of Antebellum Childrearing." While this narrative is correct about the waning influence of the Calvinist notion of "infant depravity," it does not account for the emergence of a secular theory of boyhood depravity. This term no longer carried its Calvinist connotation, but it nevertheless characterized a moral condition; according to many educators, the egocentric boy often showed little or no concern for others and thus was inaccessible to a moral entreaty. As scholars and historians such as Cott, Deborah Fitts, Joseph Kett, and Rotundo have shown, antebellum boys were often characterized as rude and troublesome, yet historians have not noted how thoroughly these notions permeate educational thought and domestic theory, nor have they appreciated the larger implications of these characterizations, such as the ways in which negative conceptions of boyhood were the basis for theories of boyhood discipline.[10] Many of these tutelary complexes, especially texts published in this period, played an important role in disseminating and enforcing the notion of boyhood depravity. If antebellum culture spiritualized women and girls, celebrating their unique fitness for the job of domestic nurturer by virtue of their naturally refined sensibility, it physicalized boys, making them the objects to be refined.

Critics have shown the many ways in which antebellum conceptions of domesticity negatively impacted the lives of girls and women, and these same theories, although clearly benefiting boys and men in many ways, likely adversely affected boys' lives when it came to management practices.[11] MacLeod says there is "little evidence" that "boys were punished more sternly than girls" (109). Neglecting a considerable body of educational writings and historical evidence (such as Mann's belief that the corporal punishment of girls was "exceedingly rare"), she bases her claim on a few memoirs and a misreading of child nurture literature. She says, for example, that in *The Mother's Book* (1831), Lydia Maria Child "condemned physical punishment . . . as useless" (104). But Child explicitly endorses corporal punishment for boys: "If a boy is too bad to be governed by any other means than flogging, and is too strong for you . . . tell his father, or his guardians, of his disobedience, and request them to punish him" (31). And historians of education and childhood in the nineteenth century also have drawn our attention to many memoirs by men in which they recall the often severe whippings they received as boys.[12] That the vast majority of educational literature shows boys as the primary recipient of harsh physical punishments suggests they may have received the majority of such discipline, and the widespread support for resolutions that outlawed corporal punishment for girls also suggests that many endorsed only the physical correction of boys. Like Brodhead, MacLeod enlists fiction as proof of her argument, but the fiction of the period is full of boys being corporally punished. There certainly were educators and authors who talked about saintly boys and mischievous girls, as well as those who condemned the harsh treatment of boys, but educational and noneducational writings reveal a far greater interest in—in fact an obsession with—misbehaving boys and their punishment.

The works of Cobb, Alcott, and Sedgwick that I explore in the final three sections of this chapter are part of this widely circulating discourse about boy-nature, a discourse apparent in novels, stories, book reviews, teacher's manuals, mother's magazines, children's magazines, and education journals written during the period in which these three reformers' texts were published. As the Roxbury Massachusetts School Committee observed in its 1846 "Report on Corporal Punishment in Schools," the connection between boy-nature and methods of boyhood discipline often did not work to the boy's benefit: many teachers "manifest an *appetite* for the rod and entertain such views of boy-nature, as to have no faith in the superiority of other influences" (cited in Cobb 260; emphasis in original).[13] This lack of faith is not surprising given how the culture often understood boys. Rotundo observes that "at the surface, the nineteenth-century middle class regarded boyhood fondly," and while poets and illustrators often described and pictured boyhood as an idyllic space (as they did girlhood and childhood), a reading of educational literature and other cultural discourses shows that, even at the surface, there was plenty of animus directed against boys (255). Boys were repeatedly characterized as "nuisances," "reckless," "depraved," "conceited," "disobedient," "mischief-makers," and "little interested in anything except what concerns the body." A review of *The Pilgrim Boy* in *The Mother's Magazine and Daughter's Friend* (1857) says this "story of the olden time . . . may be useful to the boys of our day, who despise restraint, or revel in a misjudged freedom, and . . . do as they please" (64). Similarly, a piece on corporal punishment in *The American Annals of Education and Instruction* (1836) refers to "the unruly boys of the present generation" ("Corporal Punishment" 339). An article on raising boys in *The Mother's Journal and Visitant* (1845) likewise characterizes boys as having a "recklessness of spirit" ("Training V" 181), while another educator claims, "The boy . . . when freed from the artificial restraints of the school-room . . . not unfrequently [*sic*] becomes reckless of all restraint" (cited in Cobb 256). Many male writers rejected what Foucault would call a "lyric" boyhood because such a sentimentalized representation erased the pain they suffered as a result of negative theories of boy-nature. The author of "The Profession of Schoolmaster" dismisses these kinds of representations as false, and instead sees boyhood as a period that no man "would ever want to relive": "we cannot but look upon that class of beings stigmatized by the term *boys* with some lively touch of pity" (41; emphasis in original). Other writers share this rejection: "why do we often hear . . . of the 'good old times.' . . . [T]he unnaturalness . . . [and] sufferings of such a life to a sensitive boy, no language can describe" (*An Autobiography* 7-8).

The common "boy as savage" trope brings together many characteristics typically associated with the unsentimental version of boyhood: as a "savage" the boy is immoral, immune to reason, primarily concerned with his own bodily needs, and sometimes even brutal. A writer in the *Mother's Magazine and Family Circle* (1858) argues that "boys when left to themselves, as at a public school, treat each other . . . brutally" ("Moral Discipline" 275). Echoing this belief, another calls them "the most vicious of wild beasts . . . better unborn than untaught" (Wood 51), while the author of an 1863 essay titled "Against Boys" warns, "Any idea of appeasing the boy element is, however, quite ridiculous; the animal is implacable, and, like a horse that perceives his rider is afraid of him, becomes unmanageable if petted" (85). In Sedgwick's *Home*, Wallace Barclay's father invokes this language as a justification for his excessive punishment of his son, describing the boy as a "creature who [is] the slave of [his] passions" and a "beast of prey" (17). While the notion of "man as a noble savage" posits characteristics of the savage as ideals that civilized men should aspire to, the notion of the "boy as savage" often compliments neither the boy nor the savage. Scholars who discuss the boy-savage metaphor cite its use by male authors after the Civil War as a way to dignify the boy throughout the nineteenth century, yet such was often not the case during the antebellum period. Gillian Brown says that "nineteenth-century Americans often characterized the sphere of boyhood . . . as a state of savagery," and Kidd notes that "savagery was often a less pejorative concept than we might assume, associated with self-reliance and entrepreneurial spirit" (91, 63).

Yet educators writing before and after the Civil War repeatedly employ the metaphor and its corollary notion of immorality to explain why boys would require physical discipline. Writings about corporal punishment even invoke the behavior of a "savage" as a case in which physical correction is justified. In the domestic advice manual *Gentle Measures in the Management and Training of the Young* (1871), for example, Abbott includes a fictional anecdote of a native "savage" boy who repeatedly disobeys his mother. At first, this anecdote seems out of place, for what relevance could it have to Abbott's white, middle-class readers? But understood within the frame of the boy-as-savage trope, as well as Abbott's and others' references to boys as "bodily" and "depraved," this anecdote presents an implicit theory of boy-nature and a justification for corporal discipline. *The American Whig Review*'s "Boyhood and Barbarism" appears to compare boys favorably to noble savages. But then the writer starkly shifts direction, claiming that the association between the two elevates boys only when expressed as a metaphor: "These illustrations . . . sap the theory which has just been presented. But could we show you these [boys] out of doors, and unveil their schemes . . . the balance in favor of barbarism would, we fear, be rather startling" (283). In "The Profession of Schoolmaster," the author makes it clear that negative ideas about boy-nature were closely connected to the pedagogy to which boys were subjected: we "put him into that class . . . *fera naturae* . . . and base our plans for his improvement upon the assumption of his total depravity" (41). "Depravity"—the moral condition of the "savage" and a popular word for describing boys in educational writings—placed boys, like native Americans and other "savages," in a tense relationship with domestic culture but saw them as capable of being assimilated via discipline. Dr. Samuel Taylor, head of the Phillips Academy in the decades before and after the Civil War, believed in "the total depravity of the great majority" of boys (cited in Rotundo 256). In the opening section of *The Teacher* (1856), a popular advice manual for instructors, Abbott praises schoolmasters who "think . . . before they go into their school, what sort of beings boys and girls are . . . and take care to make [themselves] acquainted with these materials *just as they are*" (27–28; emphasis in original). In a dialogue, he illustrates the case of a teacher who lacks such forethought:

> I have such boys I can do nothing with them. Were it not for *their misconduct,* I might have a very good school. . . .
> Why, is there any peculiar depravity in them which you could not have foreseen?
> No; I suppose they are pretty much like all other boys; . . . they are all hair-brained and unmanageable. [My] plans . . . would be excellent if my boys would only behave properly.
> Excellent plans . . . and yet not adapted to the materials upon which they are to operate! It is your business to know what sort of beings boys are, and to make your calculations accordingly. (29; emphasis in original)

Abbott's surrogate in the dialogue recommends the approach to boyhood discipline that angers the author of "The Profession of Schoolmaster," who criticizes teachers who have negative ideas about boy-nature and "calculate" their management strategies "accordingly."[14]

Abbott, who cofounded and taught at the all-girl Mount Vernon School as well as boys and coed schools, begins *The Teacher* with an admonition to "know" the nature of both boys and girls, but then gives boys the vast majority of his attention. The text's lengthy chapter on "moral discipline" focuses on "the inclinations of boys" to be "lax," "sly," and "mischief makers," and Abbott even selects a boy as the one "specimen" most suited to represent all childhood discipline problems. Continuing his warning to "know your materials," he says that "the first point to be attended to is to ascertain who [the likely discipline problems] are" (162). He then lists a physiognomic taxonomy of boy "characters" under an engraving of two boys fighting: the "coarse, rough-looking boy," the "sly rogue," and the "sullen and silent" boy. Almost the entire chapter explores strategies for dealing with such boys (163). When excerpts from the closing section of *The Teacher* were reprinted in the May 1839 issue of the *American Annals of Education and Instruction,* much of the opening commentary was omitted, altering the ostensible gender-neutral focus. The journal version begins, "It is of the first importance that he should become acquainted, as early as possible, with the characters of the boys, especially to learn who those are which are most likely to be troublesome. There always will be a few" (216); and it concludes, "The ways by which boys engage in open, intentional disobedience, are, of course, greatly varied" (222). These changes reinforce what was already apparent: the essay is solely an examination of boy behavior.

The fictional children Abbott features in his educational articles exemplify the ideas about gender and childhood found in *The Teacher*. In these essays, children are divided almost exclusively into bad boys and good girls; boys are described as "troublesome," "cunning and treacherous," "rude . . . and always doing wrong," and contrasted with a "fair-haired girl . . . with an air of precision and propriety" ("Advantages" 26, 25). In an anecdote illustrating the practice of emulation (motivation by reward), Abbott contrasts two "dull and coarse boys, sluggish in the mind, and little interested in anything except what concerns the body" with "two bright, and sensitive, and eager girls . . . interested in their studies . . . [and] eager for the good opinion" of parents and teachers ("Advantages" 30).[15] This characterization of girls as concerned for the opinion of others establishes them as the kind of children who could be disciplined through appeals to social affect. As a popular novelist and influential educator, Abbott embodies the cultural obsession with boys as disciplinary problems, and his writings reveal an important cultural belief and a related authorial practice.[16] First, he holds conventional ideas about the nature of boys and girls: boys as bodily, less intellectual, and prone to misbehave, and girls as moral, intellectual, and obedient. And second, his writings on discipline, although offered as non-gender-specific discussions, show only boys as serious behavioral problems.

Many articles in educational journals make claims about childhood and discipline similar to Abbott's. Although some hard-line educators endorsed the corporal punishment of girls, educational writers typically concentrated on boys and boy-nature as the crucial problems, and the ones that required physical discipline. An 1856 article in *The American Journal of Education* titled "Discipline; School Government" looks at a number of management techniques, and like Abbott's texts, uses anecdotes that almost always feature a misbehaving boy. The author argues that "when a boy can not [*sic*] be reached by other modes of discipline, and becomes difficult to control we resort to the rod" (Hamill 131). Like Cobb and Alcott, he does not say explicitly that girls do not misbehave or that they should not be physically punished; he simply never talks about them. "Confession of a Schoolmaster," which ran from 1835 until 1838 in *The American Annals of Education and Instruction,* similarly focuses on boys and dramatizes the use the rod as an appropriate disciplinary strategy in such cases. The master sees his "rigid" measures as unfortunate but necessary in a schoolroom where children "of both sexes, and all ages and habits, are thrown together" ("Errors" 30).[17] When the schoolmaster recounts his theory and practice of punishment, however, while some of the discussion refers to "the child," all anecdotes of misbehavior refer to boys. The only other episode to deal exclusively with discipline is devoted to the master's problem with a difficult boy and his recourse to physical discipline. Like many anecdotes of boys being punished, this installment narrates the process—the cutting of the switches, the classroom preparations, and the public whipping itself—as if imagining a reader who desires to see this practice in detail. And, as is so often the case in these kinds of educational articles, corporal punishment is successful: "The use of the whip, on Charles," the author notes, "seemed to have accomplished its object completely" (91). Although the master feels discomfort in having to use physical coercion, he believes it is sometimes the only way to "reach" a boy. Looking across the breadth of antebellum writings about education allows us to see that when physical discipline is the issue, boy-nature is the subject. Since boys were "depraved," "immoral," or "mischievous"—terms never generally applied to girls—they would often require a different form of punishment. The remainder of this chapter develops this picture of pedagogical culture by examining influential authors and reformers—Lyman Cobb, Bronson Alcott, and Catharine Sedgwick—whose theories and practices both recall and reinforce popular and pervasive beliefs about boy-nature and bodily discipline.

Lyman Cobb and the "Bad" Boy

> All will agree that a boy must be made to yield.
>
> —Lyman Cobb

Cobb's *The Evil Tendencies of Corporal Punishment* is the most systematic treatise on corporal punishment published in the United States during the nineteenth century. Appearing in 1847 at the height of the reform movement, it was one of the more influential works to deal with the subject; Walt Whitman and other journalists printed excerpts in newspapers, and legislators cited Cobb in attempts to outlaw the practice in schools. Brodhead calls this book "an endlessly sustained refutation of every possible argument for physical correction" (22), ignoring Cobb's repeated endorsement of numerous forms of corporal punishment for boys. "We are to . . . exercise it as an *ultimatum* or *last resort* to make a boy yield or submit," Cobb says, yet "GIRLS *should* NEVER BE WHIPPED, *whatever may be done with* BOYS" (9, 81; emphasis in original). The "whatever" includes whipping, and like Mann, Cobb provides instructions: "a *suitable* whip or light (not a *heavy*) rattan, applied to the back between the shoulders" (88). Agreeing with one of the many experts he cites, Cobb believes "there is something repulsive in the idea of a close relationship between a cane and the tender back of a little girl" (268), and while he claimed to prefer noncorporal methods, he finds nothing repulsive in the image of a rod and a boy's back: a "WILFUL [*sic*] and MALICIOUSLY *disobedient* boy" should be physically punished (31; emphasis in original).[18]

Cobb's positions on discipline are intimately connected to his beliefs about boyhood as a developmental stage that he figures as a kind of contagion. He argues that when boys are young, they, like girls, are essentially good. But often in "*boyhood,*" he says, "they become BAD" (205; emphasis in original): "many boys are rather *unfeeling,*" and "are not, at that time, suitable company for men, women, or children" (210–11; emphasis in original).[19] Cobb's ideas about boy development accord with standard nineteenth-century childrearing philosophies, which generally held that as infants and young children, boys and girls were essentially the same and therefore should be disciplined in the same ways.[20] But boyhood was a distinct stage. The boy was no longer the generic "child," for he had entered boyhood and become a discipline problem: "My boys are very loveable" one mother noted, "till they outgrow babyhood, and begin to show themselves to be boys, coarse, ungainly, and unloving" (Manners 40). While Cobb believes that moral suasion can work on some misbehaving boys, he repeatedly contrasts its successful application on girls with its heightened potential for failure on boys: "*They* [girls] certainly *can* be *persuaded* to do what is right, (whatever may be said about *boys*), without a resort to the use of the rod" (11; emphasis in original). Cobb sees boyhood as a time when boys are often inaccessible to moral suasion's social structures of affect. Because boys can be "unfeeling," they often cannot be managed with a strategy that depends on affect and an emotional connection with the mother.

Surprisingly, modern readers have overlooked the fact that *The Evil Tendencies of Corporal Punishment* is *solely* about boyhood discipline, a point that Cobb makes early: "I wish it to be distinctly understood, that, my remarks are directed entirely to the management of *boys.* . . . I will not so degrade myself as to make use of the word *girl* or *female* . . . in connexion with the subject of *flogging*" (11; emphasis in original).[21] While the text claims to be about the evil tendencies of physical discipline, it is equally about the evil tendencies of boys—their truancy, lying, cheating, fighting, and disobedience. He occasionally mentions a misbehaving girl, yet he never applies terms such as "willful" or "malicious" to girls in general, and he uses only anecdotes of "troublesome" boys to illustrate both the disciplinary strategies he recommends and those he rejects. Cobb opposes corporal punishment for girls, not because of their relative smaller size or greater risk of injury (arguments we might expect to be made but rarely were) but because they posses characteristics that make it unnecessary. In arguing against their corporal punishment, Cobb repeats ideas about girls that are recognizable as the conventions of antebellum gender discourse that I discussed earlier. Since they are "the *gentler, nobler,* and *lovelier* SEX" (81; emphasis in original), and typically have a "SENSIBILITY" that most boys do not, girls should be beyond the reach of the whip or ferule (74; emphasis in original). Such practices are not only unnecessary and detrimental to them but disastrous for the nation. "We have ... elevated WOMEN to the true and dignified station," Cobb proclaims, yet will "sink back into barbarism" if the physical disciplining of girls continues (7; emphasis in original). Girls' treatment is intimately tied to their cultural standing and the status of the United States as a civilized nation, yet the possible harsh treatment of boys has no negative implications for domestic or national structures. Indeed, it is the opposite. Cobb implies what Mann makes explicit: the corporal punishment of boys is in the best interest of home, school, and nation.

While making boys the exclusive focus of his book and issuing blanket condemnations of their behavior, Cobb dramatizes the one circumstance in which a boy should never be corporally punished. The most important criterion for determining the exception is the degree to which the boy is *"unboyish."* This exception features a boy described in the terms Cobb uses to generalize about girls and to argue against their corporal punishment—"gentler, nobler, and lovelier" and with a *"delicate* SENSIBILITY":

> a lovely boy ... of rather a delicate form and nervous temperament, failed to *pronounce* the word. The teacher said to him angrily, "Come up here." In an instant his little delicate frame was in a state of nervous tremor. ... The teacher took his thin and slender hand in his, bent it in such a manner as to expose the most sensitive part of it to the blows, and then beat it with a long, wide ferula, the dear boy, at each successive blow, repeating with piteous cries, "oh, I *will* remember." (27; emphasis in original)

Returning to anecdotes about "lovely boy[s]," "slender and delicate, but very interesting," Cobb calls scenes of their corporal punishment a *"deplorable* and AFFECTING sight" (88; emphasis in original). He appears to assume that readers share his lack of "interest" in the welfare of more conventionally masculine boys, and therefore believes that the sight of them being whipped would not generate any sympathy. Whitman makes the same assumption in his often reprinted anticorporal punishment sentimental sketch, "Death in the School-Room," which features the unjust disciplining of Tim Barker, a feminine boy similar to Cobb's: "a slight, fair-looking boy of thirteen," who was a "sickly emaciated infant" (177, 178). Barker's appearance, history, and devotion to his widowed mother mark him as a "saintly child," who Whitman says is "too unearthly fair" (178).[22] In a discussion of nineteenth-century representations of saintly children, Anne Trensky observes that "the majority ... are girls, and when they are boys they have girlish appearances and mannerisms" (389). Given the relationship between saintliness and femininity visible throughout antebellum culture, it is not surprising that writers like Cobb exempt from corporal punishment only boys who look and act similarly to girls. The fact that many parents and teachers also used violent means against less "delicate" boys fails to concern Cobb, because for him "boyish" boys have less right to humane treatment. Even though Cobb makes feminine boys the exception to his claims about boy-nature, as exceptions they speak to his belief in boyhood as a developmental stage in which boys are typically devoid of the sentiment that characterizes girls.

Bronson Alcott and the "Material" Boy

> Childhood hath saved me!
> —Bronson Alcott
>
> [Boys] deceive us.
> —Bronson Alcott

Although Cobb's text includes anecdotes of punishment, *The Evil Tendencies of Corporal Punishment* is essentially a work of disciplinary theory. Beyond brief claims about actual applications of his theory, it contains no detailed record of practice. Elizabeth Peabody's *Record of a School,* however, offers a rare sustained look at a theory in practice. Peabody's transcriptions of and commentary on Bronson Alcott's conversations with his students at the Temple School in Boston in 1834 and 1835 include numerous discussions of discipline and scenes of boys being punished.[23] When Ralph Waldo Emerson visited the school, he watched the pupils "engage . . . questions of truth" and "felt strongly" that his transcendental creed was reaffirmed: "Age, sex are nothing; we are all alike before the great Whole" (cited in Sanborn 231). Perhaps Emerson did not spend enough time there to realize that sex plays a crucial role in Alcott's teaching and his beliefs about childhood education. Alcott's transcendentalism appears to be predicated on the notion that gender is irrelevant: the child's soul is not a boy's or girl's soul, but simply a soul. So in his educational philosophy, he often speaks of only "the child." Yet in practice, as *Record of a School* indicates, though all may be "alike before the great Whole," boys and girls are different before Alcott, who makes boys' behaviors and their bodies the exclusive sites for discussions about and implementations of his beliefs about corporal punishment. Indeed, Alcott rarely mentions the faults of his female students; we rarely see them being disciplined, and they are never punished with a ferule.

Critical discussions of Alcott's educational theories often focus on texts like *Observations on the Principles and Methods of Infant Instruction* (1830) or *The Doctrine and Discipline of Human Culture* (1836), documents that do not refer to the gender of those instructed. Even critics who examine the *Record,* a text that continually discusses gender and punishment, have not looked at Alcott's obsession with boys and discipline. Most downplay his endorsement of corporal punishment, never mentioning aspects of the *Record* such as his proposed "tremendous law!" of corporal punishment for every boys' offense; McCuskey even claims that in the late 1820s "corporal punishment disappeared from Bronson Alcott's schools" (26). Critics who explore his educational theories through the lens of his domestic practice (such as Charles Strickland) similarly have not recognized how gender functions, perhaps because Alcott was strongly influenced by European philosophers and educators whose theories made little or no gender distinctions. For example, Johann Pestalozzi, a major influence on Alcott, was a Rousseauian essentialist: thus Pestalozzi repeatedly writes of "the instruction of children" and "the instruction of Man" and offers no theories that would allow us to determine if he believed that boys and girls were distinct or needed to be treated differently (26).[24] Alcott had only daughters and never punished them with a rod, as he did his male students. As Anne Boylan notes, he went to "great lengths to avoid spanking his daughters," lengths to which he never went to avoid using the rod in his school (163). It is only in the Temple classroom, then, where he instructed boys and girls together, that we can see how theories of gender and childhood learning structure his disciplinary theory.

Although it seems likely that gendered theories of discipline such as Cobb's and Alcott's might lead to a classroom practice that in some way favored girls (or at least benefited them by an exemption from corporal punishment), Alcott's beliefs, according to his male students, lead to such favoritism:

> there was a long talk about *partialities* in school, during which one of the boys expressed great dissatisfaction at the fact that there was a girl in school who was never found fault with. . . . This boy, however, said that Mr. Alcott thought she was the best person in the school;—and asked him if he did not? Mr. Alcott replied that he thought she was better than the boy, who was asking him that question. (*Record* 49; emphasis in original)

The *Record* reveals numerous instances of such *"partialities."* For instance, Alcott punishes boys when they whisper, but not girls (107). When discussing the faults in four boys' journals, he tells one that there was nothing worth reading in his, and another that his writings reveal him to be an "automaton," but then he praises two girls' journals, prompting a boy to argue—and Alcott to admit—that he knowingly did not mention problems in their journals (98).

Throughout his career, Alcott often expressed a confrontational attitude toward male students, an attitude he thought justified because of traits he believed were inherent to boys. During his tenure as superintendent of Concord schools in the 1850s, he outlined a fundamental difference between boys, who he believed invited harsh discipline, and girls, who did not need such measures: "boys . . . wait for feeling the bit, the awfulness of power, as certain proofs of authority. Girls have other ways of minding" (cited in Harding 99–100). Although the *Record* certainly presents positive interactions between Alcott and his male students, these moments stand in stark contrast to a larger disciplinary practice based on "the awfulness of power" that he felt boys often needed to experience. In fact, Alcott says about boys in general that "they interrupt us, they deceive us, they are not ingenuous, they require punishment" (141), the kinds of sweeping critical statements absent from his rhetoric on girls.

In the opening days of the Temple School, Alcott wrote of his thirty pupils, "about half are girls,—a circumstance most favorable to the exertion of a pure moral influence on the formation of character" (cited in Sanborn 178). Alcott's claim reflects Mann's, Cobb's, and the culture's belief that boys' characters could benefit from girls' "pure moral influence" and heightened "sensibility."[25] Indeed, educators often highlighted the harmful effects that boys could have on the morals of others; as *Ralph Rattler; or The Mischief Maker* (1853) warns, "A fierce lion . . . would be better than such a boy; for, at the worst, a lion can only kill the body. But a bad boy can . . . lead the souls of his schoolmates to death. . . . [E]very child . . . must avoid an *artful, mischief-making boy*" (cited in Davis 61; emphasis in original).[26] Because his male students often lack an ethical sensibility, Alcott uses physical correction to "rouse sensibility, when there was a deficiency" (143). "The ministry of pain," he argues, "was God's great means of . . . [the] elevation of character" (143).

During a conversation on discipline, one of the most discussed topics in the *Record,* Alcott tells the boys who had "been punished with the ferule [to] rise" (77). He explains to the class why their behavior had required this kind of penalty: because "boys deemed thoughts to be unreal, it was necessary, for outward things which they did believe real, to take the side of the conscience, and help to make them seem real" (77). In other words, the way to make boys understand abstract ideas—the only things that Alcott as a Platonist believes to be real—is by "a ferule to the hand." Alcott is disappointed when boys show an interest in money or prefer the "descriptive" aspect of a narrative to the "reflective" part, but he argues that this materiality can be modified or erased through dialogue or the beneficial effects of bodily discipline: "Boys came here with their fingers in their ears" and to "make them hear I would sometimes hurt the body . . . when it is necessary to reach the mind and put thoughts in it" (45). He thus articulates the idea behind Cobb's argument for boyhood corporal punishment, a notion that recalls Abbott's beliefs: because boys are often dramatically more material than girls, Alcott uses the ferule to speak to boys in their own language, that of compulsion and the body.

Alcott also shares Abbott's belief that boys are "sluggish," arguing that they "needed bodily punishment to rouse their sluggishness of mind . . . [and] on account of their obstinacy and opposition" (108). Such opposition leads Alcott to threaten his male students with a "tremendous law!" one he never mentions for girls: "every boy present who got into a lazy position, . . . were inattentive, &c. should . . . receive a blow upon their hand" (117). Unlike Cobb, he never explicitly calls the corporal disciplining of girls "barbaric" or a sign of teacher incompetence—he simply never does it. And like Mann and Cobb, he intends to control boys by keeping the threat of bodily punishment ever-present by repeatedly talking to them about disciplining their bodies. He tells his students that some of the "boys . . . make their minds the tools of their bodies, and that is very bad," seeming not to recognize that this is the very reason he practices corporal punishment on boys (75).

In what is the only widely known moment from the *Record*, Alcott employs an unusual approach in which he makes his own body a tool of class management.[27] He announces that anyone who is late from recess would be "obliged to [corporally] punish him" (141). In a three-page note—the longest note in the book—Peabody offers a description of the scene in which Alcott is hit, a practice he calls "vicarious punishment":

> Mr. Alcott, in two instances, took boys into the anteroom to do it. They were very unwilling, and at first they did it lightly. He then asked them, if they thought that they deserved no more punishment than that? And so they were obliged to give it hard:—but it was not without tears, which they never had shed when punished themselves. This is the most complete punishment that a master ever invented,—was the observation of one of the boys, at home; Mr. Alcott has secured obedience now; there is not a boy in school, but what would a great deal rather be punished himself, than punish him. (145)

Peabody anxiously defends Alcott in this note, saying in a later edition of the *Record* that this was the only instance of this type of physical discipline that occurred in the school. Perhaps Peabody is defensive because this discipline angered parents and educators, many of whom had repeatedly been critical of Alcott's beliefs and practices: "Since the publication of the first edition of this book," Peabody reflects, "there has been no recurrence of this species of punishment, corporeally."[28] Like all other scenes of physical correction in the *Record*, this one involves only males—Alcott and boy students—and rather than lead to additional incidents in which Alcott was hit by students, it simply generates more of the corporal punishment that appears so often in the text: Alcott hitting boys.[29]

One student who had been elected superintendent for the day—he was to write the names of students who had misbehaved on a slate—"begged so hard to be" physically punished for the misdeeds of the boys whose names he had recorded that, in imitation of Alcott's punishment, he was "allowed to receive the strokes" (145). The singular moment of Alcott's vicarious punishment ensures that the school's economy of physical discipline—in which only the boy body receives the "blows"—is not threatened. And it ensures, at least according to Alcott and Peabody, that boys will freely accept corporal punishment. Indeed, Peabody notes that as a result of Alcott's being hit, "there is not a boy in school, but what would a great deal rather be punished himself" (145). And such punishments continue throughout the remainder of the *Record*.

Since Alcott's project of "spiritual culture" (a phrase from the *Record*'s subtitle) is fully invested in asserting the primacy of the "realities in the mind," he teaches boys about these realities by inflicting pain on their bodies. Because boys inhabit the world of "outward things," Alcott disciplines them by speaking directly to their interest in the corporeal. Girls, on the other hand, are inherently more attuned to his sentimental project of "spiritual culture" and therefore can be reached with communal and intellectual petitions. Typical of his transcendentalism, then, Alcott maps onto boys and girls a kind of material-spiritual opposition, much as Cobb had mapped onto them an asocial-social dichotomy and Abbott a physical-intellectual dichotomy. Although Alcott never explicitly states this opposition, the *Record*'s constant references to boys' bodies and the invisibility of girls' bodies, as well as his comments about the superiority of female moral influence articulate his beliefs about the roles that gender difference plays in his classroom practice.

Alcott's interest in physical punishment seems to have had a dramatic effect on one student. When Alcott tells a boy the "shape his mind would come forth in, if [it] could take shape," the student "screamed with laughter" because Alcott described exactly what the boy had imagined: "a sword to prick all the boys with!" (109). Given Alcott's concern with boys' bodies, it is not surprising that the student would imagine a violent act against "all the boys" in which his sword represents Alcott's ferule. Although the progressive Alcott would seem to be an unlikely spokesman for conventional educational attitudes, his belief that boy-nature generates physical punishment (rather than its being a choice of Alcott to inflict it) makes him thoroughly representative. Decades after the initial publication of the *Record*, Alcott worried that reform movements might have had an adverse effect on boys. He wondered if "we are correcting the old affection for flogging at some risk of spoiling the boys of this generation" (cited in Harding 172). Alcott felt affection for corporal punishment during much of his educational career, an advocacy that is not surprising given his belief that boys "require punishment."

Catherine Maria Sedgwick and the "Boyish" Boy

> Then learn one lesson from your poor brother. Learn to dread doing wrong. If you commit sin, you must suffer.
> —Mr. Barclay in *Home*

Shortly after Peabody's *Record of a School* was published, she visited the novelist Catherine Maria Sedgwick to relay the "testimony of an intelligent, *orthodox*, factory girl" who told her that Sedgwick's recently published *Home* exemplified how they should live in Lowell, an endorsement Sedgwick believed "better than the opinion of half the ministers in New England" (cited in Kelley 150; emphasis in original). Apparently, many agreed with the mill-girl's assessment. In six years the novel went through fifteen editions and was repeatedly referred to in educational journals as a model of family management theory. Critics have traditionally understood Sedgwick and the novel as opposed to any form of physical discipline and endorsing moral suasion instead. Glenn, for instance, says that "Sedgwick's story underscored reformers' desires to discipline an individual's mind, not punish his body" (142). Historians Bernard Wishy (46), Carl Degler (91), Cott (14), Davis (47), and MacLeod (104) similarly consider this text representative of the period's endorsement of a love-centered, nonphysical regime of self-discipline. Yet the text's featured scene of punishment involves a bleeding boy, and it evinces an ideology closely related to Mann's, Cobb's, and Alcott's *orthodox* ideas of boyhood punishment.

Sedgwick, whose Unitarian-inspired domestic sentimentalism infused her most famous novels, *Hope Leslie* (1827) and *Redwood* (1824), wrote *Home* in response to a request from prominent Unitarian minister Henry Ware Jr. for a work of instructional fiction that was both "a formal tale and a common tract." Such a hybrid format, Ware noted, would be particularly effective in educating "readers by a familiar exposition of principles, and . . . a display of their modes of operation" (cited in Dewey 239). Like the *Record*, *Home* offers a theory of discipline and an examination of what that theory would look like in practice. The novel immediately announces that its imagining of New England family life should be taken, as Ware wanted it to be, as representative: "In a picturesque district . . . it matters not in which of the Eastern States, for in them all is such unity of character and similarity of condition, that what is true of one may be probable of all" (1). As the text goes on to articulate, "unity of character and similarity of condition" refer not only to geography but to the domestic relationships that the text explores. This erasing of difference allows Sedgwick to present principles that would apply to all her readers. So when she speaks about the Barclays, she is speaking to all parents about themselves and all children. For Sedgwick, to understand her treatise-novel correctly is to read it as both a representation of and a plan for a model family and the kind of discipline that will ensure such a social structure.

Throughout *Home,* Sedgwick employs conventional early- and mid-century conceptions of childhood gender, and her strict difference-based construction in the Barclay family replays a familiar binary about boys and girls, such as Abbott's "coarse boys" and "sensitive . . . girls." Speaking of the Barclays' grandfather, for example, the narrator says that "he had but two children, the one a worthless son, and the other a girl, a most dutiful and gentle creature" (2). Sedgwick wants to make sure that readers do not see her child characters as conventions of fiction that bear little resemblance to actual children, so she has a character voice her preference for "stories of real live children,—real,—not book children," implying that her characters are fully representative of such "real children," though they fully conform to fictional stereotypes of good girls and bad boys (59). When the text moves from recounting the Barclays' history to the narrative present, it begins with an examination of the children and their nature that is immediately followed by a scene of misbehavior. The children are the "hopeless" Wallace and the "affectionate" Haddy, and Sedgwick's terms for girls—"dutiful," "gentle" and "affectionate"—follow Cobb's and Alcott's characterizations. At first, Wallace's brother, Charles, would seem to complicate the binary. Unlike Wallace and like Haddy, he is patient, helps his grandmother with her knitting, and always behaves. Yet Sedgwick stresses that he is "*unboyish*" because of these behaviors (16; emphasis in original).[30] He represents an exception that, like Cobb's "delicate" boys, proves the rule that "boyish" boys—that is to say, most boys—lack the sensibility of girls. Sedgwick does not think that such boys are ultimately "hopeless" or that all boys are necessarily bad, but only that boys will present a major challenge to family government.

Angry that his sister Haddy has cut a hole in his new kite to make a ruff for her kitten, Wallace grabs the cat and throws it into a tub of hot water. His father responds quickly: "Wallace stood pale and trembling. . . . The children saw the frown on their father's face, more dreaded by them than ever was flogging, or dark closet with all its hobgoblins" (17). Implicitly invoking aspects of the boy-as-savage trope, the father says, "Go to your own room, Wallace, you have forfeited your right to a place among us. Creatures who are the slaves of their passions, are, like beasts of prey, fit only for solitude" (17). Though he is not locked in a dark closet, Wallace's punishment is extremely harsh: he spends two weeks in full isolation, unable to talk to or eat with any family member. In her commentary on Wallace's penalty, Sedgwick positions herself as a pure moral suasionist, completely against physical chastisement; like Mr. Barclay, her surrogate in *Home,* she

> held whipping, and all such summary modes of punishment, on a par with such nostrums in medicine as peppermint and lavender, which suspend the manifestation of the disease, without conducing the cure.... [T]he only effectual and lasting government ... is *self*-government. (26–27; emphasis in original)

Yet, surprisingly, Sedgwick never has the Barclays use moral suasion on Wallace—no attempt is made to address his reason or affection. The lack of such approaches, while inconsistent with Sedgwick's claim to advocate suasion, is consistent with how the father describes Wallace as a "beast" and a "creature who is the slave of his passions." It is unlikely that readers would expect reason or affection to be effective in the case of such a nature. The narrator says "A happy combination for children is there in an uncompromising father and an all-hoping mother" (18). But it is the father's "uncompromising" beliefs that are enforced.

After two weeks, Wallace rejoins the family. Yet it is not penance at the end of his isolation but rather self-inflicted wounds that serve for Sedgwick as the sign that he has been properly disciplined. When harassed by another schoolboy, Wallace wants to hit him, but refrains. As he later tells his father, "I thought just in time. There was a horrid choking feeling in my throat ... but I did not even say, 'Blame you.' I had to bite my lips, though, so that the blood ran" (22). In effect, Wallace performs a kind of corporal punishment upon himself. Although not hit, his blood flows. Like Cobb's practice of forcing angry or misbehaving boys to eat a snowball or to "sweat ... profusely" (156), Mr. Barclay's discipline, though Sedgwick and many others would not think of it as such, is physical discipline—as Alcott would say, pain can be used "when it is necessary to reach the mind and put thoughts into it" (44).

In an essay on Louisa May Alcott's endorsement of childhood fights as displaced corporal punishment, Michael Moon notes that "liberal theorists of childhood discipline made concerted efforts to repress the fact that their supposedly innovative theory and practice were rooted in violence against the physically less powerful child" (213). In other words, like Sedgwick, they found ways of getting children to do their corporal punishment for them. The advocacy of fighting as a form of corporal punishment, for example, was widespread. Addressing its boy readers, the "Benefit of Hard Knocks" in the *Youth's Companion* (1867) says that "a boy who is sent to a large school soon finds his level.... [H]e is sure to be thrashed into a recognition of the golden rule." "It is a good thing for youths to be knocked about in the world," the writer concludes: "it makes *men* of them" (7). The author connects the need for such violence to the narcissistic nature of boys: "if not all [boys], certainly nineteen-twentieths of the sum total enter life with a surplusage [*sic*] of self-conceit. The sooner they are relieved of it the better" (7). Like this form of corporal punishment and Cobb's ostensible alternatives to corporal punishment, Sedgwick's substitute for the lash is nevertheless physical correction. She presents herself as an opponent of whipping and the rod, yet she endorses corporal discipline; self-government here does not involve appeals to reason or love, but rather physical punishment. The mark of this self-directed violence is the bloody sign to his father that Wallace has been disciplined. Upon hearing of the blood he exclaims, "God bless you, my son" (22).

Home was referred to in educational journals and Wallace's punishment in particular was cited as an effective method of discipline, and such a scene would likely not have been accepted by readers if the "affectionate" Haddy or the "*unboyish*" Charles been in Wallace's place. The novel relies on a readership predisposed to believe in the moral deficiencies of boys. Sedgwick sets up Wallace's punishment with a theory of the distinctions between boys and girls, one that replays Cobb's, Abbott's, and Alcott's understanding of children and gender difference. For Sedgwick's readers, Wallace's behavior represents typical boy behavior, and so his punishment represents an appropriate response. This fictional scene's ability to embody boyhood discipline to contemporary audiences places it among the more important texts—fictional and otherwise—of the corporal punishment reform movement. The fact that this incident replays the violence against the boy body that is so crucial to the other works we have looked at shows that, despite what reformers often said, they strongly believed in physical correction as a means of disciplining boys.

Morrill Wyman and the "Unreasoning" Boy

That dreadful being—a boy.
—"Against Boys"

There also might have been some society, or some law, for the prevention of cruelty to school-boys.
—"My School-Boy Days"

In the mid-1860s doctor and teacher Morrill Wyman led a movement to reform corporal punishment in Cambridge, Massachusetts, schools. Wyman was convinced that he had the sanction of the public, for the campaign was endorsed by the citizens five to one. "A more deliberate vote could not have been taken," he proclaims; "the whipping of girls is 'shocking to the community'" (16). He also circulated a petition that had among its signatories James Russell Lowell, Henry Wadsworth Longfellow, and current and former presidents of Harvard. Like Cobb and many antebellum educators and reformers, Wyman and his followers were concerned only with shielding girls from the ferule or the whip: "let the experiment be tried of abolishing the rule authorizing corporal punishment, at least as far as girls are concerned" (48). "With regard to boys," however, he argues that "such reserved force may be desirable and necessary" (44), echoing a phrase that Alcott uses in the *Record* when he says that hitting boys is often "necessary and desirable" (3). Wyman notes with satisfaction that corporal punishment is no longer practiced in the navy, merchant marines, prisons, or reform houses, and that husbands can no longer hit their wives, nor masters their apprentices. Even the worst case in an insane asylum does not need it: "Certainly, if an unreasoning lunatic can be governed without whips, they can be dispensed with in the case of a reasoning girl" (6). But whips, switches, rulers, and rods cannot be dispensed with in the case of boys, who apparently—and inexplicably—represent a disciplinary problem more challenging than that of an "unreasoning lunatic." Wyman makes the boy the sole possible recipient of corporal punishment, the only figure beyond the reach of affective discipline and persuasion.

The "*distinction of sex,*" as Wyman calls it, like Mann's "differences . . . which individualize the sexes" is the critical factor in discipline, and Wyman is specific about what this distinction entails and its origin in sentimental ideology (37; emphasis in original):

> Why should not girls be treated as boys? Because girls are not boys. Every parent having children of both sexes, knows that they have moral characteristics which at once distinguish them. . . . They are . . . more sensitive in feeling . . . [have a] delicate sense of propriety . . . , [are] gentle, docile, confiding, and affectionate . . . [and have a] woman's refined sensibilities. (32–33)

For Wyman, moral suasion will always be an effective discipline for girls, because as "reasoning," "moral," and "affectionate," they will respond to appeals based upon those traits. Wyman's "distinction of sex" closely follows beliefs about gender held by writers like Mann, Abbott, Cobb, Alcott, and Sedgwick. Though Wyman writes after these educators, he can serve as the most concise spokesman for antebellum reformers on children and punishment: "Why should not girls be treated as boys? Because they are not boys." Difference determines discipline. Like the others, he certainly believed that boys could be reformed. But many educators believed, as Wyman did, that corporal punishment was an effective tool in bringing about a change in boy-nature, a tactic they were decidedly unwilling to remove from the disciplinary arsenal.

From Jacob Abbott's *Rollo's Philosophy: Water*, 1842.

Chapter 3

"The Medicine of Sympathy"

Mothers, Sons, and Affective Pedagogy in Antebellum America

> It is important that the son be as much as possible with the mother.
> —"Training of Boys II"

> Good mothers alone make good men.
> —E. N. Kirk

> A boy . . . does not readily find the medicine of sympathy.
> —Lydia Sigourney

As we saw in the last chapter, debates about discipline often centered on the respective merits of two approaches: corporal punishment and moral suasion. Many educators argued that physical discipline was particularly effective with boys because hitting a boy was speaking to him in a language he could understand: that of the body. The success of moral suasion, however, was not so assured. It could work only if both participants in a domestic disciplinary encounter—typically the mother and her child—possessed the ability to sympathize with each other. If one couldn't "feel" for the other, then persuasion was impossible. The omnipresent antebellum image of the mother as a "fountain of sympathy" should have been reassuring to those interested in affective pedagogy. But many maternal advice writers challenged this belief about maternal affect; they were eager to show that the "all-sympathizing" mother was a sentimental fiction, arguing that mothers often needed the most basic of instructions on how to generate and perform sympathy in the management of children.[1] Antebellum writings on the mother-son bond expose a fear about the consequences of boys' nature, for if boys were "mischievous," "troubled," and motivated only by self-gratification, how could maternal sympathy—which relies on the moral nature of both the authority and her charge—be effective in managing them? As Foucault observed, the celebration of sympathy has been central to a discipline based upon "the affective intensification of the family space" (*Discipline* 109). It is easy to see, then, why domestic advice writers would be concerned, for they argued that the mother-son relationship was the affective familial bond most crucial to domestic and national stability.

Critics often discuss the mother-child relationship without making the kinds of distinctions between male and female children made by many antebellum women writers. These authors saw the category of "the child" as complicated by gender and they revised sentimental conventions about the natures of mothers and of children. Like corporal punishment theorists, they discussed crucial differences between the affective capacities of boys and of girls, noting that such distinctions were essential to mothers' approaches to discipline, even in ways that many mothers did not recognize.[2] Among the numerous texts I explore, the writings of Harriet Beecher Stowe and Lydia Sigourney perhaps best represent this revision. Stowe's *Uncle Tom's Cabin* (1852), which in many ways exemplifies the dominant form of antebellum sentimentalism in its celebration of the efficacy of domestic affect and motherhood, narrates the failure of maternal sympathy as a tool for managing boys. Possibly the period's most dramatic commentary on the limits of sympathy, the novel features two idealized sentimental mothers who raise the text's two most troubled sons. Like *Uncle Tom's Cabin,* Sigourney's *Letters to Mothers* praises "mother love" as a powerful and redemptive social force, yet she shows it to be a fiction that bears little if any connection to the presence (or absence) of pedagogical sympathy within boyhood management. She believes that when a son is the disciplinary object, most mothers simply do not act in accord with the convention of the "all-sympathizing" mother.

Along with their interrogation of ideas about maternal sympathy and boys, Stowe, Sigourney, and the other writers I examine make varied and contradictory claims about the nature of sympathy itself. Some believed it flowed naturally from mothers to all children and was therefore the most accessible and potent form of discipline. Others agreed it was an involuntary response but made an important qualification: it typically manifested itself only within the mother-daughter relationship. Mothers, they claimed, had an inherent tendency to disidentify with boys; given that the nature of boys was so different from that of girls and women, mothers distanced themselves from sons. These writers believed, however, that mothers could learn to generate sympathy, that it could be authentically performed if mothers recognized its disciplinary benefits. Though it might seem paradoxical given the many sentimental depictions of sympathy as natural and involuntary, these authors understood it as a learned, rational response to the problems of child management.

When Joanne Dobson said "sentimentalism . . . takes as its highest values sympathy, affection, and relation," she made a familiar association between sympathy and sentimentality, one that sees the former as intrinsically allied to the latter: discourses of sympathy are always about sentimentality because sympathy is the affective force that brings the world into accord with the objectives of sentimental ideology (283). Studies of nineteenth-century culture almost always conceive of sympathy in this way, but I argue that many domestic theorists wanted to sever this association. They endorsed sympathy as a child management tool, while simultaneously revising or even completely dismissing sentimental beliefs about the nature of mothers and sympathy. Critics have said that that culture fully embraced these beliefs (especially during the antebellum period), but the writings I look at undermine this critical position; they represent a widely disseminated approach that competes with sentimental claims in debates about affect and child management. For many writers, sympathy had little or nothing to do with sentimentality.

☞ ☞ ☞

In the eighteenth and early nineteenth centuries, most American theorists of domesticity and childhood pedagogy believed—as John Locke and others had argued—that the father was responsible for his children's moral education. But in the decades before 1850, "the custody of children was transferred . . . officially from male to female," and the theoretical and practical implications of this transfer were developed throughout maternal advice literature, a body of writing instrumental in shaping women's beliefs about motherhood (Ryan, *Empire* 56). Given antebellum domestic ideology's tendency to figure the mother as the locus of familial sentiment, it is not surprising that maternal affective pedagogy—the management of children by appeals to their moral and emotional bonds with the mother—occupies center stage in advice literature's theorizing of affective discipline. Ideas about mothers' sympathy are expressed within this literature in discourses that I call "pragmatic" and "sentimental." Pragmatic discourses typically appear in educational journals and advice writing, and they examine the relationship between white mothers and their children by focusing at length on particular disciplinary approaches. Articles such as "Mothers, Do You Sympathize with Your Children?" (1856), "The Comforts of Playing 'Hookie'" (1856), and "What Is to Be Done with Charley?" (1860) outline the skills that a mother needs to teach her child and suggest numerous forms of motivation and discipline. The five-part epistolary series "Training of Boys" published in 1845 in *The Mother's Journal and Family Visitant*, for example, details the "moral and physical training" of sons; it discusses "boy-nature" and how to create a domestic environment that adapts to this nature and show mothers how to use an affect-based discipline ("Training I" 117).

Perhaps the most popular way of talking about maternal sympathy embodies a mode of thinking about culture that in studies of the nineteenth century has been called "sentimental." Such ideology is visible in the popular lyrical encomiums to "eternal mother love" and the "hallowed" mother-child relationship that often appear in novels, poetry, sketches, and women's magazines. Sentimental discourses tend to be less explicitly instructional than pragmatic ones, and they always celebrate the mother's capacity to generate sympathy and govern children with it: "What a fountain of love is a mother's heart," an author in *The Mother's Magazine* writes in language typical of sentimental discourse, "and how it pours out its streams upon her offspring . . . how tender her sympathy in his misfortune" ("A Mother's Love" 115).[3] The ability to sympathize is seen, like mother love itself, as "unquenchable" and inherent to women. The author of an essay in *Godey's Lady's Book* entitled "The Mother's Love" refers to this love as an "instinct . . . that we have no power to control or subdue," which "imbibes the mind with equal tenderness for her infirm child . . . as for him who gives early promise of personal as well as mental beauty" (Ellis 163). These writers felt that mothers were equally likely to sympathize with healthy or sick children and with sons or daughters.

I am not setting up sentimental and pragmatic discourses as opposites; rather, I am saying that they approach the mother-child relationship at different levels of specificity and are typically in conflict in ways that are revealing. Writers of these discourses often—but not always—want the same outcome: for mothers to sympathize with sons. Both discourses on the management of girls propose that mothers naturally felt affection for daughters and that a discipline based on sympathetic identification would therefore be the most successful method. Indeed, as many critical examinations of female bonds have shown, antebellum culture expected that women and girls would "establish positive affective relationships."[4] "The entire lifeworld of middle-class daughters," historian Nancy Theriot notes, "encouraged intense identification between mother and daughter" (63). "The identification of women with the heart" meant that women and girls were defined "in relationship to other persons" and that the ability to sympathize would likely be directed at those most capable of offering sympathy in return (Cott 165).[5] As many scholars have also noted, children's texts of the period endorse this notion of girls' nature by encouraging girls to be motivated through "affiliation" and boys by "achievement" (Cott 72).[6] The affective, other-directed nature of women and girls mandated that they use their heart-sanctioned moral superiority to influence men and boys because, as one woman exclaimed, "[W]hat a savage creature would man be without the meliorating offices of the gentle sex!" (cited in Cott 163). Of course, most advice writers hoped that mothers would develop a strong connection with their sons. Yet, as Theriot observes, because of the widespread belief "that the sexes were so different from each other," many girls and women worried that close bonds between members of the opposite sex "were rare" (79). Elizabeth Barnes has noted that the production of sympathy depended upon a "recognition of likeness" (*States* 92), and many writers argued that mothers believed they were fundamentally different from their sons, a difference that precluded identification.

Though sentimental and pragmatic discourses typically agree about mothers' inherent ability to sympathize with daughters, in theories of boyhood management, these two discourses are often completely at odds. Mary Ryan suggests that "the sexes intersected in such a way as to create, at the level of ideology at least, a tight knot between mother and son" (*Empire* 58–59), but pragmatic ideology insists the opposite was true. The mother-son bond is almost always figured as the most unstable family structure. Pragmatic writers offer two distinct objections to sentimental discourse: some claim that mothers are inherently unsympathetic with boys yet can learn to use sympathy when managing them, while others argue that the use of sympathy with boys is at best ineffective (boy-nature is such that they can't respond to it) and at worst dangerous (boys will manipulate it to avoid punishment).[7] While pragmatic discourses occasionally portray a mother as unsympathetic toward her daughter, they almost never suggest that mothers possess a natural tendency to be so.

Paula Bennett has said that the second half of the century witnessed "profound changes [in] women's self-construction" that revised the "sentimental discourse" of writers including Sigourney (592).[8] As I show, however, Sigourney and many other pragmatic authors constantly critique and reimagine popular definitions of women and sentiment, especially those about mothers and sympathy, even during the antebellum period. Although "the boy" was celebrated in sentimental sketches and poems (as "the child" and "the girl" were), in educational discourses (as we saw in chapter 2) boys were repeatedly characterized as "mischievous," "troubled," and "depraved." Sympathy, as David Marshall notes, depends on one's "capacity to feels the sentiments of someone else," thus making the narcissistic and materialistic boy inherently a troubled category (3). The anecdotes of misbehaving boys that appear in advice literature rarely depict them producing shame, contrition, or tears—emotional responses that figure a child as capable of acknowledging a breach of familial bonds and her own moral negligence. And it should be noted that while many of the authors explored in this chapter echo the widespread negative attitudes about boys and boy-nature seen in chapter 2, other authors do not.

In "Mothers, Do You Sympathize with Your Children?" a piece in a popular 1856 collection *The Mother's Rule,* a boy misbehaves in ways typically associated with the limited emotional range of boys: he "has an irritable temper. A trifle would make him angry, and then would come an outburst of passion" (127). Like an animal, the boy is easily triggered and has difficulty recognizing that his own desires should be subordinated to the desires of others and the needs of family order. Another essay in this collection contrasts the mothers of the two discourses and connects their ability to sympathize to their notion of boy-nature. The mother of the sentimental imagination—"the ever-youthful mother . . . whose heart is ever ready with its hearty, warm, abundant sympathy"—is set against the kind of mother often found in pragmatic discourses, one who cannot identify with boys" ("The Bright Side" 196). Echoing the notion of gender difference endorsed by the woman who believed men and boys would be "savage creature[s] . . . without the meliorating offices of the gentle sex," she exclaims that "*All* boys [are] noisy savages" and "are, as a matter of course, to be snubbed, and stinted, and *put down!*" (196; emphasis in original). It is important to note that the only generalization about gender that she makes involves boys; although the mother says some girls are "frivolous," she emphatically states, "*All* boys are noisy savages," simplifying boys' emotions in order to justify her disciplinary "course." Her ideas about girl-nature do not lead to a discussion of any discipline that might result from these traits, whereas her beliefs about boys are connected to an endorsement of repression: since boys can't respond to maternal sympathy, they need to be "snubbed . . . and put down!"

Though the harshness of this mother places her on the extreme end of bad mothering as found within pragmatic discourses, she nevertheless represents one of its central tenets, a belief found throughout antebellum culture: mothers often fail to sympathize with boys because they believe boys, like savages, are either devoid of morality or possess a sympathetic nature far less developed than in girls.[9] While nineteenth-century adult males are often characterized by their capacity for reason, this was decidedly not the case with boys, for boyhood was a distinct stage. The boy was not yet a man, but he was also no longer the generic sentimental "child"; he had entered boyhood, becoming unreachable through emotional bonds, and therefore a chronic problem for maternal affective pedagogy.

Laura Wexler has argued that any "enlargement by sentimentality of the percentage of the population who can come 'inside' the magic circle of domesticity still leaves behind the vast numbers who cannot qualify for entry under moral standards" (17). And it was precisely on the grounds of such standards that some argued boys could not always participate in a domesticity created by sentiment—boys had a limited capacity to reproduce in themselves the emotions of others. Wexler sees forms of sentiment as allied with the project to acculturate "savages," yet she doesn't note that antebellum boys were often described as "savage" in pedagogical theory, a popular trope that, as we have seen, had implications for boys' discipline and acculturation. Though the treatment of white boys was far removed from that of marginalized nonwhite groups, the metaphor suggests a kind of cultural stigma attached to boys that was similar to one often attached to Native Americans. As I noted in the last chapter, scholars who discuss this metaphor cite its use by post–Civil War male authors as a way to celebrate the boy, yet such examples do not represent antebellum uses. Brown and Kidd are certainly correct that the late century believed "savagery was often a less pejorative concept than we might assume" (Kidd, "Boyology" 63), yet antebellum educators and mother's advice writers had a different agenda when they used the metaphor. They repeatedly invoked it to justify corporal punishment for boys and to explain why boys could be immune to affective appeals. In the "Training of Boys" series the author worries that readers might find the very discussion of sympathy "incongruous with my general subject" of managing male children, an understandable concern given that boys' discipline was often identified not with "moral suasion" but with corporal punishment ("Training IV" 164).

While I am not equating the social status of boys and Native Americans, I am suggesting that the parallel between them is meaningful to women's advice authors. For many, this nature means that boys' participation in "the family circle" is a complicated question in a way that girls' involvement is not. They want to see that mothers, to adapt Stowe's famous words, "felt right" about boys in the ways that Stowe and others wanted them to feel right about slaves or other marginalized figures such as asylum patients, Native Americans, or prisoners, all of whom are not part of the world of white middle-class authors. When the figure is a boy, who, as a future man, appears to be the least marginalized figure in antebellum culture, the parameters that often define domesticity and what it excludes—such as race or class—disappear. The ostensible goal of affect-producing narratives such as *Uncle Tom's Cabin* and Sedgwick's *Hope Leslie* was to humanize others and present them as objects worthy of white sympathy and a place in American public life. Similarly, boys were characterized by pragmatic writers as both central and liminal figures—both within and yet somehow at the edge of domestic life—and often unfairly cut off from mothers' sympathy and alienated from home, a separation that only sympathy could undo.[10]

Many advice writers understood this alienation as a problem, and this belief about boyhood and domesticity challenges the critical view represented by Rotundo. The physical and ideological exile of boys from women's spaces and women's sympathy, he says, was solely intended for boys' and society's benefit.

They were left alone to explore "boy culture," a carefully constructed masculine world outside of, and antithetical to, the domestic "circle," a masculine world whose rules prepared boys for a place in public life and for the competition of the market (337). Rotundo and many scholars cite the relationship between boys and maternal authorities visible in Huck Finn's and Tom Sawyer's desire to escape the "sivilizing" influence of women as representative of the relationship between boyhood and the domestic endorsed by authors and educators throughout the century. Yet mothers' journal writers often criticize genteel culture for sometimes banishing boys to "the streets, that mamma and sisters might play on the piano and write letters in peace" ("What Is to Be Done" 15). In "Look at the Results" (1843) the author argues that not only do many mothers and sisters attempt to exclude boys from their sanctioned place in domestic life, but that every family member can follow suit by displaying "a want of *consideration*" when dealing with boys (56; emphasis in original). She tells an anecdote about the mistreatment that boys often suffer: immediately upon entering his house, a dirty and disheveled boy is chastised by the servant and his sister, threatened with a whipping by his mother, and scolded by his father. The author, who claims to have observed this scene, lectures mothers on how to be affectionate to neglected boys and "win [their] kind feelings" (58). The debate about discipline represented by the conflict between the views of this author and the family she discusses shows that antebellum beliefs about boyhood masculinity are a contested site within, not outside of, domestic spaces and theory; rather than always celebrating boys, they express contradictory and often condemnatory ideas about them.

Lydia Sigourney was deeply interested in boys and showed more concern for them than did many educators and authors, and her *Letters to Mothers* (1838) was one of the most popular of the numerous antebellum maternal advice books to counsel its readers about boyhood management and sympathy. In the opening of Letter XI, "Idiom of Character," it appears as if Sigourney is going to construct an individualized, gender-neutral disciplinary theory, one aware of the "different dispositions of each subject" (118). It soon becomes clear, however, that her theory is based on "the barrier which an Unerring Hand erected between" the natures of both boys and girls and on a key belief about maternal nature: mothers have difficulty providing "affectionate mother[ing]" to boys (121). Sigourney cites a poem that evinces a typical characterization of boy-nature and its uneasy relationship to maternal discipline:

> boys are driven
> To wild pursuits, by mighty impulses.
> Out of a mother's anxious hands they tear
> The leading-strings. (122)

Although the word *savage* is not mentioned, her language invokes the content of the trope. Like the savage, the "wild" boy is not controlled by reason; instead he is "driven . . . by mighty impulses," and his actions tend toward expressions of violence, as he "tear[s] / The leading-strings." Because of this aggressive and physical nature, "in the discipline of sons," she warns, "mothers need a double portion of the wisdom that is from above" (121). This stands in stark contrast to the way Sigourney figures mothers and daughters, repeatedly saying that their sympathetic relationship flows from female nature itself and is reinforced by participation in activities that take sympathy as the primary subject: together they "visit the aged, go on errands of mercy . . . [and] sit by the side of the sufferer" (120). With girls, sympathy comes naturally, but with boys, it must be calculated. The mother needs to train herself how to "keep hold on his affections" by demonstrating affection for him herself (123).

In pragmatic writing like Sigourney's, then, sympathy becomes denaturalized. It doesn't arise spontaneously from the mother as sentimental discourse claimed; rather it must be learned or unlearned and consciously employed or rejected. The "Training of Boys" reveals a deep anxiety about sympathy that is not immediately apparent in the writings of Sigourney and others, an anxiety that reflects sympathy's intense valorization throughout antebellum culture. Something that can be so transformative, so powerful a means of control, could if misapplied be destructive; although sympathy could have a "salutary influence . . . on boys" ("Training IV" 164), but "even this best principle," the author warns, can "degenerate into a morbid tenderness, subversive of the best interests" of boyhood discipline ("Training III" 148). Calculating the proper amount of sympathy to use on a boy was the mother's difficult task, one that presented numerous problems as the mother struggled to find the precise mean between a "morbid tenderness" and a "cold and distant manner" (148). When a sentimentalized sympathy produces too great an identification with the disciplinary object, it fails to fulfill its promise to curb the excesses associated with the savagery of boyhood masculinity, becoming the "false tenderness" that "is the fruitful source of very much of the misrule . . . unsubdued passions . . . which stalk abroad unabashed at the present day" (149).

Like the pragmatic writers discussed earlier, authors skeptical of using sympathy with boys also criticize sentimental beliefs about mothers and children. They do not argue, however, that mothers lack sympathy, but that the sympathy that comes naturally to them represents a threat to proper management; the sympathizing mother would likely be too quick to empathize with the child and so be lax in her application of discipline. For these writers, sympathy is an unreliable emotion that can negate discipline. An essay that dramatizes this concern is "The Comforts of Playing 'Hookie,'" which appeared in *The Mother's*

Magazine for Daughters and Mothers. To provoke an emotional response in readers accustomed to images of bodies in pain, it begins with a picture of a "poor" suffering boy followed by a series of questions interrogating the reader's reaction to the image. The first question asks, "Have you any sympathy with this poor boy?" and worried that readers might answer yes, the author quickly undermines any identification by showing it to be dangerous (91). The boy has skipped school and, though he shivers in the cold, does not deserve any mother's sympathy. The author talks to the boy, modeling the way that mothers should manage misbehaving sons and warning them that boys can and frequently do manipulate maternal affect. Questioning the authenticity of the boy's "sorry looks," she views them as a performance for mothers; his appearance of suffering and remorse seems to be an index of genuine contrition but is marked as false, just as to respond to it would be "false tenderness." For her, the sole sign of repentance would be for the boy to "run home [and] take a whipping" and not to hope that his performance will moderate or eliminate the stern discipline that he deserves (92). The author of "Training of Boys" sees only excessive sympathy as a "morbid tenderness" that could impede discipline, yet this author views even the slightest amount of sympathy with the disciplinary object as harmful. She rejects any affect-based discipline for boys.

Not only is corporal punishment endorsed in "The Comforts of Playing 'Hookie,'" but more important, it is coupled with the denial of sympathy, a disciplinary tactic the mother in "The Bright Side" implies is foremost in her arsenal when she recommends "snubbing" boys. Whereas affective pedagogy was supposed to situate the disciplinary object within familial bonds as a way to control him, here the denial of sympathy becomes a form of discipline. Tellingly, this piece appears in a section of the journal called "The Family Circle," a recurring feature that often dramatized principles of domestic discipline by offering anecdotes of family life. For this author and many others we have explored, the boy's participation in the family circle is a vexed issue, and the withholding of sympathy essentially bans him from affective domesticity. She believes that the boy's "sorry looks" expose a weakness in the claims of those who endorse affective discipline; if mothers can't distinguish between a boy's real and performed suffering—and boys were often described as "deceitful"—then affective discipline cannot succeed. Boy-nature is more powerful in its ability to deceive than maternal sympathy is in its capacity to govern.

As a writer acutely aware of the connection between sentiment and suffering bodies like the one in "Comforts," Catharine Sedgwick understood the effect that such an image could have on readers. Elizabeth Barnes has noted that nineteenth-century readers were trained "to put themselves in the character's position in order to experience the full effects of the punishment meted out," and Sedgwick worries that the opening scene of punishment in her novel *Home* could trigger exactly this kind of identification between maternal reader and disciplined boy character (608). In the last chapter, I discussed this scene as one of corporal punishment, and it is worth returning to it here briefly to see how it comments on the relationship between maternal affect and boys. Unlike the author of "Comforts," Sedgwick is not concerned that boys will manipulate maternal sympathy, but rather that such sentiment will compromise punishment. She fears, as does the author of "Comforts," that her readers might empathize with Wallace Barclay because of the stern discipline that his father orders. So she quickly counsels them to think of him not as a child, but as a body infected with "moral consumption" (17). This rhetorical move depersonalizes Wallace, reducing him, as other writers reduced boys, to a complex of urges and desires unmediated by a moral sense ("driven by mighty impulses," as Sigourney's poem described them). Thus she attempts to diminish, if not completely erase, the possibility of identification with him.

Sedgwick wants readers to agree that stern punishment is inarguably the correct treatment for this body's disease and therefore should be administered quickly and without reservation—and repeated by mothers when dealing with their sons. During his two weeks of disciplinary isolation, Wallace is not allowed to talk to any family member, a punishment difficult to imagine Sedgwick advocating for girls, whom she describes, in terms familiar from sentimental ideology, as "gentle" and "compassionate." Sedgwick's endorsement of isolation recalls Cobb's belief in boyhood itself as a kind of contagion, for which he also recommends separation: in boyhood "many boys . . . are not, at that time, suitable company." The harshness of Sedgwick's treatment of Wallace suggests not only the value she places in swift and stern punishment, but more importantly it displays her opposition to the sympathetic disciplining of boys, an opposition rooted in widespread beliefs about boys as emotionally coarse and not always worthy of experiencing the social bonds and communal activities that define domestic life. And Sedgwick calls the only consistently kind boy in the novel "*unboyish*," fully severing any connection between boys and sympathy. When Sigourney laments that "a boy . . . does not readily find the medicine of sympathy" and another writer worries that boys " do not find sympathy" ("Training of Boys V" 181), perhaps they are thinking of the unsympathetic pedagogy of advice writers like Sedgwick.

☙ ☙ ☙

No matter what approach writers take to questions of maternal sympathy and boyhood discipline, they justify their position by discussing what they believe to be the domestic and national benefits. Boys are at the center of these debates because they are the future patriarchs, and affective discipline could generate in them the moral sentiment they lacked and would need as men. As essays in mothers' magazines and advice books repeatedly remind readers, "good mothers alone make *good men*" (Kirk 167; emphasis in original). The belief that only mothers possess the ability to create moral sons serves as the moral to nearly every discourse about maternal sympathy and the mother-son bond, such as "A Mother's Love," a short piece in *The Mother's Magazine* that celebrates the capacity of the maternal "affection" a boy experiences when young to discipline him when he assumes "the duties of manhood" (4).[11] John Abbott sums up the power of the mother-son bond by citing the damage caused when it is severed: "when a son leaves home, and enters upon the bustling world, many are the temptations which come crowding upon him. If he leaves his mother . . . he will most assuredly fall before these temptations" (*The Mother at Home* 15). "On the Preparation of Young Men for the Perils of Our Cities" in *The Mother's Magazine* (1841) suggests to mothers that the sympathetic management of boys will assure that when they leave home they do not participate in the "vice" that "is beginning to stalk unabashed" (10). Interestingly, the author invokes the association between boys and savagery: "Kindness has tamed the most savage animals" and "is wonderfully effective" with boys (11). The heart and mind of a boy who is thus managed, she notes, will not be "vitiated . . . by [the] baleful circumstances" he will encounter in America's urban spaces (11). Indeed, these writers believe that maternal sympathy is the most powerful of all familial pedagogical tools, an always present antidote to the powerful forces that threaten domestic order.

But if maternal sympathy can produce such powerful, lasting results, its absence can be equally profound. "The mother," Catharine Beecher warns in *A Treatise on Domestic Economy* (1842), "forms the character of the future man . . . for good or evil" (67), and Sigourney likewise proposes that bad mothers are responsible for bad men, such as Benedict Arnold, and good mothers for good men, such as George Washington. The writer who called excessive sympathy a "morbid affection" thought it dangerous precisely because its use would sanction "improper conduct" and eventually lead to "bloody duel[s] and cruel murder[s]" ("Training IV" 166). In "What Is to Be Done with Charley?" an article in the *Mother's Magazine and Family Circle* (1860), the author tells mothers to guarantee their "Charley" a domestic space of his own in order to avoid such outcomes. In this piece, as we have observed in other maternal advice writing, the alienation of boys from the domestic circle is depicted with alarmist rhetoric about the resulting violence. Boy-nature was such that, if not governed within the confines of the affective family, a boy—and by extension his social world—would simply be "doomed" (16). Criticizing the kind of nonaffective mothering endorsed by bad mothers like the one in "The Bright Side," the author argues that "many a hard morose, bitter man has come from a Charley turned off and neglected, and many a personal heartache has come from a Charley left to run the streets," a heartache that only sympathetic mothering could prevent (15). Mother's advice writers typically believed that when the maternal bond with a boy was strengthened and sympathy productively employed, the possibility of raising a bad son was eliminated—a right-feeling mother would always raise a right-acting son. A strong sympathetic bond, they argued, could always counteract the outside forces that threatened his development. As one man wrote: "I feel I owe it . . . to a pious mother who . . . like a guardian angel hovers over my heart to restrain me from evil" (cited in Lewis 64).

Yet the most popular novel of the period makes a case that complicates both sentimental and pragmatic claims about the effectiveness of maternal sympathy. Harriet Beecher Stowe's *Uncle Tom's Cabin* argues that even a pious mother who embodies sentiment offers no guarantee of producing a morally upright son. The son of such a mother is the novel's, and perhaps the period's, greatest villain. Stowe recognizes that white male power, ambition, cruelty, and callousness bring into being the kind of material and moral conditions necessary for slavery, and *Uncle Tom's Cabin* everywhere critiques these forces and depicts their damaging effects. She nevertheless gives the crucial role to mothers and their pedagogy. In the final chapter, "Concluding Remarks," she says that if they "had all felt as they should . . . [their] sons . . . would not have been the [slave] holders" (624). It is not only that mothers needed to feel right, but as domestic theorists often said, that the affective bond mothers created with their sons would model the way a boy should feel about others. Yet the boyhood narratives of *Uncle Tom's Cabin*'s two most prominent slave owners—Augustine St. Clare and Simon Legree—show that even perfect mothers, those capable of immense sympathy with slaves and sons, can fail. Part of the power and horror of Stowe's examination of motherhood is that the text's most intelligent and demonic slave owners have its most idealized mothers.[12]

Stowe's characterization of St. Clare's mother evinces what Eva Cherniavsky has called "essential motherhood," the ideology of sentimental writings about the mother. "*She* was *divine!*" St. Clare exclaims, and "as far as I could ever observe there was not a trace of any human weakness or error about her . . . [and everybody] say[s] the same" (333; emphasis in original). St. Clare's mother was an "angel," "a direct embodiment and personification of the New Testament—a living fact . . . to be accounted for in no other way than by its truth" (333). Stowe wants readers to understand a crucial point: this mother is not the cultural fiction of sentimental maternal encomiums, but a "living fact," a literal and true realization of the loving, sympathizing mother.

St. Clare's relationship with his mother replays the close affective tie that many advice writers believed could be so effective in managing boys, and the bond between them was reproduced in their bond with their slaves: they "formed a committee for a redress of grievances" and tried to ease the abuse of slaves by St. Clare's father's cruel overseer (336). While they were occasionally successful, his father, an aristocrat with "no human sympathies beyond a certain line in society," eventually asserted his patriarchal right to determine how the slaves would be treated (335). And St. Clare's twin brother, Alfred, followed the father's beliefs and felt "no possible sympathy" with his brother or with the family's slaves (334). Stowe notes that, as twins, the brothers "ought to resemble each other" (334), but this again points to her recognition that mothers do not have the authority that sentimental discourse—and even Stowe herself—often ascribes to them.

In spite of this flawless mother, St. Clare—perhaps Stowe's most eloquent critic of slavery—becomes complicit in its operation. Though his mother has the primary responsibility for his moral development into his late boyhood, she ultimately is unable to see that he truly "feels right" about slavery. Here the ideal mother leaves unfulfilled the promise offered by the sentimental discourses that created and celebrated her: the promise that she would raise a moral son. St. Clare offers a compelling critique of the period's beliefs about maternal training, one that contradicts Stowe's claims in the "Concluding Remarks" but accords with the story Stowe creates for the brothers:

> What remained for her but to train her children in her own views and sentiments? Well, after all you say about training, children will grow up substantially what they are by nature, and only that. From the cradle, Alfred was an aristocrat; and as he grew up, instinctively, all his sympathies and all his reasonings [*sic*] were in that line, and all mother's exhortations went to the winds. (337)

Nature, class, and male influence supersede maternal sympathy.

Stowe's most compelling portrait of a mother and son and her strongest revision of sentimental claims are visible in the relationship between Legree and his "gentle" mother. Stowe describes Legree's boyhood mothering as similar to St. Clare's: he was raised "with prayers and pious hymns. . . . Far in New England that woman had trained her only son, with long, unwearied love" (528). Yet Legree, like St. Clare, follows the trajectory of his cold, unfeeling father, upon whom his mother "had wasted a world of unvalued love" (528). Despite his mother's training, the "magic of the real presence of distress" that transforms Stowe's Senator Bird as he witnesses the suffering of the fugitive slave, Eliza, is lost on Legree (156). He eventually rejects his mother and is never reconciled with her. Although she is dead, her powerful presence is still with him; but instead of providing the lifelong moral guidance that advice authors claimed this presence would, the "angel" of sentimental discourse becomes a ghost, an echo of unrealized maternal power, who haunts Legree as well as the discourse that created it, "turn[ing] things sweetest and holiest to phantoms of horror and affright" (529). Legree is tormented by his rejection of his mother, imagining a "pale mother rising by his bedside" in retribution (529).[13]

Stowe provides these two male characters with a history that details their boyhood bonds with their mothers, and she is a sentimentalist insofar as she celebrates "essential motherhood" and argues for the social benefits that follow from proper maternal bonding with sons. Critics have rightly noted that Stowe's text valorizes mothers and their power to effect change, and the novel has many examples of strong motherhood; Mrs. Shelby, Rachel Halliday, Aunt Chloe, Mrs. Bird, and others influence husbands and sons, "rul[ing] more . . . by persuasion than command" (143). Mrs. Shelby, who is never described in the sentimentalized language used for Legree's and St. Clares's mothers, is able to raise a model son, George, whose final act in the novel is to free his slaves. Yet when presented with antebellum culture's ultimate challenge of raising abolitionist sons, Stowe's ideal mothers (Legree's and St. Clare's)—the ones who should be the most effective according to Stowe's and the culture's sentimental discourse—are surprisingly ineffective. While readers—and mothers in particular—would probably have been appalled by St. Clare's cynicism and horrified by Legree's cruelty to his slaves and his rejection of his perfect white mother, they certainly might have been terrified by Stowe's two portraits of sentimentalized yet ineffectual motherhood. Stowe's dramatization of the powerlessness of maternal sentiment reminds us that, as Glenn Hendler has argued, questions of sympathetic identification were complicated by authors throughout the century ("Limits" 694).[14] In *Uncle Tom's Cabin*, the power of maternal affective pedagogy is fully undermined by the corrupting influence of the "peculiar institution."

Although Stowe believes that these mothers are, as St. Clare notes, without "a trace of any human weakness," it is possible that she did not fully consider the ways in which her descriptions of these mothers and sons conflicted with the claims of domestic ideology about sympathy and the mother-son relationship. Typically, pragmatic discourses revise sentimental writings by arguing that mothers are not icons of "affection" and tend not to sympathize with boys. But by placing two sentimental mothers in a narrative that celebrates their seemingly inexhaustible sympathy with their sons *and* represents its impotence, Stowe offers perhaps the most devastating critique of sentimental discourses found in antebellum writing.

The author of "Training of Boys" warned that excessive sympathy could create "a morbid tenderness, subversive of the best interests" of both the mother and her disciplinary charge ("Training III" 148). Perhaps unintentionally, Stowe seems to suggest that the excessive sentiment St. Clare's mother directs at her son may in some way be responsible for his failure to adopt an abolitionist position. St. Clare himself says of his boyhood, "[T]here was morbid sensitiveness and acuteness of feeling in me" (334), the kind of perversion of sentiment that some pragmatic writers saw as the outcome of an improperly performed sympathy; such "an acuteness of feeling" tended to manifest itself as a narcissism that precluded identification with others. Though it might seem incongruous with Stowe's praise of St. Clare's mother and maternal sentiment, her narrative nevertheless rejects domestic ideology's belief that if a mother learns to calculate and employ sympathetic management, she can be certain of an ethical son. In a description of the "unusually gentle and sympathetic" Mrs. Bird, who is "the most indulgent and easy to be entreated of all mothers," Stowe says that maternal sympathy possesses a kind of instability that can allow it to devolve into its opposite, in the same way that the ideal mother could generate the cruelest overseer (143). Bird's extreme tenderness can quickly become an "inexplicable" kind of rage: "anything in the shape of cruelty would throw her into a passion, which was the more alarming and inexplicable in proportion to the general softness of her nature" (143).

It is unlikely that Stowe wants readers to believe that these two ideal mothers should be held accountable for the actions of their sons. Yet the novel dramatizes a fear that forces beyond a mother's control can negate the effects of even the most perfect mother's sympathy, a fear that undermines Stowe's belief in the spiritual redemption promised by the sentimental power of maternal love. In her pioneering work on Stowe's novel, Jane Tompkins claims that *Uncle Tom's Cabin* is "the *summa theologica* of nineteenth-century America's religion of domesticity . . . [and] the story of salvation through motherly love" (*Designs* 125). Tompkins centers on mothers like the Quaker Rachel Halliday, whom she calls Stowe's "God in human form" (142). It is true that the novel exalts Halliday as a mother whose household and domestic ideology represent a kind of a matriarchal utopia, yet Tompkins does not mention the two mothers I examine, figures who complicate her argument. Indeed, Stowe specifically calls St. Clare's mother—and not Halliday—"God in human form": she is "a direct embodiment and personification of the New Testament." Despite this mother's Christ-like status, she fails to deliver on the promise of salvation. Tompkins and many since her have seen the novel's endorsement of maternal sentimentality as representing a way for Stowe and women readers to access a form of power tied to beliefs about sentimentality. Hendler has called *Uncle*

Tom's Cabin an "apotheosis" for "the culture of sentiment" in nineteenth-century America (*Public Sentiments* 3), yet I argue that Stowe's celebration of sentiment is destabilized by narratives of idealized mothering that suggest the best of mothers can raise the worst of sons.

⁂

Boys were guaranteed a central role in antebellum domestic and public life, but perhaps—if many writers' concerns reflect actual conditions—only when they were no longer boys. The boyhoods of male characters like those in Stowe's novel and the boys in pragmatic discourses show that this stage was considered a crucial time for the affective molding of a male's domestic, social, and political character. But writers did not agree about the disciplinary value of many forms of management used in boyhood, especially sympathy: some praised it as the most successful (though underused) kind of discipline, others rejected it as ineffective and endorsed corporal punishment because it spoke directly to boys' physical natures and desires, and yet others warned that all maternal sympathy was dangerous—either boys would cleverly manipulate it to avoid punishment or the sympathizing mother would withhold the stern discipline a boy deserved.

This diverse field of reactions reveals extensive anxiety about the relationship between boys and their mothers, showing just how troublesome interactions between maternal emotion and boy-nature could be. Like the novels examined in chapter 1, writings about affective discipline demonstrate that boyhood should not be seen simply as a stable component of domesticity or as its male-only counterpart. The conflicts between sentimental and pragmatic discourses show that mothers' advice writing figured the mother-son bond and sympathy as ideologies subject to constant scrutiny and widespread disagreement. Not surprisingly, these arguments circulated around antebellum culture's cherished sentimental convention of the "all-sympathizing mother" and the less than ideal boy.[15]

From Louisa May Alcott's *Little Women, Part Two*, 1869.

Chapter 4

"Wake Up, and Be a Man"

Little Women, Shame, and the Ethic of Submission

> "Now be a man." How often have we heard the above sentence uttered to a boy.
> —"Now Be a Man."

> The majority of young men . . . hop[e] . . . to become a good citizen, husband, and father . . . [and go] into business.
> —Rebecca Harding Davis

> Justice has never been done to the sweetest and most attractive side of her nature—her real love for boys, which sprang from the boy nature that was hers in so marked a degree.
> —Alfred Whitman

During the past twenty-five years, *Little Women* has been at the heart of the feminist project of reading texts by nineteenth-century American women. A primary reason for the extensive interest in Alcott's novel is its discussion of the cultural spaces women occupied, or were excluded from, during the mid- and late-nineteenth century. Although critics have disagreed about the novel's pedagogical content—whether it "seeks a new vision of women's subjectivity and space" or argues for a "repressive domesticity" (Murphy 564)—it nevertheless offers us a complicated and compelling picture of Alcott and her culture's understanding of girls and women. Yet an important story within *Little Women* remains largely untreated in criticism, one that will affect our understanding of the novel's exploration of gender: that of the male protagonist, Laurie. Although critics have done important work by drawing our attention to Alcott's exploration of patriarchal structures and their disciplinary effect on girls and women, they have not looked in any detail at her concurrent examination of their effect on boys and men.

In many ways, Laurie's story resembles the narratives of numerous mid- and late-nineteenth-century middle-class young men as well as the descriptions of such boys' lives found in advice and conduct manuals. Like the struggles of the March girls, Laurie's struggle and ultimate submission to cultural expectations for young men recount a typical confrontation with the limitations of gender roles. Throughout *Little Women,* Laurie is subjected to a version of what critics have often described as the "ethic of submission," a pedagogical ethic usually deemed relevant only to girls' and women's lives because only they were expected to submit to patriarchal authority: "American women," Tompkins has famously argued, "simply could not . . . [rebel] against the conditions of their lives for they lacked the material means of escape or opposition. They had to stay put and submit" (*Designs* 161). For Tompkins and many critics after her, this ethic meant that girls and women were expected to conform to narrow roles (dutiful daughter, caring mother, obedient wife), in contrast to boys and men, who were free from such limitations.[1]

In Alcott scholarship, the view of submission as a gendered phenomenon goes back to critics such as Nina Auerbach, Judith Fetterley, and Patricia Spacks, who, in her landmark work *The Female Imagination,* takes *Little Women*'s heroine Jo at her word when she says "Boys always have a capital time," forgetting that the narrator and even Jo herself realize that this is often not the case (100).[2] Ann Murphy's "The Borders of Ethical, Erotic, and Artistic Possibilities in *Little Women*" represents an influential example of scholars' claims about gender and the novel. Her discussion of "female subjectivity" and "sisters' pilgrimage" are based on the assumption that male subjectivity and male pilgrimage always have a fundamentally different structure than those of women. This assumption, however, does not take into account Laurie's life as the novel portrays it. Murphy's argument that the text is about the "cultural limitations imposed on female development" (565), though certainly true in one sense, seems incomplete because it erases the ways in which Laurie's development is impeded by similar limitations. The text repeatedly shows how his tutor, grandfather, and the March girls seek to control his development through a pedagogy of shame. Indeed, the novel stages numerous conversations between Laurie and other characters in which his disciplining is the subject. The girls, for example, frequently "lecture" him (150, 408, 420), talk about how and why they will "manage" him (211, 296, 342, 407, 456), and stress that he not be a "disappointment" to those who care about him (409). Such conversations occur dozens of times, but typically go unmentioned in scholarship even though they shed considerable light on the novel's approach to discipline. Given the presence of these conversations, I think it is accurate to say that the novel is almost as interested in Laurie's growth and self-sacrifice as it is in Jo's, an interest that should not be surprising given the attention Alcott pays to boys throughout her writing.

Although critics have begun to question a gendered understanding of submission as it applies to men's and boys' lives, in Alcott studies it remains a prevalent assumption; Jo's story is seen as a paradigmatic example of this ethic, while the ways in which Laurie's story parallels hers are neglected. Only Elizabeth Keyser and Anne Dalke have noted that *Little Women* dramatizes Laurie's struggle with patriarchal expectations. Keyser observes that Laurie "exemplifies . . . the masculine plight," yet she does not explore at any length what "the masculine plight" is, how Laurie represents this dilemma, or what cultural beliefs shape it (*Whispers* 66–67).[3] Dalke mentions that Laurie's narrative parallels those of the girls, but does not examine this similarity or discuss its significance (573).[4] Jan Susina's "Men in *Little Women*," the only article in the collection *Little Women and the Feminist Imagination* that focuses on male characters, takes a dismissive view of Laurie and his significance in the novel. Calling him an "awful character," an "unrealistic figure," an "eternal boy," a "token male," and not "a real boy," Susina sees Laurie as a mistake: "I certainly don't want to be Laurie" (169). Following earlier critics, he thinks of Laurie as an undifferentiated "fifth sister," but this overlooks both the complexity of Laurie's life and Alcott's interest in how his life dramatizes problems that boys faced.[5]

But Alcott saw herself as an author who celebrated, defended, and explained boys and their lives to a culture that she believed often mistreated and misunderstood them. For her, Laurie's experiences are conditioned by the kinds of patriarchal and materialist ideologies that affected girls' lives. The specific ideologies are, of course, historically contingent; Laurie, for example, is allowed and encouraged to attend college, but Jo is not. For boys, though, the pressure to live up to the standards and achievements of other males (especially the pressure to succeed in the market) and the shame they feel when they fail, have, in some sense, always circumscribed their field of possibilities, as it circumscribes Laurie's.

Using studies of masculinity in America during the nineteenth century by Rotundo, Michael Kimmel, Judy Hilkey, and others, I examine Laurie's capitulation to materialist pressures in the form of his grandfather's desire that he become a merchant and the way that Amy March functions as the grandfather's agent. By repeatedly questioning his masculinity, Amy shames Laurie into acting in accord with his grandfather's wishes, a disciplinary approach that recalls Rollo's father's shaming of his son and the shame Abbott and many others used to motivate boys.[6] In an essay published in *The American Journal of Education* (1855), for example, the author says, "An appeal to a boy's sense of shame, or to his manliness, may often be made with success" (Hamill 128). He refers to an incident in which he was able to get a boy to take an exam simply by saying, "Albert, I want you to be a man, and . . . pass your examination" (129). Once we understand Laurie's story as submission brought about by a pedagogy of shame, we can then revise the conventional critical position that only the "feminine quality of self-denial" is "the novel's . . . message" (Gaard 5).[7] In order to understand more fully what *Little Women* has to say about gender, shame, and discipline, we must recover Alcott's narrative of masculine self-denial.

⁓ ⁓ ⁓

Perhaps critics have not explored the parallels between Laurie's and the March girls' narratives because Alcott often celebrated boyhood in her letters and journals and set it in opposition to her life as a girl and a woman, a life filled with restrictions and disappointments. The joy and freedom she could not imagine for herself, she sometimes imagined as the province of boys. In October 1860, for instance, Alcott saw the Prince of Wales while he was on a tour of the United States. "Boys are always jolly," she mused, "even princes" (*Journal* 100). Possibly in part because of such idealizations, critics believe that Jo articulates a truth about boyhood when she says that "boys always have a capital time." But in *Little Women,* Laurie's story shows us that Alcott's ideas about the lives of boys are more complex, and the text rarely makes any idealizing claims about boyhood. Laurie is definitely not "always jolly," and, puzzled that he could be wealthy and sad, Jo exclaims, "Theodore Laurence, you ought to be the happiest boy in the world" (52). Laurie's unhappiness results from his place in a world of men and the concurrent pressure of proving himself a man to the novel's characters. As Kimmel notes, this pressure is a defining feature of American masculinity in the nineteenth century (*Manhood* ix), the era that the historian Joe Dubbert calls "the masculine century" (*A Man's Place* 13).

Gilded Age success manuals for young men published around the time of *Little Women* often depict a boy's life as fraught with anxiety. They present him as prone to worrying and suffering from "dissatisfaction with . . . [his] destiny" and "spells of melancholy" (cited in Hilkey 76). Similarly, Alcott introduces us to Laurie as a lonely, frustrated young man. Unlike the nurturing domestic circle of the March girls and their mother, Laurie's world is an isolated male enclave composed of his grandfather and his tutor, John Brooke, both of whom are grooming him for a life he does not want. During a game called "rigmarole," Brooke relates a thinly veiled allegory of Laurie's submission and his role in it. As a knight, Brooke must "tame and train" Laurie, "a fine, but unbroken colt" who is a "pet of the king," Laurie's grandfather (127). Although Laurie eventually goes to work for his grandfather, he desperately wants "to enjoy myself in my own way": "I'm to be a famous musician myself, and all creation is to rush to hear me; and I'm never to be bothered about money or business, but just enjoy myself, and live for what I like" (29, 142).

In spite of these fantasies, Laurie knows that his future involves a different kind of "capital time" than Jo thinks boys always have, namely one devoted to "money and business." As Dubbert observes, men "were expected to cash in on . . . opportunities to maximize their gains and minimize their losses" and not, as Laurie says, "live for what [they] like" (15). His grandfather fears that Laurie wants to pursue a materially unproductive, and therefore unmasculine career: "His music isn't bad, but I hope he will do as well in more important things" (55). What is important for his grandfather is that Laurie succeeds in business, as he had. His grandfather echoes a sentiment that popular writer T. S. Arthur expresses to his readers in *Advice to Young Men on Their Duties and Conduct in Life* (1852): "As respects music . . . if a young man have any taste at all in that way, he ought to cultivate it." Arthur goes on to say, however, that boys should devote themselves to "graver pursuits" that will help them succeed in the market because "entering business is the most important act of a young man's life" (65, 152).

It seems likely that Laurie's desire to be a musician and not a merchant would have met with a stern response not only from his grandfather but from many parents. Antebellum conduct books and Gilded Age success manuals never acknowledged art as a viable career for middle-class young men. Rather, these manuals endorsed typical preindustrial occupations, such as farmer, craftsman, and shopkeeper (Hilkey 110). Even the boys' fiction of the period rarely portrayed artistic occupations as possible careers for middle-class boys. Vocations such as musician—and the arts in general—were thought of as "less manly" because, as entertainment, they were outside the rigors of the marketplace. "Aesthetic contributions" to culture, Dubbert notes, were devalued compared to the contributions of businessmen and "men of action" (30–31). William Dean Howells, a contemporary of Alcott, learned to his dismay that a career in the arts was seen as a "female" vocation: "To pursue his interests," Rotundo observes, Howells "had to divide himself into male and female halves that could only flourish in different social realms" (170). In an 1878 manual, *Success in Life, and How to Secure It: or Elements of Manhood and Their Culture,* William Owen expresses the standard position on the relative value of the arts, a view similar to Laurie's grandfather's desire that Laurie do "well in more important things": "Let poets and preachers, [and] artists . . . bestow more time on material matters . . . and let our schools and colleges remember to make men—stalwart, invincible *men*" (cited in Hilkey 109; emphasis in original).[8]

Norms of masculinity, as Kimmel and others have argued, are often created and enforced through the pressures placed on boys and men to reproduce behaviors that usually either explicitly or implicitly involve capital.[9] Throughout the nineteenth century, boys were often expected to enter their fathers' businesses, and *We Boys,* a novel released by Alcott's publishers Robert Brothers in 1876, dramatizes this expectation. The narrator talks about the occupations of his and his best friend's fathers: "My father is [a] cashier . . . and I do think a cashier's is the stupidest business!" (7). But in the epilogue we learn that both boys—now men—have the same jobs as their fathers. The same kinds of sentiments are held by Laurie:

> I ought to be satisfied to please grandfather, and I do try, but it's working against the grain, you see, and comes hard. He wants me to be an India merchant, as he was, and I'd rather be shot; I hate tea, and silk, and spices. . . . Going to college ought to satisfy him, for if I give him four years he ought to let me off from the business; but he's set, and I've got to do just as he did, unless I break away and please myself, as my father did. (144)

But this dream of breaking away, Alcott says, is difficult for both sexes to realize; pleasing oneself is, to use one of her favorite phrases, an "air castle" that must be abandoned by little men and women alike. Here, as elsewhere, Alcott dramatizes a central claim of many critics who study masculinity: culture has its designs on male fulfillment, too.[10] Therefore, like many fictional and real young men, Laurie is not free to pursue the career he wants, for it would be "working against the grain" of cultural expectations.

Dubbert's and Hilkey's studies of advice literature for young men shows that manliness was synonymous with success in the market. A boy knew that he would never be viewed as a man unless he was fiscally productive; as success manuals repeatedly announced, "character was capital" (Hilkey 126).[11] That a career as an artist would be counterproductive has already been forecast in the story of Laurie's father, a musician who "please[d him]self" and ran away, only to end up dead (144). The narrator never tells us how and why he dies, but the implication is that his death is a consequence of his career choice. Had he become an India merchant—as Laurie's grandfather surely would have wanted—a different outcome is easy to imagine. Though still only a young man, Laurie has been initiated into the male world of negotiation. He trades four years of his life in order to escape becoming an India merchant—a bargain that does not pay off as he had hoped.

Although many boys and men probably fantasized about "breaking away," the pressure placed on them to succeed in business meant that most could not and did not "break away." In reaction to pressure and violence directed at him by his grandfather, Laurie tells Jo he wants to run away to Washington. "What fun you'd have!" Jo replies. "I wish I could run off, too. . . . If I was a boy, we'd run away together, and have a capital time; but as I'm a miserable girl, I must be proper, and stay at home. Don't tempt me, Teddy, it's a crazy plan" (212–13). In spite of the romance of escape, she believes that Laurie's interests are best served by remaining, so she orchestrates a truce to keep him at home. Critics tend to take Jo's comment as reiterating a cultural truth: boys can run away, but girls must submit. Ann Murphy, for instance, claims that "as a boy, Jo would be . . . able to . . . 'run away [with Laurie] and have a capital time'" (577), even though the text tells us in no uncertain terms that Laurie cannot run away. Early in the novel, Jo identifies with Laurie's desire to escape and encourages him "to sail away in one of your ships, and never come home again till you have tried your own way" (144). Toward the novel's end, the notion of a ship voyage returns, but with an important difference: "Laurie says [to Amy] he feels as if he 'could make a prosperous voyage now with me aboard as mate'" (438). As we saw in chapter 1, in Optic's novels the ship metaphor at first suggests a movement into a life of adventure but then articulates a transition into the adventures of domesticity that Laurie embraces.

Running away is not an option for him, as it often was not for middle- and upper-class young men, for they typically were not the ones who went out west in search of gold or to sea in search of whales.[12] Rather, they grew up to raise families and hold respectable middle-class positions; as Rotundo observes, parents discouraged a "bold and daring code" for boys and young men and instead endorsed "the cautious, abstemious ethic of the clerk" (43). Alcott herself often wished to run away, but she learned through her father, as Laurie learns through Jo and later Amy, to embrace the doctrines of duty, labor, and submission. In a journal entry of August 1850, Alcott said of teaching, "School is hard work, and I feel as though I should like to run away from it. But . . . [I] do my best" (63). Although contemporary readers must have identified with Jo and Laurie's desire to escape, they most likely agreed with Jo and Alcott that a boy must "do [his] duty" (145).

John Crowley and others have argued that Laurie wants to run away in order to escape domesticity, and a great deal of critical work on nineteenth-century canonical texts has similarly characterized male escape fantasies as defined by a longing to be free from women and the home.[13] Novels such as *Moby-Dick* and Cooper's Leatherstocking tales were canonized by critics who felt that these texts advocated an ideal American manhood by celebrating the protagonist's flight from "feminizing" civilization and his refusal to submit to the "bonds" of domesticity. Feminist scholars rightly faulted these critics' endorsement of the flight trope as misogynist, yet they repeated the critical assumption that domesticity was, invariably, the crucial problem for men, the sole aspect of their daily lives that they wanted to escape. Although it is true that escape fantasies could be driven by an urge to reject what some men felt as the confines of domesticity, recent scholarship on masculinity has drawn our attention to the ways in which men have constantly fantasized about escaping the pressures of the market and what Thoreau railed against as the "curse of trade [that] attaches to business" (143). It is more accurate and helpful to see Laurie's desire for flight as representing the anxiety many boys and men felt trying to live up to ideal male behaviors and roles. And Jo tells Laurie's grandfather that his resistance is not to domesticity but to business: "He won't [run away] unless he is very much worried, and only threatens it sometimes, when he gets tired of studying" and preparing for his career (215).

Crowley goes on to suggest that Laurie has an "impulse to escape the civilizing force of" domesticity because he is "completely surrounded by the woman's sphere" (393, 394). Yet it is male vocation and violence he wants to flee. In the early part of the novel, and by implication for many years before the action of the text begins, Laurie has been completely surrounded by men in a way that suggests his boyhood has been a kind of imprisonment: Mr. Laurence "keeps his grandson shut up when he isn't riding or walking with his tutor, and makes him study dreadful hard" (21). The narrator describes Laurie's "sphere" in bleak terms: "it seemed a lonely, lifeless sort of house; for no children frolicked on the lawn, no motherly face ever smiled at the windows, and few people went in and out, except the old gentleman and his grandson" (47). Rather than wanting to escape domesticity, he yearns for it, saying to Jo:

> "I beg your pardon for being so rude, but sometimes you forget to put down the curtain at the window where the flowers are; and, when the lamps are lighted, it's like looking at a picture to see the fire, and you all around the table with your mother; her face is right opposite, and it looks so sweet behind the flowers, I can't help watching it. I haven't got any mother, you know;" and Laurie poked the fire to hide a little twitching of the lips that he could not control. (50)

The picture Laurie draws here evokes the conventional domestic tableaux of so many Victorian novels and prints, an image that encodes the values of domesticity: children gathered around their mother in a scene lit by the glow of a fire. Later, Laurie again imagines his place in the domestic using another visual genre, the landscape:

> "Here's a landscape!" thought Laurie. . . . It *was* rather a pretty little picture; for the sisters sat together in the shady nook, with sun and shadow flickering over them. . . . A shadow passed over the boy's face as he watched

them, feeling that he ought to go, because uninvited. . . ."May I come in, please?" (139)

Far from escaping domesticity, Laurie knows that his life will be intimately involved with it. Though some men and boys could and did flee what these images represented, escape into solitude (best represented by the misanthropic nomadism of Daniel Boone) or into male community (the whaling ships of *Moby-Dick*) was a notion of male possibility more fantastic than real.[14] Alcott shows such masculine worlds as unsatisfying ideals and instead advocates a notion of male behavior that was more generally endorsed. Writing shortly before *Little Women* was published, the popular lecturer and conduct book author Josiah Holland summed up what middle-class culture expected of its boys: "One of the first things a young man should do is to see that he is acting his part in society. . . . [Y]ou can have no influence unless you are social. . . . The revenge which society takes upon the man who isolates himself, is as terrible as it is inevitable" (Titcomb 63–69). To be "social" meant to play a part in marriage, domesticity, and the marketplace. To embrace these structures, then, was the conventional expectation for young men.[15]

❦ ❦ ❦

In a crucial and often-cited scene in *Little Women,* Mr. Bhaer convinces Jo to give up her dream of earning a living as a "sensational" writer. The scene begins with Jo's defense of sensation stories, but after listening to Bhaer's attack on such "trash," she feels "horribly ashamed" (356). The shame Jo feels from seeing herself through, as she puts it, his "moral spectacles," causes her to throw all her "lurid" stories into the stove (356). Though these stories are profitable and give her the opportunity to experience imaginatively a life she is denied, Jo must stop writing them because such a profession is incompatible with the way in which the novel conceives of "womanhood" (356). Thus Mr. Bhaer acts as a kind of enforcer for the text's values, shaming Jo into sacrificing her desire. But rarely referred to are those scenes in which Amy, acting like Mr. Bhaer, shames Laurie into giving up his dream of life as an artist, and the moment in which Laurie, imitating Jo's destruction, destroys his own manuscripts. The striking resemblance between these scenes clearly shows that Alcott wants to draw our attention to the similar sacrifices that boys and girls must make in order to fit into narrowly defined adult roles.

To make Laurie into a man, Amy constantly reminds him of his distance from cultural ideals of masculinity. Elaine Showalter observes that Mr. Bhaer, Jo's German husband, is "unconfined by American codes of masculinity" (xxvii). Yet I argue that Alcott shows us how Laurie, as an American boy, is all too confined by such codes; and Amy sees it as her job to awaken the sleeping "young knight" from his boyish illusions and bring him into conformity with these norms.[16] She even concludes her sermon to him on manliness and responsibility by promising, "I won't lecture any more, for I know you'll wake up, and be a man" (411). As Jo's "lurid" literary aspirations are in conflict with the way *Little Women* imagines her as a woman, so too are Laurie's boyish artistic dreams incompatible with the way it imagines him as a man. In this section of the novel, Amy and the narrator share a discourse that connects boyhood to dreaming and manhood to waking from these dreams, a shared language that suggests how Amy acts as a voice for the novel's values.

An essential part of Amy's shaming of Laurie involves renaming him; as his friends had called him "Dora" to emphasis his failure to measure up to their standards of masculinity, Amy calls him "Lazy Laurence" to feminize him by emphasizing how unindustrious, and therefore unmanly, he seems to her. Laurie's new name comes from Maria Edgeworth's didactic tale "Lazy Lawrence," published in a popular collection called the *Parent's Assistant*.[17] The story features two boys, Jem, a model of masculine ambition, and Lawrence, a model of idleness. Like Laurie, Lawrence dreams, dismisses ambition, and enjoys "amusements," but he eventually converts to the ways of industry, following the protagonists in Abbott's and Optic's novels. As Rotundo observes, one of the key

> deficiencies of character that [was] thought to cause failure . . . was laziness. Again and again we have heard men exhort one another to "industry," "persistence," "hard work." . . . Each of these popular phrases stood not only as an exhortation to positive behavior, but as a warning against negative behavior. (179)

Amy's appeal to Laurie to be industrious, then, represents a typical exhortation to be successful, but also a warning that if he continues on his present course he will be perceived as a failure. Like a success manual come to life, Amy attempts, as H. A. Lewis attempted with his advice manual *Hidden Treasures* (1887) to "awaken dormant energies in ONE PERSON who otherwise might have failed" (cited in Hilkey 75; emphasis in original).[18]

Though the name "Lazy Laurence" implicitly feminizes him, Amy tries to make her assault on Laurie's masculinity explicit: "instead of being the man you might and ought to be, you are only—" (408). But before she can finish, Laurie interrupts her. He likely believes that she would conclude with "a boy," "a girl," or "a woman," and in fact she soon says, "Aren't you ashamed of a hand like that? It's as soft and white as a woman's, and looks as if it never did anything but wear Jouvin's best gloves" (408). A physical sign of manliness was roughness, typically visible in a hand that has been shaped by labor. Daniel Boone's nineteenth-century biographer Timothy Flint, for example, railed against men who lacked the "manly hardihood" of the pioneers, calling them "effeminate spirits, the men of soft hands" (cited in Kimmel, *Manhood* 61). Even if it would not literally rough up his hands, Laurie's position as an India merchant would be a job that made something happen, that would make a man out of him. Laurie is beginning to realize that he cannot become the kind of man that his culture and Amy demand if he continues to pursue his "effeminate" art.

Amy uses her own art to further convince Laurie that he has yet to act "manfully." She shows Laurie

> a rough sketch of [him] taming a horse; hat and coat were off, and every line of the active figure, resolute face, and commanding attitude, was full of energy and meaning. . . . [In] the rider's breezy hair and erect attitude, there was a suggestion of suddenly arrested motion, of strength, courage. (411)

The image contains numerous codes of the "real man" as Amy and the novel conceive of him: active, resolute, in command, and sexually powerful.[19] Amy's image recalls those offered in success manuals in which writers often connect success and metaphors of sexual potency. William Owen, for example, argues that "Unless man can erect himself . . . how poor a thing is man" (cited in Hilkey 149). Amy's "suggestion of suddenly arrested motion," too, is typical, for according to Hilkey, the manual writers believed that "only the virile could succeed, and then only by holding their inner powers in reserve for use at just the right moment" (149).[20] Even the kind of sketch Amy draws encodes manliness; it is "rough," in contrast to Laurie's "soft" feminine hands. She tells him that this picture represents him "as you were" and then compares it to a picture that could have been an illustration of Edgeworth's "Lazy Lawrence." But it is clear that Laurie never was such a man. Amy makes this claim in order to shame him by calling his virility into question. As she had used Edgeworth's story as a model for Laurie's life, she uses her drawing to teach him "a little lesson."

When Amy says to Laurie, "[I]nstead of being the man you might and ought to be, you are only—," he concludes for her with "Saint Laurence on a gridiron" (408). The narrator tells us that this insertion "blandly finish[es] the sentence," but Laurie's invocation of one of the most famous Christian martyrs should not be so easily dismissed. That Laurie sees himself as Saint Laurence, a martyr who was burned to death, implies that he recognizes the renunciation of his "boyish passions" as a metaphorical death, a sacrifice for the greater good of domesticity. The process of converting lazy Laurie into a man, the process that Amy begins, he concludes with a literal act of destruction, as he destroys his manuscripts: "He grew more and more discontent with his desultory life, began to long for some real and earnest work. . . . [T]hen suddenly he tore up his music-sheets one by one" (422). Laurie's destruction of his manuscripts and the fiery death of his patron saint both refer to Jo's similar act of martyrdom: the extinguishing of her desire by burning her sensational tales. And it is crucial to realize that Amy's shaming of Laurie (which echoes the dozens of lectures he has received from other characters) inspires the destruction of his music. Playing on the fears that, as Kimmel notes, have "haunted" American men, fears "that they are not powerful . . . or successful enough" (*Manhood* 8), she repeatedly calls Laurie's masculinity into question and invokes "Lazy Lawrence" to rewrite his life to coincide with that script whose ending he provides by following its narrative of idleness to industry: "I won't be a humbug any longer" (422).

But Laurie knows that simply destroying the manuscripts is not enough. The best way to prove to Amy and his grandfather that he is not a "humbug" is to do what men do: get a job. As critics have shown, male identity in the nineteenth century was intimately connected to work, and Laurie knows that if he fails to work he will be seen as insufficiently masculine, as weak and feminine. He sends Amy a note addressed to "Mentor" from "Telemachus" in order to acknowledge the success of her "little lesson": "'Lazy Laurence' has gone to his grandpa, like the best of boys" (412). Although Laurie literally goes to see his grandfather, the metaphorical "going" is most important. He has finally left his boyhood "air castles" behind and submitted to his grandfather. Like "the best of boys" he embraces the values of the patriarchy and abandons idle dreams in favor of "earnest work." The boy who earlier said he never wanted to be "bothered about money or business" now exclaims, "I'm going into business with a devotion that shall delight grandpa, and prove to him that I'm not spoilt. I need something of the sort to keep me steady. I . . . mean to work like a man" (457).

This is perhaps the novel's most compact formulation of the cultural connection between masculinity and productivity: to be a man is to work. Acting as Mentor, Amy is (to adapt the title of Edgeworth's collection) the "culture's assistant"; she enforces its codes of masculinity. As Mentor educates Telemachus, Amy teaches Laurie that he can prove himself a man by putting his boyhood fantasies of self-fulfillment behind him. And given her use of Edgeworth's text in enforcing these codes—a use Laurie acknowledges when he says, "'Lazy Laurence' has gone to his grandpa"—it is clear that Laurie cannot rebel "against prescribed texts" (B. Clark, "Portrait of the Artist" 81). In fact, "Lazy Lawrence" acts as the master narrative behind Laurie's story, his conversion from idleness to industry. Rather than rebel against this text, Laurie embraces its dictates and decides to "work like a man."[21]

It is curious that, although Laurie is wealthy, he and Amy believe so strongly that he must work. But as Francis Gund wrote in 1837, "business is the very soul of an American: he pursues it, not as a means of procuring for himself and his family the necessary comforts of life, but as the fountain of all human felicity" (cited in Kimmel, *Manhood* 24). Like Amy, success manual authors worried about the boy who already had wealth, believing that he was likely to lead a life of "emasculated idleness and laziness" (cited in Hilkey 91). Jo had expressed this concern in an earlier "lecture" to Laurie:

> Just be a simple, honest, respectable boy, and we'll never desert you. I don't know what I should do if you acted like Mr. King's son. He had plenty of money, but didn't know how to spend it, and got tipsy and gambled, and ran away, and forged his father's name, I believe, and was altogether horrid. . . . I sometimes wish you were poor. I shouldn't worry then. (150)

At the close of one of the novels we examined in chapter 1, Oliver Optic says of the protagonist something that Amy would likely say of Laurie as *Little Women* ends: "even though not now required to work, he was constantly employed in some useful occupation . . . he was no longer an idler" (*Work and Win* 287).

Amy thinks she is preparing Laurie to "be a man" (411) so that he will be a suitable partner for Jo, but the novel has already told us that this pairing is not a possibility. Instead, she prepares him to fill the prescribed categories of businessman, husband, and father, the roles he ends up playing in her life. As a young woman named Mollie Clark said to her suitor in the year *Little Women* was published, "I often think it is so different for men from what it is with us women. Love is our life [,] our reality, business yours" (cited in Rotundo 168). This perception, Rotundo argues, "was constantly reinforced by the people who made up a man's social world" (168), just as Amy, Jo, and his grandfather reinforce it for Laurie. When Laurie marries Amy, he submits to convention, becoming a husband and accepting the reality of a life of business.

Many critics have suggested that Jo's marriage to Mr. Bhaer is a kind of punishment and a way in which her ambitions are tamed by the narrative; rather than marry the attractive young Laurie, she ends up with the fatherly older man.[22] Yet Laurie's marriage to Amy—the most traditional of all the March girls—instead of to Jo could similarly been seen as his punishment for desiring something other than the conventional expectation. But, of course, Amy's conventionality is the point. Laurie's decision to marry her signifies that he has proven his manhood to all of the novel's characters, and because Amy has invested the time to convert him from a boy to a man, she is rewarded for it. Thus Laurie, like Jo, accepts the novel's expectations for his gender by embracing domesticity and business.[23]

Unlike Laurie, the boy protagonists in the novels of Twain, Aldrich, and other boy-book authors spend much of their time away from the domestic and are often free from the kind of pedagogy of shame practiced in *Little Women*. When scholars discuss Laurie, they often contrast the kind of masculinity he embodies (or lacks) to that of the boy-book's hero, seeing Laurie as androgynous and the bad boy as hypermasculine.[24] Both Laurie's and Jo's androgyny, critics argue, are prominently signaled by Alcott's choice of names, each of which is typical of the other's gender. Yet to see Laurie (who is also called Teddy) as a "fifth sister" is to miss that he frequently serves as an object of desire for the March girls, and perhaps more importantly, that he is figured in a way that anticipates the "good bad boy" of the boy-book:

> Being only a "glorious human boy," of course he frolicked and flirted, grew dandified, aquatic, sentimental or gymnastic . . . talked slang, and more than once came perilously near suspension and expulsion. But as high spirits and the love of fun were the causes of these pranks, he always managed to save himself by frank confession, honorable atonement, or the irresistible power of persuasion which he possessed in perfection. In fact, he rather prided himself on his narrow escapes, and liked to thrill the girls with graphic accounts of his triumphs. (238–39)

Such a description recalls Tom Sawyer or *The Story of a Bad Boy*'s Tom Bailey, who describes his young self as "an amiable, impulsive lad, blessed with fine digestive powers and no hypocrite. . . . In short, I was a real human boy" (Aldrich 7–8).[25] Like Laurie, the bad boy often commits pranks yet always receives forgiveness; Tom Sawyer, for example, continually misbehaves, yet his Aunt Polly "ain't got the heart to lash him, somehow" (10). Similarly, the March girls call Laurie a "bad boy" (207, 213) but feel "that it was impossible to frown upon" him (210).[26]

Laurie's theatricality also identifies him as a literary precursor to Tom Sawyer, and this theatricality is tied to a masculinity that is clearly defined as heterosexual (Laurie acts to "thrill the girls") and that lacks the kind of ambiguity associated with androgyny. Laurie exhibits the kind of romantic posturing that characterizes bad boys like Sawyer, who goes to Becky Thatcher's house, lies underneath what he believes to be her window, and revels in the fantasies of a wounded lover—all of which evoke Laurie underneath Meg's window:

> Laurie . . . seemed suddenly possessed with a melodramatic fit, for he fell down upon one knee in the snow, beat his breast, tore his hair, and clasped his hand imploringly . . . and when Meg told him to behave himself . . . he wrung imaginary tears out of his handkerchief, and staggered round the corner as if in utter despair. (225)

It is true, of course, that Laurie operates in a fictional and moral context different from that found in *Tom Sawyer*, and it is far easier to imagine Laurie making a "frank confession" than to imagine Tom making an "honorable atonement" for any of their pranks.

Although Laurie anticipates the "good bad boy," he differs from this character type in ways that speak not only to Alcott's moral concerns but to her interest in making Laurie a compelling fictional boy by giving him a complex social character. She allows him to negotiate a number of boy-girl relationships and male expectations, and would likely argue that by portraying boyhood as closely intertwined with domestic concerns she has created a more realistic representation of boys' experiences than the one depicted by the late-century authors we often call "literary realists."[27] Thinking about Laurie not as a male March sister but as a kind of bad boy within a girls' novel allows us to see that, not only does *Little Women* show a similar narrative of development into adulthood for each gender, but it examines problems exclusive to boyhood, offering a more nuanced exploration of the ways that boys relate to other boys, girls, women, adult males, and the home environment than do many other novels of the period.

As a part of this exploration, Alcott's narrative about boyhood uses not only a familiar character type from boys' fiction but other conventions central to the genre, perhaps the most prevalent of which is a violent confrontation between males. Prior to Stephen Crane, few American writers on boyhood narrated this physical violence in any detail, but the vast majority of nineteenth-century books that feature boys, even such seemingly innocuous texts as Abbott's novels, include scenes of boys fighting each other (or being hit by authority figures) or threats of them being "thrashed."[28] As critics have shown, violence is one of the most significant ways in which male-male relationships are defined and male character created, not only through displays of power but by the feelings of shame that violence engenders in the boys who suffer from it. In canonical boy novels like *Ragged Dick* (1868), *The Story of a Bad Boy* (1870), *Adventures of Huckleberry Finn* (1884), and Howells's *A Boy's Town* (1890), violence helps to establish hierarchies and prepares boys for the environments they will face as adults.

When we first meet Laurie, he tells Jo about a fight he had with boys who mocked his name, Theodore, by calling him Dora. When Jo asks how he got the boys to stop referring to him in this way, he replies, "I thrashed 'em" (28).[29] By fighting, he proves to them (and to Jo by recounting the incident) that he has right to be addressed as he chooses, and he renames himself Laurie in an attempt to assert himself and to recapture patriarchal authority by referencing the family name, Laurence (27). (Amy explicitly undermines Laurie's claim to the associations of this name when she recasts him as "Lazy Laurence," as the boys had renamed him Dora.) After Laurie tells Jo the story, she recounts a similar incident: "I can't thrash Aunt March" (who called her Josephine), "so

I suppose I shall have to bear it" (27). We know, of course, that Jo would not thrash anyone, and we also know that Laurie's grandfather has "lectured and pummeled" him, something he finds very difficult to bear.

While Jo does not believe that the grandfather possesses a capacity for violence, Laurie understands how aggression functions to generate humiliation and obedience in a boy's world: "he privately thought she would have good reason to be a trifle afraid of the old gentlemen if she met him in some of his moods" (51). And later, we learn that his grandfather, perhaps in one of these moods, resorts to violence when Laurie refuses to answer a question: "I've been shaken, and I won't bear it!" "If it had been anyone else" Laurie says, "I'd have . . . I'll allow no man to shake *me*" (211; ellipsis in original). The violence directed at Laurie by his grandfather is the physical analogue to his disciplining by shame, and his response to violence is typical of fictional boys who wish to punish those who have shamed them or assaulted their masculinity: "I'll thrash him with my own hands" (214).

But he never does. Instead, he submits to his grandfather's will just as he later submits to Amy's shaming. Judith Fetterley has famously noted that the martial context of the Civil War (the period during which *Little Women* takes place) provides a metaphor for the personal conflicts in Alcott's life that the novel portrays ("Alcott's Civil War" 370).[30] Yet, for Alcott, the physical aggression in Laurie's story is not a metaphor. Violence had a real presence in nineteenth-century boys' lives, so she gives it an important role in Laurie's story. And Amy's discipline and the violence of Laurie's peers and grandfather ultimately serve the same pedagogical purpose: they function as part of the long initiation and awakening into manhood that is boyhood.

⁂

In an essay on the significance that *Little Women* has for readers in the twenty-first century, Christy Minadeo sees the novel as valuable for what it tells us about the experiences of girls, especially the ways in which they struggle with cultural discipline. "The trajectory of girls' lives," she argues, "remains carefully defined, and that is why *Little Women* remains relevant to contemporary readers" (200). But the violence, pressures, and expectations faced by Laurie are absent from her essay. She mentions him only in passing—he is not the subject of a single paragraph. To talk about *Little Women* and gender without including Laurie denies him, Alcott, and us his story. Alcott could have written a very different narrative, one in which Laurie's life was more like Huck Finn's than Jo's.[31] He could have "always had a capital time," perhaps even running away to the capital as he wanted. But like many boys and young men, Laurie was not Huck Finn.[32] He couldn't "light out" for the territory because there was another kind of "capital time" awaiting him because of his family's status and history: life as a merchant. Critics have frequently invoked Huck Finn's narrative as a point of contrast to the March girls' lives, saying that Huck "may very well be a metaphor for white, middle-class male America" (Murphy 567). But if Huck is a metaphor, it is perhaps more aptly for the dreams of American boys, young men, and adults who wanted to escape the pressures and responsibilities of their work, but like Laurie, were expected to accept their role. The parallel between Laurie's and Jo's conformity to expectation makes it clear that he is as crucial to *Little Women*'s exploration of gender as are the March girls. As a novel about Laurie's and the March girls' submission, *Little Women* remains relevant to us as a story of how both boys and girls confront cultural limitation.

From Francis Forrester's *Dick Duncan*, 1860.

Chapter 5

"What Our Boys Are Reading"

Lydia Sigourney, Francis Forrester, and Boyhood Literacy

> Is it to be expected that we can read about a . . . man, and at the same time be uninfluenced by him? It were impossible.
> —William Alcott

> Great harm . . . is done to boys . . . by the nervous excitement of reading.
> —William Graham Sumner

> The librarian and the trustees often talked to the boys found with such trash kindly and pleasantly, telling them of the dangers of reading the stuff.
> —*The Library Journal*

In his semiautobiographical novel *The Story of a Bad Boy,* Thomas Bailey Aldrich describes a moment when the young protagonist, Tom Bailey, discovers a trunk of books in the family home: "I subsequently unearthed another motley collection of novels and romances, embracing the adventures of Baron Trenck, Jack Sheppard, Don Quixote, Gil Blas, and Charlotte Temple—all of which I fed upon like a bookworm" (39). For scholars familiar with Susanna Rowson's sentimental novel *Charlotte Temple* (1794), the fact that the hero of a quintessential boys' story (and an inspiration for Mark Twain's Tom Sawyer) would mention this book in the same breath as these adventure narratives—let alone "feed upon it"—might come as a surprise, going against what we expect a boy to have read and enjoyed. When critics talk about boys and literacy, they often focus on fiction by men and overlook stories by women as well as nonliterary texts. Aldrich mentions that Bailey reads history, a genre of particular interest to many authors and educators, who believed that historical narratives had an "ennobling" effect on boys.

Reading has long been talked about in studies of nineteenth-century culture and of children's literature as a way to discipline adult and child readers in general or women and girls in particular, but it has received less attention as a source for ideas about disciplining boys.[1] In a recent volume, for example, Ana-Isabel Aliaga-Buchenau helpfully looks at female readers and fiction but gives little time to boys' reading as theorized throughout novels, short stories, book reviews, essay collections, children's periodicals, and conduct manuals. Like many critics, she argues that boys' novels create and reinforce affirming notions of male authority and privilege, yet she overlooks vigorous debates about the possible negative effects that numerous kinds of reading could have on a boy's subjectivity. While literary critics tend to study the reception of novels, nineteenth-century theorists of reading were interested in travel, science, biography, and especially history, and they argued at length about which would be best or worst when it came to molding the masculinity of boy readers.[2]

Though I explore theories of disciplinary literacy that appear in educational periodicals, advice materials, and boys' novels such as Francis Forrester's novel *Dick Duncan* (1860), the first section of this chapter returns to the writings of Lydia Sigourney, an extremely popular poet and author of advice manuals, exemplary memoirs, and children's literature who spent a great deal of time writing for boys and thinking about their pedagogy, aspects of her career that have been almost completely ignored.[3] An important theorist of antebellum domesticity, Sigourney conceives of the boy not as a figure who stands in opposition to the domestic and its virtues but as a critical part of a home-centered value system that endorses masculine self-sacrifice and social obligation. Reading Sigourney's work on boyhood literacy helps us to complicate our use of the boy as a foil against which we can discuss the girl, and it allows us to see boys as carefully defined products of domestic theory, an act of definition in which nineteenth-century women like Sigourney play a prominent role.

This chapter looks at two writers—one male and one female—but does not argue that men endorsed a kind of reading that Sigourney and other women rejected. Numerous positions were articulated in debates about literacy, and though many males favored what I call "heroic imitation"—an approach to reading in which boys consume narratives about historical figures and replay their typically masculinist attitudes or actions—others were either critical of this model or endorsed it only in a very limited way. I have selected Sigourney and Forrester because both confront the idea of heroic imitation and examine the reading of history, and both practice an oppositional way of responding to a number of popular antebellum literary and cultural fictions about boys. As a writer acutely aware of the diverse ways that cultural expectations shaped and limited the lives of women, Sigourney argues that boys' reading, especially popular genres such as history and biography, often advocates a repressive pedagogy and sanctions what she sees as harmful norms of boyhood masculinity. Because the beliefs of Sigourney and the educators she engages were in wide circulation, she is perhaps the figure best able to help us understand what was at stake in debates about cultural literacy.[4] The discussions of reading in her work and the numerous writings about boyhood literacy published throughout the culture from 1820 on attest to the importance given to reading, which was seen as perhaps the principal source for a boy's ideas about his own masculinity.

⁓ ⁓ ⁓

In an 1853 biography of her son Andrew entitled *The Faded Hope*, Sigourney offers Andrew's short life—he was born in 1830 and died shortly before his twentieth birthday—as a study in cultural literacy. Sarah Robbins says that *The Faded Hope* presents the kind of "literacy [that] molded [Andrew's] character . . . as an ideal for other American youth to emulate," and while his reading habits were put forward as exemplary, the material he read was often criticized by his mother (4). Sigourney believes that certain narratives profoundly harmed Andrew, but she alerts readers to his experiences because she wants to make a larger argument about boys and reading. She does not worry that improper reading would make a boy "unmanly"—as some advice writers did—but that often-endorsed kinds of reading would make a boy want to be too manly; that is, they would encourage him to emulate an ideal of masculinity that was socially irresponsible and ultimately self-destructive. Sigourney is deeply invested in the way that what Robbins calls "mother-lead literacy" could be challenged—and even fully undermined—by forces beyond a mother's control, much as Stowe had worried that the affective mother-son bond was vulnerable to other influences (5). Indeed, *The Faded Hope* offers one of the period's most detailed, and saddest, looks at boyhood and literacy.

Opening with a postmortem portrait of Andrew and ending with the narration of his death, *The Faded Hope* chronicles a boyhood ultimately overshadowed by the notions of manhood that discipline her son. Sigourney wrote the biography to tell of Andrew's boyhood, the illness that kept him from reaching adulthood, and the important role played throughout his life by books. At the age of seven he wrote in his journal, "This is my birthday. Now, I am a boy" (*Faded Hope* 47). Andrew recognized what his culture had taught him: boyhood was a crucial developmental stage, one complete with its own set of expectations and pressures. He begins his assent to these expectations by making himself into the boy that he believes his culture wants him to be, even though, as we will see, such dictates conflict with other desires he has. While we have long been interested in the initiation from boyhood to manhood, Andrew's comment alerts us to another crucial, if less studied, moment of male transition, the movement into boyhood itself. Andrew Sigourney realized—though he would not likely have been able to express it as such—that he was operating under a code of boyhood masculinity, one largely created through and embodied in his reading.

This was "an age of books," conduct author Daniel Eddy proclaimed, and thus an age in which literacy would be a primary method of disciplining boys like Andrew (34). Authorities such as Eddy warned boys to pay careful attention to what and how they read, and William Alcott agreed, arguing that boys must read systematically, avoiding "licentious" material and looking for lessons about self-governance. In his approach to reading, Andrew was the ideal reader as imagined not only by Sigourney but by nearly all educators and conduct book authors. His reading was systematic, he read numerous genres, and he always "patiently reflected" on the material's moral content. Indeed, Andrew was obsessed with books, keeping a journal in which he listed the texts he read, often supplying annotations. Andrew's love of reading inspired him to write poetry, a practice that conflicted with his desire to be perceived as masculine. He "steadily imbibed the impression," Sigourney laments, "that it was not manly to write verse, and therefore, as he desired to be manly not visionary, he performed a crusade against his native taste" (*Faded Hope* 181).

This crusade of self-repression followed from Andrew's longing to become conventionally male in the ways that boys' reading—especially histories—depicted exemplary masculinity: "he conceived a desire of future distinction . . . the not unlikely effect of . . . studies, which create an admiration for heroes" (182). For Sigourney, to be "visionary" meant to see beyond conventional prescriptions for male behavior, and she hoped that Andrew's desire to imitate the heroes of his reading "might be modified, and pass away" (182). But unfortunately for her it did not. Her maternal influence was not able to modify the dictates embodied in his reading, especially those about disciplining the self and avoiding "effeminacy," two key tenets of boys' reading. Andrew made his sole goal attending West Point, "commenc[ing] a course of self-discipline and hardship," walking over twenty miles a day, and "despising all . . . indulgence as effeminacy" (182). In many ways, these expectations remained constant through the century; as we saw in the last chapter, *Little Women* depicts the pressures that Laurie feels to live up to masculine expectations that conflict with his "visionary" notions about himself. Laurie eventually enters his grandfather's business although, like Andrew, he wants to pursue the arts, preferring to be a pianist and composer instead of a merchant. Both knew, as most boys did, that the arts were typically thought of as "less manly" because they were not productive of capital in the ways that a man needed to be.

In trying to understand her son's fetishizing of the masculinity promised by the military life, Sigourney looks to "the tales of Washington" that inspired Andrew (182). This recourse to reading as an explanation for her son's behavior is not surprising. Not only did the culture at large obsess over the effects of children's reading—with commentary on the subject in both boys' and girls' advice books, children's magazines, educational journals, and elsewhere—but Sigourney herself was deeply invested in literacy, writing over a hundred essay for boys, many of which she later collected into readers. In arguing that stories about Washington could harm boys by causing them to view certain pursuits as insufficiently manly, Sigourney is criticizing a staple of boys' reading. Two best sellers of the first half of the nineteenth century, Mason Weems's *The Life of Washington* (1800) and Jared Sparks's *The Life of George Washington* (1837), appeared on many educators' reading lists for boys, and short pieces about Washington that were based on these biographies and that celebrated him as an exemplar of masculine ambition appear throughout children's magazines.[5]

In an essay on Washington in *The Boy's Book* (1843), Sigourney focuses not on his political and military achievements, but on the domestic implications of his life, in particular the ways in which his relationship with his mother could serve as a model for boy readers. "Some of the most interesting" aspects of his life," she says, "are those "that connect him with his mother" ("Filial Virtues of Washington" 65).[6] Sigourney certainly knew that many of the male authors who wrote about Washington were not particularly concerned with this relationship. Weems claimed that his biography stresses the "private virtues" of Washington—what he calls the man "below the clouds," but as historian Peter Onuf notes, "in truth, very little of the *Life* fulfills this promise" (x).[7]

Many educators argued that boys' reading should primarily consist of the kind of biographical and historical texts that Sigourney saw as potentially dangerous. Though most advice writers did not completely oppose fiction, they claimed that novels (as well as short stories and poems) could have a bad effect on boys, so along with numerous educators and reviewers, they told boys to focus on history and biography. Popular advice author and novelist T. S. Arthur says that "books of facts . . . should make by far the larger portion of" the reading of boys and young men; "History [and] biography" he goes on to note, "furnish the mind with the main facts the boys need to know" (*Advice* 45). The reverend Joel Hawes tells his readers to "give an important place to historical reading . . . [which is] replete with the most interesting and profitable lessons" (107).[8] Like Arthur and Eddy, Hawes believes that "*biography* . . . is a kind of reading [that] furnishes lessons of wisdom and prudence . . . inspiring in the reader a love of what is . . . excellent" (108–9; emphasis in original). In a section of his advice book entitled "Pernicious Literature," Rufus Clark worries about the corrupting effects of fiction, but heartily endorses the "truth . . . that history can impart" (99), and Eddy notes that history, science, and philosophy can "amuse, instruct, and benefit" boys in a way superior to other genres (93). In an expanded section on books in the second edition of his conduct manual, he amplifies his suggestion that a boy's reading center on American history writers such as Bancroft and Prescott (191). Eddy and these advice writers rarely worry, as Sigourney and others do, that reading histories and biographies by Bancroft, Sparks, or Weems could have anything other than ennobling consequences for boys like Andrew.

When Andrew tells his mother that he was rejected by West Point and that his dream to live out the historical narratives he read while young was over, "the paleness as of the grave passed over [his] lip and brow" (195). This description displays the kind of foreshadowing typical of the sentimental narratives that Sigourney often wrote; readers know that a character described in this way will likely die before the story ends. Sigourney's phrase intimately connects Andrew's disappointment to his death, making the latter appear to be the almost inevitable result of the former. In a poem probably written when Andrew was still an infant, she tells a story about boyhood reading that strangely foreshadows Andrew's death:

> I saw thee scan the classic page . . .
> And marked thy strong and brilliant mind aroused to bold pursuit
>
> . . .
>
> I shrank with secret fear,
> A shuddering presage that thy race must soon be ended here.
>
> ("Death of a Beautiful Boy" 13–18)

Since Andrew, like the boy in the poem, could not become the "man" that his boyhood reading—the "classic pages" of history—demanded he be, his race would end: he would not reach manhood. In popular American sentimental novels like *Charlotte Temple,* the sickness or death of the female protagonist signals the price she pays for operating outside of accepted moral boundaries. But in *The Faded Hope*—a kind of sentimental and moral biography—Andrew's sickness does not follow from any violation of cultural norms but rather exposes the "sickness" of the norms themselves and the pressure they place on the disciplinary subject. Put in terms of another affective narrative, Andrew dies of a broken heart: the pain he feels at being unable to become a true man is unbearable, a pain he finds unspeakable. "From that hour [of his rejection by West Point] the subject," Sigourney says, "was never mentioned between them" (195). And even in the final throes of consumption, Andrew remains true to another historical narrative of masculinity: the stories about the Spartans that had taught him "to meet disappointment manfully" (195). "Yielding to sickness, or accepting care," he believed, "savored of effeminacy," an attitude that saddened Sigourney, who deeply wanted to care for her son (211). Even while Andrew is dying, he relies on the kind of martial narrative that Sigourney attacked in her essays for boys.

The Faded Hope is Sigourney's most personal criticism of norms of masculine literacy, but in the decades prior to its release, she had published numerous pieces in children's periodicals that expressed with equal force her antipathy toward popular ideologies of masculinity. In 1839 she published *The Boys' Reading-Book; in Prose and Poetry, for Schools,* a collection of her writing that she later revised into *The Boy's Book*. *The Boys' Reading-Book,* she said, "was written with care, aiming to enforce such principles as seemed to me vitally important," the kind of domestic values that she felt were lacking in other essays and collections (*Letters of Life* 343).[9] Some of the pieces in her readers had originally been used as lessons for Andrew, who was eight when her first collection for boys appeared. When Sigourney discusses *The Boys' Reading-Book* in her 1866 autobiography *Letters of Life,* she imagines Andrew, her "boy-pupil, my faded hope," reading with her and "pausing to ask some question" (343). Thus, at the same time that Andrew "conceived a desire of future distinction" and began to "perform a crusade against his native tastes," Sigourney was writing, publishing, and even using as lessons for him stories such as "John and James Williams," a tale about the dangers of embracing the narratives of manliness advocated in biographies, adventure stories, and popular histories, a tale that failed to have the effect on Andrew that Sigourney had wanted.

As *The Faded Hope* connects "the tales of Washington" with Andrew's desire to pursue a military life and his subsequent death, "John and James Williams" connects historical writings and the death of James Williams. To ensure that readers do not miss the cautionary thrust of Sigourney's narrative, the end of the opening paragraph announces the piece as an essay on literacy: "Both were fond of books, but their taste and dispositions were different," a crucial difference that preoccupies the narrative (132). Consistent with the dramatic polarities that often structure Sigourney's narratives, one kind of reading leads to contentment, the other to death. When Sigourney revised and republished "John and James Williams" as an illustrated book titled *The Farmer and the Soldier* (1836), she noted that she reissued it to critique a widespread advocacy of a historical-military disposition, hoping to get this attack into greater circulation. Both versions of the story, she believed, would show a boy "the false glory that sometimes surrounds" historical figures (*Letters of Life* 335).

The thirteen-year-old James brags, "I mean to be a soldier. I have lately been reading . . . a good deal of Bonaparte," and the mention of Napoleon is calculated, for Sigourney certainly knew that he was one of the most popular models of manhood celebrated in fictions, histories, and conduct manuals for boys (*Farmer and the Soldier* 5).[10] Dubbert notes that Napoleon repeatedly appears throughout nineteenth-century writing as a symbol of ambition and mastery, and Judy Hilkey shows that his story represented an approach to life that many believed was necessary if a boy were to succeed in the marketplace; one manual even refers to the model successful male as a "Napoleon of the Mart" (cited in Hilkey 79).[11] Advice material for boys and essays about literacy often encourage readers to admire the ambition, "bold pursuit," and industry of male historical figures, but Sigourney claims that Napoleon's narrative is dangerous because his life represents the inversion of a healthy masculinity: "The *end of a life was the test of its goodness*," she notes, and Napoleon's imprisonment and death clearly embody the sickness of Napoleonic masculinity ("Napoleon" 6; emphasis in original).[12] Napoleon represents ambition, autonomy, and mastery, three traits that many endorsed but that Sigourney and others questioned as suitable values for boys.

Speaking as a surrogate for Sigourney, John Williams rejects Napoleon as an icon, but James, having fully "imbibed" the value of ambition that Andrew Sigourney would, dismisses his brother's concern: "John,—your ideas are very limited. I am sorry to see, that you are not capable of admiring heroes. You are just fit to be a farmer" (*Farmer and the Soldier* 7).[13] The story then abruptly shifts to the distant future, as John wonders about the fate of his brother, who has been gone for fifteen years. At that exact moment, James returns from fighting in an unnamed foreign war, saying, "I have come home to you, to die" (10). Like Andrew Sigourney, James never attains the ideals represented in his boyhood reading despite continual attempts: "he had ventured everywhere with the bravest, into deepest danger, seeking everywhere, for the glory, which had dazzled his boyhood, but in vain" ("John and James Williams" 135). In *The Farmer and the Soldier,* Sigourney lengthens the attack on books as it appeared in "John and James Williams," rewriting her narration about James's boyhood and putting it in the voice of the weary and repentant soldier: "That glory which dazzled me in my days of boyhood, and which I supposed was always the reward . . . continually eluded me" (14). Thus, James's desire to live up to and live out a masculine fiction by creating a life that mirrored the adventures of his reading causes his death, just as Sigourney would later believe it caused Andrew's.

In "John and James Williams," *The Farmer and the Soldier,* and *The Faded Hope,* Sigourney repudiates the belief that biographical and historical reading reward boy in culturally desirable ways; indeed, she claims the opposite. She wrote the *History of Marcus Aurelius, Emperor of Rome* (1836)—portions of which she used in Andrew's education—as a corrective to the damage caused by popular histories of military figures: "I had long been solicitous of selecting some era which might serve to imbue the young mind with a love for historical knowledge, yet leave it undazzled by the pomp of military achievement" (*Letters of Life* 339). Like the farmer, Aurelius represents for Sigourney an antidote to the "dazzling" seduction presented by the conventional heroic narratives. In spite of his considerable accomplishments, what matters for Sigourney is Aurelius's devotion to what she called the "family circle": "when a child, he was . . . attentive to his mother . . . [and] when a boy, he was careful to teach and protect his sister" (98).[14]

According to many of her critics and admirers, Sigourney was popular because her writings expressed conventional values in a literary form palatable to her genteel readers. Many claim that her children's literature in particular simply replays a host of long-standing attitudes to childhood and education; her biographer Gorton Haight, for example, spends a great deal of time showing the similarities between her didactic works for children and those of her contemporaries.[15] But when it came to boys' reading, Sigourney was enmeshed in a complex and far-reaching debate involving a number of positions, and as a mother concerned about the fatal power that reading exercised on her own son, she was a less conventional and more engaged theorist of her culture and of masculinity than we may have supposed. This way of looking at literacy, I argue, reflects conventional nineteenth-century beliefs about how boys were affected by the historical and fictional adventure narratives they consumed. Although these narratives might appear to early twenty-first-century readers as solely empowering for the boys who read them, Sigourney and many other writers believed differently.[16]

※ ※ ※

In "John and James Williams," Sigourney argues that the story of Alexander the Great represents a historical narrative as suspect as Napoleon's. She worries that boys would try to imitate the behaviors and beliefs of Alexander, whose ideas about ambition and adventure are antithetical to Sigourney's communal, other-directed domestic ethos: "Try to form a correct opinion of the great men of whom you read," Sigourney warns in the closing of *History of Marcus Aurelius* (118). Adventure narratives are generally characterized as endorsing the kinds of patriarchal impulses that Sigourney opposed, but this view oversimplifies how authors—especially those who write boy's adventure and history—imagined these books would be interpreted by readers. These writers did not want or expect a boy to imitate historical figures but to draw an abstract lesson about how these figures' lives could be applied to their own. They often wanted their stories' morals to be directed not at any kind of actions in the world—heroic or otherwise—but toward sentiments within the self; they saw the adventure novel, and even the historical narrative, as ultimately a personal and domestic genre emphasizing the values of work, self-sacrifice, and social obligation.

Published decades after Sigourney's writings for boys and reprinted the year *The Story of a Bad Boy* was first published, Francis Forrester's boys' novel *Dick Duncan* (1860) thematizes the moral value of reading history and, like Sigourney, Forrester employs the story of Alexander.[17] Under the names Francis Forrester and Lawrence Lancewood, minister, newspaper editor, and author Daniel Wise wrote dozens of children's books from the 1850s through the 1880s. Though his writings were not as popular as Sigourney's, Forrester's novels represent a kind of well-received, didactic boys' story produced before and after the Civil War, a type that has been neglected in the study of boys and their literature in favor of boy-books. Although we might expect a fundamental change in attitudes about the disciplinary purpose of boys' reading during the course of the decades since Sigourney's first boys' reader appeared in 1839, I would argue that no major shift is visible; popular novels like Forrester's share attitudes toward the moral imperatives of literacy similar to those found in the writings of Sigourney and many others. Forrester believed his fiction was unburdened by the didacticism found in earlier works and thus was able to speak more meaningfully to boys about their masculinity. Yet his novels' "purpose" was essentially that of Sigourney's stories and histories. Forrester writes that his intent

> is to sow the seed of . . . manly character. . . . [and] exhibit the virtues and vices of childhood, not in prosy, unreadable precepts, but in a series of characters which move before the imagination as living beings do before the senses. Thus access to the heart is won by way of the imagination. (i)[18]

He endorses historical narratives like that of Alexander and recommends a kind of imitation of such "manly" role models—a celebration of historical reading that might at first appear to put him at odds with the stance taken by Sigourney, yet he ultimately endorses the values that she does.

Forrester and Sigourney advocate a position regarding masculine achievement and adventure narratives taken by male and female writers throughout the nineteenth century. Like Sigourney, Forrester doesn't expect or want readers to copy any given actions or to adopt a martial worldview, so he rejects heroic imitation. He makes it clear that the success narrative of a historical figure is valuable *only* as a metaphorical trajectory for a boy's moral growth and his eventual disciplining into suitability for domestic culture; in other words, just as figures like Alexander the Great conquered others, so must the boy conquer himself. This interpretation of heroic action is made repeatedly throughout *Dick Duncan,* as Forrester never leaves it as a metaphor for readers to unpack themselves. The novel argues that literacy—and the reading of history in particular—is a basis for a boy's ideas about self-governance, and the text shows that a boy's willingness to engage in the right kind of reading proves that he is on the way to "conquering" himself.

Dick Duncan articulates a theory of how boys' historical and fictional adventure narratives were consumed in the century: the moral content of the stories was interpreted as a personal mandate for the boy reader's self-improvement. Forrester's beliefs about the ethical value of adventure narratives agree with those held by many popular authors like Oliver Optic and Horatio Alger who argue that the trappings of adventure should be used in boys' fiction as a way to make the moral purposes of their narratives palatable to readers. Sigourney did not use historical narratives in exactly the same way as Forrester, but she certainly would have agreed with his belief that the goal of literacy was to educate boys in the primacy of self-governance and social responsibility.

The opening of *Dick Duncan* situates Forrester's story within the adventure tradition, but the novel ultimately reimagines the adventure ethos as a part of its critique of boyhood literacy. Guy Carlton (whose name evokes the aristocratic names of numerous adventure protagonists) is late for a meeting of the archery club (inspired by stories about Robin Hood) because he is deeply involved in reading the "adventures" of Rollin's *Ancient History,* a text that, like the biographies of Washington discussed earlier, frequently appears on educators' book lists for boys. That Guy reads this text to other characters each day identifies him as the novel's model boy. When he reads aloud "Rollin's account of Alexander," the narrator comments that he has "as interested a group of listeners as ever gave attention to an orator; the military adventures of the great Alexander charmed their imaginations" (57), just as they "dazzled" the boyhoods of Andrew Sigourney and James Williams. Guy is "glad [the boys are] pleased . . . [and] think[s] Rollin's *History* the most interesting book [he] ever read," and Forrester must think so, too, because the book and scenes of reading it structure the text (15). Indeed, he refers to it throughout the book in commentaries on the adventures that the boys have undertaken. Guy's and the other boys' pleasure is intimately connected to activities like reading that have a clear disciplinary value, just as the father of Abbott's Rollo believed.

Guy already embodies the novel's ideals of masculinity, but Dick, who as the book tells us "loves mischief," does not. Dick is offered as a typical boy, one whose boyish spirit must be eradicated. The heroines of many girls' novels, such as Louisa May Alcott's *Jack and Jill* (1880) and Susan Coolidge's *What Katy Did* (1872), suffer an illness that becomes an occasion for the protagonist's transformation, and Forrester figures Dick's boyishness as a sickness that must be cured. Guy reads to the confined Dick every day, and as a result "Dick began to give attention to reading himself. To the surprise of everyone he one day said to his father, 'Pa, I wish you would get me Rollin's *Ancient History*. . . . I want to read it through'" (89). His father replies by repeating advice manuals' dictate to read systematically as a form of discipline: "Well, my boy, if you promise to read it through steadily, I'll get it" (89). Dick's "eagerness" to pursue a disciplined regime of historical reading proves that he is beginning to govern himself: "I'll read some in it every day" and "leave off my tricks" (90).

Though Dick says he will attempt to lead a life modeled on Alexander's, Forrester wants to ensure that his readers understand the very limited form of imitation that the narrative sanctions. Dick's Uncle Morris articulates exactly how boys should replay Alexander's accomplishments: "Keep up the conflict with your evil habit, however, and you will live to be a better man than Alexander the Great," to which a puzzled Dick replies, "[T]hat can hardly be, sir . . . he was a great conqueror and I shall never command a corporal's guard, much less a grand army" (149). "Quite likely. Yet if you conquer yourself," his uncle insists, "you will achieve a greater conquest than the subjection of empires" (149). *Dick Duncan*'s representative boy needs to be "conquered" just as *Little Women*'s Laurie is "tame[d] and train[ed]" by his tutor, who describes his charge, in the animalistic terms often associated with boys, as an "unbroken colt . . . who was freakish and wild" (127). Jane Tompkins tells us that references to horse-training in Susan Warner's *The Wide, Wide World* (1850) represent the kind of "sexual style" of discipline indicative of Warner's and the culture's figuring of male-female relationships in terms of female submission to patriarchal values (600). But as Forrester and Alcott show us, male and female writers also use such figurative language, without the sexual content, to characterize the process of breaking boys, of eradicating the kind of traits they possess at the beginning of these novels.

In keeping with the revision of adventure tropes that runs throughout *Dick Duncan*, self-discipline becomes meaningful to boys as "self-conquering." A key purpose of disciplinary literacy was to prepare a boy for the difficulties he would face as a husband, father, and worker, and conquering the self was viewed as both an end in itself and the necessary first step to success. As the novel closes, the once playful Dick settles down, devoting himself to work and abandoning the belief, one held by Jacob Abbott's Rollo and many other popular fictional boys, that boyhood should be a space in which play is free from any notion of utility. Despite its adventure trappings, *Dick Duncan* is not so much a novel of adventure as it is a novel of reform. Rather than functioning as the antithesis of domestic novels like *Little Women* or girls' books by Martha Finley, Susan Coolidge, and others, it is a companion text, one equally interested in the disciplining of its readers. Forrester believes that the scenes of historically related play, adventure, and reading in *Dick Duncan* will keep boys interested in the narrative so that they can learn the real lesson, which is always self-discipline.[19]

As Forrester's novel ends, Dick has to "leave off" mischief and play as a sign to others of his personal transformation. Though his sense of play makes him compelling as a literary character, it must be eradicated so the stage can be set for his adulthood, and when this transformation happens, he and his book ultimately become less interesting. Lynne Vallone has argued that girls' play—which she sees as the opposite of boys' adventure—"has an elegiac quality" (22). We know, she says, that girls' play contains within it the values that guarantee its end, for it will be replaced by the restrictive obligations of womanhood for which the play acts as preparation. Yet *Dick Duncan* ends with a sober and chastened "Richard Duncan," who has taken to reading Rollin's history to signify his intent to shed his spirited boyishness and abandon the play that defined him. In this way, his narrative follows the plot of many popular girls' and boys' novels: just as Dick Duncan becomes Richard Duncan, Alger's Ragged Dick becomes "Richard Hunter, Esq.," leaving nearly all of his ragged qualities behind as he moves toward "respectability" by becoming a clerk in a counting house.[20]

Throughout both of these narratives, the main characters' pranks and jokes cannot last. Initially, Ragged Dick's humor has an edge—perhaps unintended—of social satire. While a poor street boy he constantly mocks capitalism and the wealthy. But when he enters business, he must—as a member of the system—leave much of this humor and political critique behind. And even that which remains has lost it force, for in "rising upward"—the path of all Alger, Forrester, and Optic heroes—Dick has refuted his earlier criticisms of capitalism and proved the essential fairness of the system: it will allow any determined boy to succeed. Forrester's novel ends with Dick Duncan losing an archery contest, for middle-class respectability demands that he never become anything like a Robin Hood–esque adventurer. As the book closes, Dick is crowned as a metaphorical "knight of industry" and predicts his own future as a less than knightly "merchant" (254, 256). Thus the heroic language of the novel is completely stripped of any traditional heroic significance. In this way, *Dick Duncan* replays Sigourney's boys' stories by rejecting the notion that readers should emulate real-life and fictional adventure heroes. Sigourney's narratives, along with Alger's and Forrester's novels, are fictional counterparts of the popular conduct books for boys and young men that offer themselves as preparatory guides for the "battle of life" and argue that if a boy is to possess a healthy masculinity, he must distance himself from play, pleasure, adventures, and most importantly, from his desires.[21]

❦ ❦ ❦

In Twain's *The Adventures of Tom Sawyer* (1876), we do not see the boys reading books, as we do in *Dick Duncan,* but we often see them talking about and imitating the exploits of characters in adventure stories. In this way, *Tom Sawyer* can be seen, like Sigourney's stories and Forrester's novel, as modeling a theory of boyhood reading. Unlike Sigourney and Forrester, however, Twain advocates a form of literacy in which boys replay the adventure narratives they consume. Indeed, critics such as Elizabeth Segel have read Twain's novels and similar boy-books as offering a liberatory mode of reading in which boys are free to act out any narrative they choose, especially those that signify their present and future power. Tom, for example, models himself and his play after the adventure fiction he reads and is allowed to live a boyhood in imitation of it—his life is "play" based upon reading. But the critical belief that adventure fictions such as Twain's boy novels, *Robinson Crusoe, Treasure Island,* or the books that Tom read were universally endorsed as appropriate reading for boys is inaccurate, and such a claim pays insufficient attention to the period's long-running debates about boys' reading. In his often-reprinted *The Boy's Guide to Usefulness* (1844), William Alcott, for example, recognizes that *Robinson Crusoe* "has a charm for many" but rejects the possibility that it could have any beneficial effects: "I have seldom know a boy made better or more contented by it" (113). He says that a boy's desire for "adventure and incident" can easily be satisfied by the kinds of travel narratives endorsed by many educators.

"The Voyage of the Salt Mackerel" (1872), a serial published in *Robert Merry's Museum,* is a travel and adventure narrative that, like *Tom Sawyer,* can be read as a metanarrative on reading, but here the author takes a stance similar to Sigourney's and William Alcott's but opposed to Twain's. Adventure stories, he tells us, have "fired [the main characters'] young hearts with a desire for . . . adventure, and they have run away," a journey that nearly ends in the "appalling calamity" of the boys drowning at sea (Barnard 246).[22] In a similar cautionary tale published in the *American Messenger,* a boy who wants to imitate the stories he reads goes to sea and, like Andrew Sigourney, "dies of consumption" (cited in Nord 115). Nineteenth-century sociologist William Graham Sumner describes the kind of adventure stories published before and after the Civil War as "intensely stupid, or spiced to the highest degree with sensationalism," and he attacks the belief that adventure narratives are beneficial to the creation of an ennobling boyhood masculinity: "sensational tales' views of life . . . are so base and false as to destroy all manliness and all chances of true success" (681).

In *Eight Cousins* (1875) Louisa May Alcott launches into a lengthy attack on "sensational" reading for boys (especially male-authored adventure narratives) that resembles the complaints of Sigourney, William Alcott, and Sumner.

She refers to Oliver Optic—whose books she calls "*optical* delusions"—but the criticism is directed against all "fashion[able] . . . popular stories" (201; emphasis in original).[23] The attack is staged as a debate between a mother, who voices Alcott's rejection of such texts, and two boys, who crave them. The boys argue that the books are valuable because of their realism and appealing protagonists, while the mother claims that these stories and their heroes offer fantasies with no relevance to the current or future lives of readers, few of whom will "defeat pirates, outwit smugglers, and so cover themselves with glory, that Admiral Farragut invites them to dinner, saying, 'Noble boy, you are an honor to your country!'" (201). Aliaga-Buchenau says that "only when women identify with protagonists" did "critics . . . perceive such identification as dangerous" (50–51). Yet this is perhaps Alcott's greatest concern: the boy reader will identify with the "appealing" hero and try to imitate his actions, a practice that she believes guarantees future disappointment and failure. And William Alcott expresses the fear of reader-adventure protagonist identification even more strongly: "is it to be expected that we can read about a . . . man, and at the same time be uninfluenced by him? It were impossible" (113). Like Sigourney and William Alcott, Louisa May Alcott sees the ideologies of ambition and independence embodied in these narratives and their heroes as insidious and "unnatural." She criticizes them as "sensationalistic," a charge leveled against boys' novels for their failure to follow the trajectory of a typical boy's life:

> Even if the hero is merely an honest boy trying to get his living, he is not permitted to do so in a natural way, by hard work and years of patient effort, but is suddenly adopted by a millionaire whose pocket-book he has returned; or a rich uncle appears from sea, just in the nick of time; or the remarkable boy earns a few dollars, speculates in pea-nuts or neck-ties, and grows rich so rapidly that Sinbad in the diamond valley is a pauper compared to him. Isn't it so, boys? (*Eight Cousins* 202)

Many critics claim that adventure narratives and the culture for which they were produced always endorse an ideology of unrestrained capitalism and masculine ambition, but this is certainly not the belief held by Forrester, Sigourney, or Alcott, who says these narratives give "boys such wrong ideas of life and business" by emphasizing ambition and material gain over the domestic virtues and familial obligations (202).[24]

Alcott employs the century's dominant metaphor for characterizing the process by which "wrong ideas" are internalized by readers: reading as ingestion. Aliaga-Buchenau argues, as Stephen Mailloux and many others have, that while males "were supposed to be able to handle the dangerous influence [of books] because of their strength"; the weakness of females meant that they could suffer serious moral harm (49).[25] This may be true for adults, yet we should not assume that the culture theorized adult males and boys in the same ways. In fact, boys, like girls and women, were seen as weak and prone to moral "sickness," desiring stories that were bad for them: "You have laid out a hard task for yourself," Alcott says, "in trying to provide good reading for boys who have been living on sensation stories. It will be like going from raspberry tarts to plain bread and butter; but you will probably save them from a bilious fever" (*Eight Cousins* 206). And here again, literacy is tied to the creation of a healthy masculinity: "they will be the manlier men," Alcott believes, by "feeding upon" the right kinds of texts (208). Sigourney, too, uses a version of this metaphor in her discussion of Andrew's unhealthy ideas about masculinity; he steadily "imbibed" harmful notions, and his death from consumption was likely caused by consuming dangerous reading. William Alcott offers a similar warning to his boy readers when he asks them "why then would you feast your mind on food which . . . will be as poisonous . . . as bad food is to the body?" (115).

Mailloux and others have argued that nineteenth-century writers believed that the weakness and irrationality of females meant that women could be negatively affected by the consumption of harmful texts. Yet, as I discussed in chapter 2, the popular metaphor of the "boy as savage" and the descriptions of boys as "depraved" characterize boys as irrational, or at least less rational, than girls. And this characterization underlies educators' beliefs about boys' responses to various kinds of reading. In an 1879 address to a Massachusetts library association, *Atlantic Monthly* editor Thomas Wentworth Higginson says that educators believed boys would be hurt by "sensational" writing because they are convinced "that boys are totally depraved" (358). These kinds of descriptions of "boy-nature" were widespread throughout the culture, so it should come as no surprise that boys would be seen as likely to suffer ill effects from reading. Sumner, for example, believes that a "great harm . . . is done to boys . . . by the nervous excitement of reading," (684–85), and many other writers, such as William Alcott, agree: "what thus affects his imagination is apt greatly to 'wear and tear' the nervous system" (118). Educators repeatedly assume that boys lack the kind of natural sentiments that would allow them to make correct moral judgments about a book or to resist its pernicious effects. Indeed, for many advice writers, boys' natural depravity draws them to depraved reading material. Higginson's comments alert us to the ways that theories of boyhood masculinity and boy-nature are connected to theories about discipline and reading, just as they are tied to ideas about the mother-son affective bond and boyhood corporal punishment.

Alcott and her fellow children's literature authors who attack "sensational" stories for boys offer criticisms of these narratives strikingly similar to those made by Mark Twain and many late-century realist writers. These writers argue that such texts represent a romanticized and therefore counterproductive worldview, with plots based on unlikely adventures and excessive coincidences, and narratives that promise unrealistic futures to well-behaved readers. Like Alcott, Twain, especially in tales like "The Story of the Good Little Boy Who Did Not Prosper" (1875), mocks the naïve wish-fulfillment of boys' stories. Critics repeatedly pair Twain and Alcott to show how differences in their positions on any number of questions are symptomatic of larger cultural and gender divides, Yet the similarity in their attitudes toward boys' novels show that issues of boyhood—as articulated both by "literary" and "popular" writers—offer an important place to look as we continue to revise narratives of nineteenth-century literary production and reception, especially those based on familiar classifications of authors, either by gender or by perceived literary seriousness. Though different in many ways, Lydia Sigourney and Francis Forrester agreed that the notion of heroic imitation was an irresponsible form of interpretation and should not be encouraged by authors. They were deeply invested in questions of boyhood literacy and shared beliefs about the relationship between a boy's masculinity and his reading of fiction and history. Indeed, many popular female and male authors writing before and after the Civil War insisted that reading was as contested an issue as any other form of discipline for boys.

Coda

"REAL BOYS" OF THE TWENTIETH AND TWENTY-FIRST CENTURIES

Educators, Academics, and Sociologists on Boyhood

> Just as planes and ships disappear mysteriously into the Bermuda Triangle, so do the selves of girls go down in droves.
> —Mary Pipher

> Boys today are in serious trouble. . . . Many of our sons are in a desperate crisis.
> —William Pollack

In *Good Girl Messages: How Young Women Were Misled by Their Favorite Books,* Deborah O'Keefe surveys girls' literature from the nineteenth century on, showing the ways in which it offers limiting ideas about female experience, ones that reflect widespread cultural narratives about girls and femininity. Written for a general audience, O'Keefe's book doesn't challenge critical assumptions about this literature; as she says herself, its "opinions" are often "not particularly controversial" (13). Rather, it offers a well-organized history of the plots, tropes, and character types that have dominated this fiction, and it examines the consequences that the constant repetition of these narrative elements has had for girl readers. O'Keefe's analysis of the pedagogical content encoded in fictions of boyhood, however, is less helpful. Her argument repeats a recognizable formula, one that I refer to earlier in this book: girls' books preach passivity and self-denial, while boys' books (and even boy characters within girls' books) represent and promote masculine adventure and autonomy.

Like the literary critics I talk about in chapter 1, O'Keefe consistently erases the line between fiction and life: what happens in these stories represents what happens in girls' lives. For instance, she contrasts two scenes of horse-riding injuries from the work of mid-twentieth-century novelist Dorothy Lyons to illustrate the different expectations for boys and girls. Connie's injury is nothing more exciting than a "painful limp" (cited in O'Keefe 65). She can't engage in the kind of free-spirited riding that leads to a boy's wounds, which the novel graphically describes:

> [His] shirt was soaked with blood across his middle. Blood was running down his chin from his cut lip. All down the right side of his hip . . . the flesh was raw. . . . The heel of his hand was covered with tiny cuts and abrasions into which gravel and dirt was ground. But what boy knows when he has had enough? (cited in O'Keefe 65)

It is true that the injuries in this scene result in part from the fact that the boy is encouraged to be more adventurous than Connie, but does the association between boyhood and adventure always work to a boy's advantage? It is easy to imagine what Lydia Sigourney's answer would have been to this question. It would have been helpful if O'Keefe had asked the same questions about the representations of boys that she asks about images of girls: could this scene, for example, (and the many like it in boys' books) represent an injurious ideal of masculinity that might have consequences for boys? Like the scar on the face of boyhood icon G. I. Joe, the wounded male body often serves as a badge of courage, a fact that certainly has not always been a good thing for boys and men. Maybe books have done boys a disservice by failing to teach them how to recognize when they have "had enough."

By setting in opposition the kinds of messages in literature for girls and for boys, O'Keefe, like many before and after her, unfortunately ignores (and even seems to reject) the possibility that young men could be as strongly misled by their favorite books as girls have been, a possibility that worried many nineteenth-century authors like Sigourney and Alcott. Literary and cultural fictions about boys who wound themselves to prove their masculinity, who spurn community and embrace alienation, or who, like Andrew Sigourney, embrace a notion of masculine achievement they are emotionally or physically unable to attain, may not equip boys to lead the kinds of lives they want. And as *Boys at Home* shows, these kinds of narratives of masculinity have a long history in American writing and a strong presence throughout all kinds of literature for and about boys in the nineteenth century.

In the last thirty years, literary critics, sociologists, and educators have devoted a considerable amount of time to valuable studies of gender and pedagogy in girls' texts, putting these findings in the larger contexts of literary history, curriculum design, teachers' classroom practices, parental beliefs about gender, and media representations of childhood.[1] These studies, like O'Keefe's survey, rightly look in detail at the effect that these ideas of femininity can have on girls, yet unlike Sigourney's work, few address in any detail the possibility that conceptions of masculinity might have an array of possible effects on boys. In *Girls: Feminine Adolescence in Popular Culture and Cultural Theory,* Catherine Driscoll says that her book "rarely mentions boys . . . [in order to] duplicate in reverse the dominant mode of studying youth" (7). While many foundational studies of adolescence have taken a male-centered approach (e.g., G. Stanley Hall's 1904 *Adolescence*), in much of the literary-historical work on the nineteenth century produced in recent decades, boys of all ages have often been, surprisingly, at the margins. Christine Griffin follows Driscoll by claiming that girls "remain relatively invisible" in studies of adolescence, but searches of reference databases for scholarly books and articles reveal that in the areas of both nineteenth-century literature and children's literature, studies of girls and young women outnumber those on boys and young men by more than ten to one (30).[2] This disparity certainly suggests that more work is needed before we can begin to believe that we understand boyhood—and therefore girlhood and childhood—in the period.

Though nineteenth-century boyhood remains a relatively understudied area, contemporary boyhood has received significant attention in the popular media in the last decade. Although this interest began as an aspect of the men's studies movement that emerged in the mid-1970, boyhood gained a kind of cultural prominence in the mid- and late 1990s, with the release of Michael Gurian's *The Wonder of Boys: What Parents, Mentors and Educators Can Do to Shape Boys into Exceptional Men,* Christina Hoff Sommers's *The War Against Boys: How Misguided Feminism Is Harming Our Young Men,* and William Pollack's *Real Boys: Rescuing Our Sons from the Myths of Boyhood.* Pollack's text, perhaps the most widely discussed book on the "boy crisis," looks at conventions of masculinity, exploring what he calls the "Boy Code," a set of ideas he argues has harmed boys' social and private lives (xxv).[3] Pollack's work is a response to Mary Pipher's influential *Reviving Ophelia: Saving the Selves of Adolescent Girls,* which received substantial attention for its claim that girls undergo a crisis during adolescence and "become 'female impersonators' who fit their whole selves into small, crowded spaces" (22). Pipher seems unconcerned about boys and rarely considers the possibility that they might suffer similar problems. Boys are rarely discussed in any detail, and the familiar binary logic of her argument is based on the assumption that boys are encouraged to realize their "authentic selves," while girls are forced to become impersonators. Pollack offers a kind of corrective to *Reviving Ophelia* by making an argument similar to that of Pipher (who writes the foreword to Pollack's book)—calling boys "beleaguered Hamlets"—but both writers ignore the relational nature of gender codes and how looking at one set of gender norms can shed light on the other.

Christina Hoff Sommers's widely reviewed *The War against Boys: How Misguided Feminism Is Harming Our Young Men* followed in the single-sex mode of Pollack and Pipher and suffers because of this approach. She targets these writers and especially Carol Gilligan, the scholar who first advocated the theory of "girlhood crisis." The American girl, Gilligan warned, "is in danger of drowning or disappearing," a danger that Sommers dismisses (cited in Sommers 4). Sommers notes the questionable interpretation of data upon which Gilligan's work is based, but her advocacy of boys as a way to critique feminism leads to a wholesale rejection of Gilligan.[4] For me, much of Gilligan's argument is suspect because of overreaching generalizations about a crisis and the way she pathologizes girls. Yet Sommers's argument is suspect because she accepts a purely biological basis for boy behaviors and does not give nearly enough attention to the diverse cultural factors—the kinds of pressures that Gilligan focuses on for girls—at work in their making. Only feminism, Sommers believes, has harmed boys. She ignores the many long-standing patriarchal myths—enforced by men and women as well as boys and girls—about what it means to be a boy and a man, the kind that Louisa May Alcott and Sigourney explore at length. Sommers concludes by saying that "one of the more agreeable facts of life is that boys will be boys," but exactly what forces beyond biology make a boy who he is go uninvestigated (213). Most nineteenth-century educators, as we have seen, take a more nuanced view and recognize the invocation of "boys will be boys" as an attempt to shut down conversations on boyhood pedagogy or as a way to diminish or ignore the effects of imperatives of masculinity. Though these educators share with Sommers certain beliefs about boy-nature and biology, they were far more concerned with the role played by any number of forces at work in the construction of boyhood.

Although dedicated to the study of boyhood, most of the boy crisis books pathologize their subjects, seeing boys as alienated, depressed underachievers, under assault either by a feminized pedagogy or by cultural norms. Sommers, Pollack, and Gurian have generally been greeted with disapproval in academic circles. Kidd, for example, offers a sustained critique of "boy crisis" books, exposing a reliance on a biological understanding of boys, a yearning for a lapsed utopian space of boyhood free from feminism, and "racist and sexist impulses" ("Boyology" 67). This kind of critique is developed at length in the collection *What about the Boys? Issues of Masculinity in Schools*. This collection is important because it emphasizes issues of race, class, and sexuality and thus complicates the picture offered by crisis books, which rarely acknowledge that their concern is primarily middle-class heterosexual white males. Despite *What about the Boys?*'s sensitivity to these issues and its insistence "that all boys are not the same," the collection's introduction falls back on familiar claims about boyhood and privilege like those by O'Keefe and many literary scholars: "boyhood . . . means entitlement" and "in short, boyhood is the entitlement to and the anticipation of power" (15). Given the diversity of boys the collection studies—boys who have dramatically different kinds of lives and experiences under a host of masculine codes—such a claim is puzzling. In the tradition of some of the literary critics I have talked about, a linage that looks to Twain's *Tom Sawyer* as the key text of American boyhood, the editors associate this privilege with an essential freedom, and they disassociate boyhood and manhood: "Boyhood is . . . freedom from manhood's responsibilities" (15). But do all boys in all situations really experience this privilege and freedom? Aren't boys often concerned with enacting aspects of adult masculinity during their boyhoods? Don't all sorts of norms of masculinity tell boys that acting like a boy—and not a man—isn't enough? In making broad generalizations, *What about the Boys?* unintentionally invokes the "competition" mode of the crisis books, in which one gender always has it worse than the other. Just as in O'Keefe's study, in *What about the Boys?* boyhood and girlhood are locked in competition—and there is always a clear winner and loser. This kind of rhetoric surfaces only occasionally in the collection, but it stands out because the essays otherwise level a devastating critique at the blind spots and generalizations of the crisis book and pop sociological rhetoric about the dilemmas of boyhood.

Recent studies of masculinity offer an approach that can help us to move away from commonplace ideas about boyhood found in popular and scholarly writings, for these studies have reoriented not only how we think about males but how we understand issues of domesticity, sentimentality, discipline, and the relationship between public and private spaces, issues equally relevant to the study of boyhood. And this reorientation is driving a steady increase in the number of literary studies of boyhood published in the last five years—such as Kidd's *Making American Boys: Boyology and the Feral Tale;* Annette Wanamaker's *Boys in Children's Literature and Popular Culture: Masculinity, Abjection, and the Fictional Child;* and Lorinda Cohoon's *Serialized Citizenships: Periodicals, Books, and American Boys, 1840–1911*—and perhaps inspire authors to move away from the cross-gender antagonism that has defined boy and girl crisis books. I wonder what kinds of interesting and unusual claims could be made if we had a more involved understanding of how pedagogical issues play out for both boys and girls. I am not arguing that a book on gender must equally address both genders—this book would not satisfy this standard—but I would like to see more studies that examine boyhood and girlhood together and go further in this direction than I have.

Reading nineteenth-century girls' and women's novels in the wake of more than three decades of feminist scholarship, we can no longer come to these texts with the belief that they are uninteresting productions of the historical moments that they represent, that they simply embody either a repressive or liberatory pedagogy, and—perhaps more importantly—that they have a transparent relationship to the cultural debates about gender in which they are embedded. So when we look at *The Adventures of Tom Sawyer,* Alger's *Ragged Dick,* Abbott's *Rollo at Work* and *Rollo at Play,* Optic's novels, representations of boys in girls' novels, or notions of boy-nature within educational discourses, we should move beyond the binaries and competition of the crisis books and ask about boyhood the same kinds of questions asked by scholars of girlhood, ones that recall issues that Lydia Sigourney explores when trying understand her son's life: What narratives about masculinity are directed at boys? How are these narratives connected to larger debates about children? How are forms of boyhood masculinity related to adult masculinities? And we should also ask questions that interrogate scholarly assumptions: What roles do boys play within our current narratives of domesticity and sentiment? How do issues of boyhood play out in writing for different audiences—boys, girls, children, and perhaps even adults? What authors and archives of material (literary and otherwise) should we examine in order to investigate boyhood and childhood pedagogy in more productive ways? When critics argue, as many have, that only "girls' stories are about accommodation," we should turn such claims into a question: what are the narratives that boys are asked to accommodate? (R. Saxton 22).

While writing *Boys at Home,* I often found myself returning to Lydia Sigourney and Louisa May Alcott as inspirations for a balanced critical disposition. They were concerned about the effects that patriarchal ideologies had on girls and women, but they were deeply interested in boys and the many ways in which the culture thought about the education of males. They recognized specific ways in which boys were entitled and empowered, but they seldom made blanket claims such as "boyhood meant entitlement," seeing such generalizations as of little use when trying to develop the specifics of an effective pedagogy. Sigourney and Alcott believed in biological differences between the genders, as do many of the boy crisis book authors, yet neither of them were ultimately invested in biological explanations. Instead their writings display a host of different management strategies that they hoped would bring about the same goal: the creation of a healthy boyhood masculinity. And most relevant for critical examinations of boyhood in the twenty-first century, Alcott and Sigourney believed that a boy is constantly acted upon and profoundly shaped by the fictions produced by the culture in which he finds himself.

Notes

INTRODUCTION

Literary Critics and "The Boy"

1. A widely held position sees the period's sentimentalism as synonymous with its beliefs about domesticity, but as my chapter on maternal sympathy in particular shows, I do not equate the two. And the chapter on physical discipline demonstrates that while many depictions of boys accord with sentimental characterizations of childhood, many do not. For a valuable discussion of the relationship between these two ideas in early American literature, see Marion Rust's "'Into the House of an Entire Stranger': Why Sentimental Doesn't Equal Domestic in Early American Fiction."
2. The term "boy-book" typically refers to a group of post–Civil War novels by Twain, Aldrich, Warner, Howells, and a few others. I use the phrases "boys' fiction," "boys' novels," or "boys' stories" to refer to other literary works for boys. For a general discussion of texts that fall into the boy-book category, see Jacobson's *Being a Boy Again* 1–24. Her book is a valuable psychological study of the conditions of authorship and the personal uses of boyhood by writers after the Civil War, and she explores the way "a particular crisis in male adulthood" is "the motive and shaping force" behind each of the stories that she discusses (24).
3. For representations of gender difference in Louisa May Alcott's novels, see the descriptions of one of the March sister's male and female twins in *Little Women*, chapter 45. "The Little Women Series" includes children's novels published from 1868 to 1886: *Little Women, Little Men, Jo's Boys, Eight Cousins, Rose in Bloom, Under the Lilacs, An Old-Fashioned Girl,* and *Jack and Jill.* See also Alcott's autobiographical sketch "My Boys" in the first volume of her *Aunt Jo's Scrap-Bag* (1872). For my account of boyhood in Alcott, see *The Louisa May Alcott Encyclopedia* 40–41.
4. For an examination of the gender differentiation that accompanies the movement into boyhood and girlhood from "infancy" (the common term for the period from 18 months to 5–6 years), see Reinier 56–60 and 125–34. See also Kett 11.

5. See Kett 11–37 for a discussion of "the language of age" in late eighteenth- and nineteenth-century America.
6. Driscoll almost exclusively emphasizes distinctions between the genders; see, for example, 113 and 257. Jerry Griswold's *Audacious Kids: Coming of Age in America's Classic Children's Books* looks at conventions of plot and character shared by boys' and girls' books but is, like other such studies, not interested in pedagogy.
7. Similarly, Caleb Crain's *American Sympathy,* a study of literary representations of male friendship in the eighteenth and nineteenth centuries, looks mostly at adults.
8. See, for example, Abbott's "Advantages" 25–30.
9. The dual audience of numerous popular books and periodicals like *Oliver Optic's Magazine for Boys and Girls* suggests that many writers believed boys and girls should read educational materials that advocate the same personal and social standards for each gender. No lengthy study of this material has been undertaken, and it is frequently overlooked in scholarly discussions of literature, education, and gender, which typically focus on gender-specific publications, such as girls' advice manuals.
10. In a study of the acculturation of American children from 1775 to 1850, Jacqueline Reinier explores gender differences that, I argue, are connected to the different kinds of disciplinary strategies to which boys and girls were subjected.
11. For information about Alcott and Optic's relationship and the growth of the gender-specific children's book series, see Wadsworth and Gleason.
12. This passage from MacLeod is also cited by Ann Murphy in her essay on differences between nineteenth-century Bildungsromans for boys and girls (567). For representative arguments about the ways in which boys' novels are essentially absent the pedagogy that informs girls' texts, see Avery 189.

CHAPTER 1

Work and Play, Pleasure and Pedagogy in Nineteenth-Century Boys' Novels

1. For a detailed study of the reception history of these two novels, see Beverly Lyon Clark, *Kiddie Lit* 77–101.
2. Elizabeth Segel's essay on gender uses Twain's novels and Stevenson's *Treasure Island* as representative of the content of books for boys, yet such an argument is complicated in productive ways when we examine Abbott, Optic, Forester, and women writers for boys.
3. Other recent collections on childhood or masculinity, such as Levander and Singley's *The American Child* (the essays by Brown and Dawson

that I talk about appear in this volume) and Adams and Savran's *Masculinity Studies and Feminist Theory,* either repeat the narrative of an essential distinction between nineteenth-century American girlhood and boyhood or they overlook questions of boyhood masculinity altogether. These omissions reflect, I believe, a reluctance on the part of criticism to take childhood as a whole as a serious subject of inquiry, as Clark eloquently demonstrates in the introduction to *Kiddie Lit.*

4. For influential accounts of play, see Callios's *Man, Play, and Games,* Huizinga's *Homo Ludens: A Study of the Play Element in Culture,* and Winnicott's *Playing and Reality.*

5. Elizabeth Smith's "Childhood's Laugh," an 1846 poem in the sentimental tradition of the other poems I cite, laments the changes that take place when a boy ages and suffers from the responsibilities of manhood:

> . . . how smart he was, and witty when a child—
> And retrospective sighs are heaved, so sadly boys are changed
> Since they along the forest way, or by the seashore ranged. (22–24)

6. Gillian Brown says that "childhood can never be the impermeable zone that adults so persistently desire it to be" (36). But while she emphasizes representations that depict childhood as a discrete and idyllic space, most nineteenth-century writers believed it was a permeable and tense developmental stage in which adult intervention should be constant.

7. I am not arguing that all of Abbott's novels are domestic novels, only that a number of them reflect the setting and values of many girls' novels. Abbott's Rollo travel narratives, for example, would not fall into this category. Although Alger's *Ragged Dick* is often classified as an adventure novel, it too shares many values with traditional domestic fiction.

8. *The Adventures of Tom Sawyer* features scenes of corporal punishment, and while such discipline never seems to bother Tom, his peers in other boys' novels are often deeply affected by it.

9. See the extensive bibliography of reviews in Darling 277–424.

10. Abbott often uses Rollo's actions as occasions to generalize about boy-nature, saying that boys are "lazy" and "unreasonable," while the only girl in the novels, Lucy, is responsible and "reasonable." See *Rollo at Work* 31, 35, and 55, and *Rollo at Play* 75–76, 106, and 180.

11. In books like Abbott's, fathers and adult males are far more present than they are in boy-books, and they often intervene to enforce the novels' beliefs about discipline.

12. Sections of *Rollo at Work* and *Rollo at Play* were published as chapter books. A portion of *Rollo at Work* was issued as *The Two Wheelbarrows* in 1855, and it included a new frontispiece that depicted boys and a wheelbarrow.

13. Although Jonas is too invested in his work ever to crack a joke, boy characters are sometimes quite funny. The humor allowed protagonists

such as Tom Sawyer and Alger's Ragged Dick has been seen by critics as another key point of contrast between girls' and boys' texts. Yet writing for boys often warned them, as conduct manuals did girls, not to "laugh at, or repeat, any rude jest or foolish story," or to say "silly . . . words" (*Useful Lads* 76, 77). In *The Diving Bell* (1851), a book in the *Uncle Frank's Boy's and Girl's Library* series, Francis Woodworth takes a typically moderate view toward humor and boys' reading. Although he endorses "funny" books, he prefers stories in which humor is connected to information that can inspire "reflection." Woodworth worries about books that emphasize entertainment over instruction, believing that a combination of the two is best, and he cites as a model Abbott's novels, which is not surprising given the way that Abbott's links pleasure and usefulness (16–28). Conduct manuals for boys often connect these ideas as well; see, for example, Hawes's *Lectures to Young Men on the Formation of Character* (1851) 50–51. For more on boy language, see W. W. Everts's *Manhood: Its Duties and Responsibilities* (1854) 29–31, and John S. C. Abbott's *The School-Boy* (1839) 178–79.

14. *Robinson Crusoe* is the ur-text for many nineteenth-century American boys' novels. It was endorsed by educators because many of its adventures are scenes of Crusoe at work, replicating the domestic environment and its values, and much of its readerly pleasure is tied to such scenes. See Mott 32–33.

15. Abbott, Hall, Optic, and Josiah Holland (writing as Timothy Titcomb) use the metaphor of the "ship-as-life" to make the same point about boys' social responsibility and self-sacrifice. See, for example, *Rollo at Play* 184; Hall *Familiar Talks* 60–61; and Titcomb 69–70.

16. A number of interesting essays on *The Adventures of Tom Sawyer* argue that its scenes of play are sometimes linked to pedagogy and adult activities, as they are in *Little Women* and other girls' books: see Robinson, Oriard, and Cox 127–55. The critics I talk about in this chapter do not mention these essays, perhaps because they are not explicitly about gender.

17. See Saxton 4–17 and Stern 166–99.

18. Gillian Brown opens her essay with an anecdote of play in the real world as a way to connect literary ideas about boyhood to realities of childhood. For her, fictional narratives are important because they mirror children's lives, a belief held by all of the critics I discuss.

19. Howells's *A Boy's Town* is, in part, an explanation of boy-nature that accords with earlier representations in Twain and Aldrich.

Chapter 2

"Desirable and Necessary" in "Families and Schools"

BOY-NATURE AND PHYSICAL DISCIPLINE

1. In *Domestic Education* (1840), Heman Humphrey makes a claim typical of New England reformers. He believes that moral suasion is the preferred method but recommends physical correction as a necessary option: "that [educational theory] which allows and even enjoins corporeal [sic] punishments . . . is the best" (56). Tellingly, when he offers an instance of the kind of childhood "perverseness" that requires physical correction, it involves a boy (see 55–60). See also Northend 59.
2. Historian Deborah Fitts notes that Mann endorsed the use of female teachers as a way to control boys who had disrupted or closed schools. I would argue that this disciplinary tactic fits into the larger context of how Mann and others understood boys, and it relates to his advocacy of corporal punishment for boys.
3. Critics and historians have often not noted that prominent educational reformers including Lyman Cobb and Mann opposed abolishing the practice for boys, nor have they looked at movements, like those in Boston during the late 1830s, that sought to ban only the physical correction of girls (see Williams 259).
4. Like Brodhead's study, Peter Messent's argument about corporal punishment in *The Adventures of Tom Sawyer* follows Foucault, showing how the novel replays what Brodhead claims is the mid-century rejection of corporal punishment.
5. For an essay on the development of antebellum printing technologies, see Zboray.
6. Page's volume was one of the more influential educational works in the century. While Page does not explicitly claim that corporal punishment should only be practiced on boys, like many pro–corporal punishment educators, he mentions it only with reference to them, implying that only boys could be so intractable as to require it. See *The Theory and Practice of Teaching* 193–207 and his short play "The Schoolmaster."
7. For a discussion of this industry and its influence, see Murray 23–50.
8. See also *Lucy at Play* (1829) 66, 70, 97; *Rollo at Play* 75–76.
9. This is certainly not to say that girls escaped physical correction. Since reformist writings are primarily disciplinary theory, these prescriptions do not necessarily reflect the actual treatment of children. It is also true that, although reformers opposed girls' receiving this kind of punishment, not all educators were reformers. Some educators made no gender-based distinctions, believing that boys and girls could be physically disciplined. The Boston grammar school masters whom Mann engaged in a long-running

public debate in the 1830s, for example, resisted any attempt to limit their ability to practice it, seeing reform movements as attacks on their authority. Yet if Alcott's text, which is theory and practice, and the anecdotes in Cobb, Mann, Abbott, and many others are any indication, a connection probably exists between the forms of discipline these authors advocated and pedagogical practices.

10. For example, see Kett 130–31, Rotundo 31, and "My Schoolboy Days." For a study of how this subject was approached in the visual arts, see Sarah Burns's essay on boyhood, sentiment, and ideology in late-nineteenth-century painting and illustration.

11. For a few of the many instances, see the collection *The Schoolmaster in Literature* (1892) and Ik Marvel's popular *Dream-Life: A Fable of the Seasons* (1851).

12. For examples, see Manning 50–57, and Mann, "Lecture" 332–33.

13. See Reinier 102–50 for an examination of strategies of childhood character formation during the period my study covers.

14. Literary representations of boys often share educational discourses' depictions of boys as behavioral problems. Gail Murray notes that mid-century fictions of childhood "dichotomize characters . . . into 'good girls' and 'bad boys'"(52). Didactic books like *Ralph Rattler; or, The Mischief-Maker* (1853), *The Village Boys; or, How to Teach Boys Not to Quarrel* (1836), and Abbott's *Rodolphus* (1852), for example, all portray the troublesome nature of boys as a problem to be solved. There were, of course, prominent "good boy" characters; Sunday School literature, for instance, often features such boys, as do many sketches in children's periodicals. Many critics refer to the hero of Abbott's Rollo series as an example of the "model boy" that authors like Twain mocked in works such as "The Story of the Good Little Boy," "The Story of the Bad Little Boy," and *The Adventures of Tom Sawyer*. Yet, as I discussed in the previous chapter, novels like *Rollo at Work* and *Rollo at Play* are structured around scenes of misbehavior. They feature a willful, lazy, and impatient Rollo constantly disobeying his parents and constantly getting punished for it.

15. Hogan claims that Abbott "flatly rejected emulation," but he rejects it only for girls (25). In "Advantages" Abbott argues that emulation can be effective in motivating "dull and coarse boys" upon whom "all your efforts to awaken a love of any intellectual pursuits are vain." He claims it can only have negative effects on "bright girls" (30).

16. Abbott briefly mentions one obedient boy type: the "quiet, sedate, cool, clear-headed" boy ("Advantages" 25). Yet his anecdotes of discipline problems almost always feature boys. "Advantages," for example, includes no anecdotes of misbehaving girls.

17. While many scholars of education and childhood have noted that some reformers sanctioned corporal punishment as a "last resort," they have not noticed that this sanction was typically gendered. Almost always, reformers talked only about boys in this context (see Hogan 32, 37).

18. Cobb offers the of use corporal punishment as a litmus test for teacher competence: "A teacher who would *strike* or *whip* a girl is certainly *unfit* to teach" (11; emphasis in original).
19. In "Against Boys" (1863) the author recommends an extreme version of the strategy that Sedgwick endorses: "If, indeed, a whole generation of boys could be brought up in solitary confinement—well secured—a reformation might be effected" (86).
20. See, for instance, "Training of Boys I" 117.
21. Brodhead, Glenn, MacLeod, Hogan, and Wishy mention Cobb's book but treat it as if it were a study of childhood discipline.
22. For an examination of Whitman's sketch, see Reynolds 75.
23. Studies of Alcott's view on education, such as Dorothy McCuskey's *Bronson Alcott, Teacher* and Haefner's *Educational Theories and Practices of A. Bronson Alcott,* tend to celebrate Alcott as a progressive reformer whose ideas anticipated later developments in classroom practice. (See, for example, Haefner 63–68; McCuskey 83; and Duck 133–88). Even Dahlstrand's biography of Alcott, which interrogates his theories in a way that Haefner's and McCuskey's do not, portrays him as a liberal reformer. While his classroom instruction was progressive in many ways, his beliefs about boyhood discipline and gender, as revealed in the *Record,* were often conventional.
24. See also Silber on Pestalozzi 194–95 and Barlow on Pestalozzi's effect on Alcott 14–136.
25. As the final form of boyhood discipline that he recommends, Cobb endorses the doctrine of "female influence," which holds that the moral character of a boy would be improved if he associates with girls: "it is the duty of every lad . . . to secure the *society* . . . of *respectable* . . . females," who will assure that he behave properly by setting the moral standard to which he should aspire (218; emphasis in original). The idea of girls as disciplinary agents receives perhaps its greatest nineteenth-century advocate in Alcott's daughter. See my discussion of Amy March and Laurie's relationship in *Little Women* in chapter 4, and the effect of Bess on the boys and young men in *Little Men* and *Jo's Boys.*
26. See also Abbott's *Rollo at Play* 21–29, 165–91.
27. Brodhead calls this scene of "vicarious punishment" a "close equivalent" to whipping scenes in the *Narrative of the Life of Frederick Douglass* (1845) and Richard Henry Dana's *Two Years before the Mast* (1840). Yet no whipping occurred at the Temple School. The only implement ever used is a ferule, and Alcott's application of it is far removed from the harshness of Douglass's whippings.
28. In the past, boys had been removed from one of Alcott's schools because of what parents perceived as either harsh or humiliating punishment; see the *Record* 80.
29. Louisa May Alcott bases a scene in *Little Men* (1871) on the "vicarious punishment" incident from the *Record;* Mr. Bhaer has a misbehaving

boy hit him six times with a ferule, a practice that another boy notes has been used in the past. Just as in the *Record,* the fictional version involves only males.

30. As if to reinforce this point, when a minor character, Harry, is introduced much later in the novel, he is described as a "good boy" who "is not like other boys" (77, 101).

Chapter 3

"The Medicine of Sympathy"

Mothers, Sons, and Affective Pedagogy in Antebellum America

1. Recent scholarship on sentiment has continued to complicate our picture of the ways in which nineteenth-century culture theorized sympathy. Essays by Roberts, Parris, and Steele look at sympathy's inability to bring about the results desired by the writers they discuss. I expand on this approach by discussing texts that critique and even fully reject popular beliefs about sympathy.
2. In the last fifteen years, a great deal of literary scholarship has studied sympathy in nineteenth-century America, but the growing body of historical work on childhood has yet to examine this emotion in any depth. See, for example, Peter Stearns's "Girls, Boys, and Emotions: Redefinitions and Historical Change," which focuses on love, anger, fear, and jealousy.
3. For an overview of nineteenth-century sentimental discourses about mothers, see Lewis's "Mother's Love" Grant 21–29, and Hays 29–39.
4. The nature of this relationship was first addressed at length in Carroll Smith-Rosenberg's influential 1975 article "The Female World of Love and Ritual." Smith-Rosenberg notes that "an intimate mother-daughter relationship lay at the heart of female" life in antebellum culture and that the "normal relation between mother and daughter was one of sympathy" (15). Although scholars have complicated many of her claims, they generally agree that her reading accurately reflects popular beliefs about this bond. For a similar reading of the mother-daughter relationship, see Welter 4–7.
5. Prescriptive literature and biographical material reveal that women believed they were more likely to receive sympathy from one of their own sex. As one man even mused, "[W]ho but a woman can know the heart of another woman?" (cited in Cott 168).
6. See Abbott's "Advantages of Discerning Peculiarities of Character in Pupils" for a discussion of gender-based discipline and motivation.

7. Even though pragmatic discourses offer a more nuanced understanding of sympathy and the mother-son relationship than their sentimental counterparts, like these discourses they typically do not record details of actual relationships, such as would be the case in letters, diaries, and memoirs. Both discourses are, therefore, largely prescriptions about child-raising. It is true, however, that authors of pragmatic discourses believe they are writing about the actual treatment of boys, and they often use real and fictional anecdotes as case studies of typical problems in mother-son interactions.
8. Parris has said that "postbellum realities" led to a revision of antebellum beliefs about the effectiveness of sympathy, though I argue that this revision had been underway for decades (25).
9. See, for example, *Lucy at Play* 66, 70, 97; *Rollo at Play* 75–76.
10. For boys as Indians and "savages," see "Boyhood and Barbarism" 278–83 and "The Bright Side" 196. For boys as slaves, see Cobb 239. For a description of boy behavior that invokes both of these comparisons, see Sedgwick's *Home* 17.
11. One writer told *Godey's Lady's Book* readers that while traveling in "foreign lands," he was strongly tempted to give in to "evil passions" but was "checked" by the voice of his sympathetic mother, "a voice which must be obeyed—'Oh do not this wickedness, my son'" ("Maternal Influence" 73).
12. In an essay on *Uncle Tom's Cabin* and domestic rhetoric, S. Bradley Shaw demonstrates that readers' familiarity with the conventions of domesticity as expressed in women's magazines shaped their understanding of Stowe's novel (74). My argument similarly places the text's ideas about maternal sympathy and the mother-son bond within the context of mother's advice magazines and books.
13. Eva Cherniavsky claims that because Stowe's Cassy, an African American, successfully "performs" white motherhood when she imitates Legree's mother, Cassy undercuts the discourse of "essential motherhood," a discourse figured as exclusively white (59). But I would argue that Cassy is only able to imitate white motherhood in the eyes of the corrupt, paranoid, and guilt-ridden Legree, and thus her impersonation represents no threat to Stowe's beliefs about white mothers. What is a threat, I argue, is the failure of Legree's and St. Clare's ideal mothers to bring about spiritual and political change through the affective mothering of their sons.
14. Kristin Boudreau explores contradictions in Stowe's beliefs that sympathy could create cross-racial identification between white readers and black characters. I argue that Stowe's ideas about same-race identification—especially between white mothers and sons—are similarly conflicted in *Uncle Tom's Cabin*.

15. Critics often try to categorize the social and psychological effects of sympathy. Whether its use within mother-son relationships was oppressive, liberatory, or otherwise could only be determined by studying cases where sufficient biographical evidence is available. I agree with June Howard, who has attempted to move criticism toward more nuanced characterizations: "a debate over whether a genre (let alone a novel) is coercive or progressive sounds thin and reductive" (92). And our ideas about what constitutes repression and liberation might not accord with those of nineteenth-century writers.

CHAPTER 4

"Wake Up, and Be a Man"

Little Women, Shame, and the Ethic of Submission

Epigraph: Alfred Whitman was a childhood friend of Alcott who served as partial inspiration for Laurie. For more information on their relationship, see my entry on Whitman in the *Louisa May Alcott Encyclopedia*.

1. See also Joanne Dobson's reference to "the cultural ethos of feminine 'obedience' and 'subordination'" (Introduction xiv).
2. Like Murphy, many critics who have examined the figure of the artist in the novel give little attention to Laurie. (See, for example, Fetterley's "Alcott's Civil War" and Clark's "A Portrait of the Artist" 95.) Despite considerable evidence to the contrary, Laurie's story continues to be characterized as one of complete freedom; see Aliaga-Buchenau 97.
3. See also Keyser's *Little Women: A Family Romance* 42–44, for a discussion of Jo, Laurie, and gender roles.
4. Anne Dalke's "The House-Band" is one of three articles devoted to male characters in the novel. Dalke examines the reciprocal process of education between males and females in order to counter Nina Auerbach's claim that the novel is about the "autonomous development of women" (571). In her extensive bibliography of *Little Women* scholarship, Ann Murphy does not include Dalke's article, perhaps because it does not address traditional feminist concerns (562–63).
5. Many other critics have expressed a similarly negative view of Laurie; Fetterley, for example, says, "If anything, Laurie is Jo's inferior" ("Alcott's Civil War" 381).
6. Shame plays an important role in the transformation that takes place in Alger's Ragged Dick. It results from his contact with Frank Whitney, the son of a successful businessman. Frank's respectability makes Dick anxious to shed his raggedness: "Frank was a tip-top boy, and he was the first that made me ashamed of bein' so ignorant and dirty" (118). Other characters and situations in the novel also reinforce Dick's feel-

ings of shame; at a dinner with another wealthy family, the Greysons, for instance, he is continually embarrassed because he has not yet learned how to act in genteel society.
7. In "Self-Denial Was All the Fashion," Greta Gaard correctly notes that "child-rearing manuals . . . emphasized [anger's] channeling in boys, but its complete absence in girls" (3). Although Laurie can express his anger at his grandfather to Jo, he ultimately must repress it and deny himself. The "dwarfing" and "diminution" of subjectivity that Gaard talks about for girls applies to him (7). In *Little Men* (the final novel in the March family trilogy) Jo makes sure the boys in her care know that the "quality of self-denial" is essential to their lives; she tells them "we will plant self-denial . . . and make it grow" (46).
8. See also Colleen Reardon's valuable discussion of Laurie and music 80–82.
9. The 1845 series "Training of Boys" in *The Mother's Journal and Family Visitant* says that when a young boy imitates his father's employment, "labor becomes insensibly incorporated among his thoughts" (182). See Rotundo 37 for a discussion about boys "imitating" their fathers' professions. See Zimet 38 for a brief examination of this idea in books of the period.
10. See Dubbert 1–11 and Kimmel, *Manhood* 1–10.
11. See Dubbert 27–28 and Hilkey 142–46.
12. See Kimmel, *Manhood* 63. *Little Men* and *Jo's Boys* (the sequels to *Little Women*) include a character named Dan, who is introduced in *Little Men* as a fourteen year old orphan and who later seeks an adventurous life by going out west. All of the characters in the novels find Dan's life the stuff of romance and therefore are attracted to him. Yet Jo's desire for him and for all boys is domestication: "if you marry and settle . . . as I hope you will" (*Jo's Boys* 67). Dan is ultimately a disappointment and source of profound sadness for Jo, for as is repeatedly noted, he cannot be trained into suitability for domestic life: "Danger and sin are near you in the life you lead; moods and passions torment you" and even Bess, a model of femininity, cannot "tame" him (122). At the end of *Jo's Boys* we learn that Dan was shot while defending the Native Americans with whom he lived. It seems fitting that Alcott associates the male who can't be domesticated with Native Americans.
13. See, for example, the discussions of Melville and Twain in Fiedler's *Love and Death in the American Novel* and Judith Fetterley's reading of "Rip Van Winkle" (*Resisting* 1–11). Fetterley correctly notes that Rip's escape is motivated by a desire to flee his wife, but it also involves a desire to get away from the pressures of work. As the narrator says, Rip wants "to escape from the labour of the farm and clamour of his wife" (32).
14. Stories about Boone were popular in the nineteenth century in part because of his strident dismissal of materialism. Although this rejection seems to place him in opposition to the more conventional promarket

attitude (an opposition Laurie shares in the first part of the novel), his popularity probably derived from the fact that he offered men an imaginative rejection of the forces that dominated their lives.

15. Holland's comments here represent the views about male submission advocated by fellow conduct manual writers Rufus Clark, Daniel Eddy, W. W. Everts, Harvey Newcomb, and the others I examine in more detail in chapter 1.
16. In a letter to Alfred Whitman, Alcott writes that "there was always something very brave & beautiful to me in the sight of a boy when he first 'wakes up' & . . . resolves to carry [life] nobly to the end through all disappointments" (*Letters* 51).
17. Amy's use of Edgeworth as a moral authority puts her in good company. Horace Mann said that "Edgeworth was 'universally acknowledged' to be the foremost writer on education since Locke" (cited in Kett 113). Alcott's father also had his students at the Temple School read Edgeworth; as shown in the *Record*, they often discussed the short moral tale "Frank."
18. As Hilkey points out, success and failure were gendered: "the equation that linked manhood with success was built upon a corollary equation that linked the feminine with failure" (155). Thus Amy's critique of Laurie participates in a conventional gendered discourse of emasculation, one that, as conduct and success manuals show, was often directed against young men.
19. Amy's emphasis on the connection between physical strength and moral character appears in advice and success manuals published during and after the Civil War. Kett says that advice author Daniel Eddy "was so convinced of the challenge facing young men in the late 1860s that . . . [he called] for physical culture [and] he lapsed into rhetorical declarations of the value of force and energy" (163), much like those in the narrator's description of Amy's drawing.
20. For a detailed discussion of this discourse in success manuals, see Hilkey 146–51.
21. Beverly Lyon Clark also argues that "other males" in *Little Women* can rebel "against prescribed texts," yet the other men—Brooke, the tutor and husband; Laurie's grandfather, the business man; and Mr. Bhaer, the wise and gentle father—are in line with conventional expectations for men ("Portrait of the Artist" 81). Laurie even romanticizes his own act of submission by figuring it in terms of one of the period's most valorized texts, that of heroic self-sacrifice: "the boy said to himself, with resolve to make the sacrifice cheerfully, 'I'll let my castle go, and stay with the dear old gentleman while he needs me, for I am all he has'" (146). He mitigates his personal loss by figuring himself as the suffering secondary character in his grandfather's narrative, which replaces his dream of a life as a musician.

22. See, for example, Spacks 101.
23. When Laurie appears in the later novels of the March family trilogy, he becomes, like many fathers in nineteenth-century novels, an often absent provider. In *Little Men,* he makes a brief but telling comment on the emotional burden caused by his vocation, a topic on which the text otherwise remains almost silent: "I get desperately tired of business" (191). Rollo's father tells his son that men expect that work "will be laborious and tiresome, and they understand this beforehand and go steadily forward notwithstanding" (Abbott, *Rollo at Work* 125–26)
24. In "The Bad Boy in Nineteenth Century American Fiction," Trensky says that the bad boy is "exclusively" the province of male writers, and does not discuss Laurie or the bad boys of any women authors (504). And Laurie is not Alcott's only bad boy; *Little Men*'s Tommy Bangs resembles Tom Bailey and Tom Sawyer: "Tommy Bangs was the scapegrace of the school, and the most trying scapegrace that ever lived. As full of mischief as a monkey, yet so good-hearted that one could not help forgiving his tricks" (28). See early critical essays on the male-authored tradition of the bad-boy book by Hinz, Hunter, and Geller.
25. In *A Book about Boys* (1869), published shortly after *Little Women* by Alcott's publisher Robert Brothers, A. R. Hope renames the "bad boy" the "real boy."
26. Despite such similarities, Susina claims that Laurie is more like the "good boy" Sid Sawyer than his brother, Tom (164). In "*Little Women* and the Boy-Book," Crowley likewise overlooks such parallels.
27. Alcott has created a far broader range of boy types than that offered by male boy-book authors, who often claim to write about the universal "boy"; *Little Men,* for example, features a large cast of distinct boy characters.
28. See Crane's "Whilomville Stories" (1900).
29. The term "thrashing" is nearly ubiquitous in boys' stories of the period. The details of fights are seldom narrated in any detail, but it is difficult to find a story in which a "thrashing" of some kind does not occur or is not mentioned.
30. See Kimmel 75–78 for a brief but valuable discussion of the Civil War and white masculinity. Stories about boys often depict large fights as military encounters, such as the snowball fight in *The Story of a Bad Boy,* which is accompanied by a map of the "battlements" (97).
31. Though *Little Women* offers a much more representative look at the cultural truths about boys and escape fantasies than other texts, for the last twenty-five years both *Adventures of Huckleberry Finn* and *Moby-Dick* have been used by critics as representative of male experiences, concerns, and possibilities in the mid- and late-nineteenth century. Critics have compared these texts to women's fictions in order to illuminate the

restrictions placed on women in light of the autonomy given to Huck and Ishmael. Yet the experiences that both these texts chronicle have limited relevance to the lives of many mid-nineteenth century boys and men. For some of the many comparisons with *Moby-Dick* made by influential critics, for example, see Tompkins, Afterword 586, 593, and *Designs* 147; Dobson, "Hidden Hand" 239; Harris, *19th-Century American Women's Novels* 20; Baym, *Woman's Fiction* 14; Ammons, "Stowe's Dream" 157; Auerbach, *Communities* 8.

32. In a famous scene in *Adventures of Huckleberry Finn*, Huck is tempted to betray Jim and send him back into slavery, but decides against it: "All right, then, I'll go to hell," he says, believing that his decision violates the principles of his culture (193). After Laurie is rejected by Jo, she asks him, "[W]here are you going?" and he answers, "[T]o the devil" (365). A fundamental difference between the characters and their authors' worldviews are visible here: Huck rebels and Laurie says he will but does not.

Chapter 5

"What Our Boys Are Reading"

Lydia Sigourney, Francis Forrester, and Boyhood Literacy

1. Critics often claim that the intent of all kinds of boys' reading is to valorize the boy as a figure of cultural mobility and power and to endorse the self-reliance and ambition that defined model men; such goals, these critics argue, differ from the repressive disciplinary aims of girls' reading. Though the particulars sometimes differed in important ways, writings about reading for boys and for girls share a surprisingly similar set of concerns; for numerous nineteenth-century examples, see material cited in Baym, *Novel, Readers, and Reviewers* 98, 170; in Machor 66, 71; and "Vicious Novels: Cause of Their Increase" (1845), "Novels and Romances" (1820), and "Reading Is Not Thinking" (1837), all of which argue that boys and girls can suffer the same ill effects from improper reading. Even essays addressed primarily to girls, such as "The Reading of Young Ladies" (1837) and Simon Brown's "What Books Shall I Read?" (1845), claim that their concerns and recommendations are equally applicable to boy readers. For some of the many critical discussions of nineteenth-century reading that focus on gender difference, see Sicherman 200–210; Golden, *Images of the Women Reader in Victorian British and American Fiction;* and Flint, *The Woman Reader.* In *Carnival on the Page,* Isabelle Lehuu examines "ephemeral paper, leaflets of memory, books in parts, and lady's books" (7), and given that the only gender-specific material she examines is intended for females, it is not surprising that she argues for a strict

"differentiation of reading by gender" (11), a claim I complicate. Although it does not discuss girls at any length, Lorinda Cohoon's *Serialized Citizenships: Periodicals, Books, and American Boys, 1840–1911* takes an approach similar to mine in that Cohoon explores the role that books played in forming boy readers into model citizens.

2. Like many essays on reading, Segel's "'As the Twig Is Bent . . .': Gender and Childhood Reading" looks productively at fiction, but does not address the many discussions of history, biography, and other genres in educational journals, book reviews, and advice manuals that are in dialogue with the texts she examines.

3. For general overviews of Sigourney in this regard, see Hovet and Kilcrup. When critics examine Sigourney's beliefs about the ways in which cultural norms affected children, they almost always study children in general or girls rather than boys. See, for example, Allison Giffen's "Dutiful Daughters and Needy Fathers: Lydia Sigourney and Nineteenth-Century Popular Literature."

4. Aliaga-Buchenau argues that nineteenth-century writers saw reading as potentially dangerous only for females, yet Sigourney and many others believed that books could be equally harmful for boys.

5. See Mott 305–6.

6. When Sigourney mentions Washington in her *History of Marcus Aurelius*, she celebrates him not as a figure of impressive political and military achievements but as a man capable of immense sympathy: "His sympathy was so great for the soldiers that tears flowed down his cheeks" when he saw the "sufferings of his army" (86).

7. Sparks's *The Life of George Washington* similarly devotes little time to the mother-son relationship; see 4.

8. Hawes was the pastor of a church in Hartford, Connecticut, and Sigourney often attended his sermons. See Haight 135.

9. Sigourney deeply believed in the values advocated by her collections, and so she published and marketed some of them herself. For information on her entrepreneurship, see Melissa Teed's "A Passion for Distinction: Lydia Huntley Sigourney and the Creation of a Literary Reputation."

10. During a game of "Truth" in Alcott's *Little Women*, Laurie says, not surprisingly, that one of his heroes is Napoleon (131). Yet Laurie becomes a merchant and not an adventurer.

11. See Dubbert 35. Even though some writers had mixed feelings about Bonaparte as a model, they believed he offered a compelling vision of manhood that should be imitated, at least partially. Interestingly, while Eddy argues that Napoleon's story shows that "earthly greatness is precarious," he also celebrates him as an example of the "advantages" of "youth," demonstrating that boys can accomplish much while young

(136). Weems opens his biography with a quotation from Napoleon on Washington: how impressive Washington must have been, the author notes, to "awaken the sigh even of Bonaparte" (1).

12. In *The Child's Book* (1844) Sigourney continues her attack on Napoleon by criticizing his "ambitious" nature and recounting his death as a lesson for her boy and girl readers (8).

13. Sigourney repeatedly celebrates the farmer as an exemplary man, praising his simplicity and humble domestic-based ambitions. See also "The Farmer" in *The Boys' Reading-Book*.

14. According to Sigourney, Aurelius possessed these traits because of the power of maternal influence: "When . . . young, he was instructed by his mother [who] took pains to teach him" to be religious, moderate, and obedient (17).

15. In a review of *The Boys' Reading-Book*, for example, a writer for the *Hartford Courant* celebrates Sigourney's story "The Only Son" as an example of the book's conventional morality. The reviewer reads it not as I do—as a cautionary tale about the negative effects that notions of manhood can have on boys—but rather as a didactic tale about sloth and intemperance: "let every boy dread the first advance of vice, for the descent is swift." Sigourney certainly intends the tale as an attack on laziness, but she sets up Frank Wilson's fall into vice as a direct result of the parents' capitulation to the pressures applied by the uncle, who endorses the kind of ideas about "manliness" that Sigourney constantly critiques. Perhaps able to see only what he expects of Sigourney, the reviewer singles out the tale's ending plea as its sole moral, ignoring Sigourney's indictment of cultural ideologies of masculinity.

16. See Machor 57 on the limitations of reading nineteenth-century fiction with twentieth-century critical assumptions.

17. Following Sigourney, William Alcott singles out "the lives of . . . Alexander . . . and Napoleon Bonaparte" as inappropriate reading (*Boy's Guide to Usefulness* 112).

18. In an 1865 magazine feature that would likely appear as highly didactic to any modern reader, the author claims that the magazine she writes for (*The Youth's Companion*) has left behind the stilted language and oppressive morality of the past: "how dreadful good boys can talk in a book; real boys never talk so. Now we make it a rule never to put anything but real boys into our stories. We have no idea of cheating you into swallowing a moral with the sugar and water of fiction" (Bonney 137).

19. While boys certainly could have read against the grain of these authors' intentions and ignored the didactic and disciplinary content, writers like Optic believed that boy readers realized adventure was not an end in itself. Examinations of children's literature often see the period immediately after the Civil War as a time of fundamental change: before the war books were didactic, and after they were not. In her 1953 history

of children's literature, Cornelia Meigs says that during this period "books for boys turned to greater realism" (265), and Ellen Donovan notes that "[f]iction written in the United States . . . for children changed fundamentally . . . with the publication of *Little Women* and *The Story of a Bad Boy*" (144). Such claims, though partially true, oversimplify the situation; though many books published after 1865 were less overtly didactic than their predecessors, books and stories for boys (and girls) with a clearly articulated moral purpose were published throughout the century.

20. Sales of novels in the *Ragged Dick* series decreased after the first book was published in 1868, perhaps in part because Dick becomes less entertaining; see Mott 158–59, 309, 321.

21. Forrester published *Forrester's Boys' and Girls' Magazine, and Fireside Companion,* which later became the periodical *Student and Schoolmate,* in which Alger's *Ragged Dick* was first serialized in 1867. Forrester released other works for a dual-gender audience, such as *Forrester's Pictorial Miscellany for Boys and Girls* (1854) and *My Own Annual: A Gift Book For Boys and Girls* (1849). These texts often endorse the same kinds of reading for boys and girls. Sigourney's advice manual *How to Be Happy* (1833) features a long list of moral values and practices that she believes boys and girls should embody and exhibit.

22. For similar warnings to boys about the danger of reading adventure narratives, see "The Arabian Nights" in *Woodworth's Youth's Cabinet* (1850) and "Booth and Bad Literature" in *The Youth's Companion* (1865).

23. For a detailed discussion of Optic's response to this attack, see Darling.

24. Book reviewers occasionally attacked Alger's novels as "sensational" because of what they believed were unrealistic plots. See reviews excerpted in Scharnhorst and Bales 34, 40, and 41. Such criticisms echo William Alcott's and Louisa May Alcott's critiques of boys' novels. Yet Alger warns boys against reading adventure novels; in a piece called "Writing Stories for Boys" he cautions, "Such stories as 'The Boy Highwayman' and 'The Boy Pirate' and books of that class, do incalculable mischief" (cited in Scharnhorst and Bales 67).

25. Stephen Mailloux frames his influential essay "The Rhetorical Use and Abuse of Fiction: Eating Books in Late Nineteenth-Century America" with comments from nineteenth-century writers on the dangers faced by females who "ingest" harmful reading materials. But he does not discuss uses of the "reading as consumption" metaphor in writings about boys. Mailloux's argument is supported by a familiar binary of boy-girl difference, represented by his setting in strict opposition *The Story of a Bad Boy* and *Little Women*. He does not mention the non-boy-books of the period, of which there were many hundreds, if not thousands.

Coda

"Real Boys" of the Twentieth and Twenty-first Centuries

Educators, Academics, and Sociologists on Boyhood

1. For a few of the many valuable studies, see Weitzman et al., Grauerholz, and Pescosolido, and Kortenhuas and Demarest.
2. Griffin's essay appears in *All about the Girl: Culture, Power, and Identity*, and the book's index is telling for its use of "boys" a category of comparison with girls. Boys are only mentioned twice: "arrest rates of" and "violence rates of" (272). In *What about the Boys?* the editors say that "the real boy crisis is a crisis of violence" (16), perhaps unintentionally relegating all other systemic problems to a status that is somehow not real. As my chapter on corporal punishment shows, many writers advocated a culture of violence directed at the boy and encouraged them to be violent against each other as a way to discipline those who showed "self-conceit."
3. Pollack's *Real Boys* was generally lauded in the press, yet it is not without detractors. In his foreword to *Reading Don't Fix No Chevys: Literacy in the Lives of Young Men*, Thomas Newkirk dismisses Pollack's claim that boys live under the tyranny of such a code (x). He is right to note that Pollack oversimplifies the emotional contours of boys' lives (as I would argue do all of the authors who see only "crisis" in boyhood and girlhood), especially in regard to his claims about boys' social experiences as defined by isolation and alienation. Yet Newkirk seems to ignore a body of work by many sociologists, educators, and masculinity studies scholars that shows how boys live in a complicated relationship to the cultural codes that tell them who they are and how they should behave. Even without all of this evidence, we should not find it hard to imagine that the things we tell boys about themselves might not always be helpful.
4. For Sommers's refutation of Gilligan, see chapter 4 of *The War against Boys*.

Works Cited

Abbott, Jacob. "Advantages of Discerning Peculiarities of Character in Pupils, and of Adapting Oneself to Them." *American Annals of Education and Instruction* 9 (1839): 23–32.

———. *Gentle Measures in the Management and Training of the Young.* New York, 1871.

———. *Letters to Mothers.* Hartford, 1838.

———. *Lucy at Play.* Boston, 1841.

———. *Rodolphus.* New York, 1852.

———. *Rollo at Play; Or, Safe Amusements.* Boston, 1841.

———. *Rollo at Work; Or, The Way to Be Industrious.* Boston, 1841.

———. "The Teacher's First Day." *American Annals of Education and Instruction* 9 (1839): 216–22.

———. *The Teacher. Moral Influences Employed in the Instruction and Government of the Young.* New York: Harper, 1856.

———. *The Two Wheelbarrows.* New York, 1855.

Abbott, John S. C. *The Mother at Home; Or, The Principles of Maternal Duty Familiarly Illustrated.* New York, 1833.

———. *The School-Boy; or, A Guide for Youth to Truth and Duty.* Boston, 1839.

Abell, Mrs. L. G. *Woman in Her Various Relations: Containing Practical Rules for American Females.* New York, 1851.

Adams, Charlotte. *Boys at Home.* New York, 1854.

Adams, Rachel, and David Savran. *The Masculinity Studies Reader.* Malden, MA: Blackwell, 2002.

"Against Boys." *The Living Age* #984 (77) April 1863. 85–88.

Alcott, Amos Bronson. *Essays on Education, 1830–1862.* Ed. Walter Harding. Gainesville: Scholars' Facsimile and Reprints, 1960.

Alcott, Louisa May. *Rose in Bloom.* Boston: Robert Brothers, 1876.

———. *Eight Cousins; or, The Aunt Hill.* 1875. New York: Penguin, 1989.

———. *Jo's Boys, and How They Turned Out: A Sequel to Little Men.* Boston: Robert Brothers, 1886.

———. *Jack and Jill.* Boston: Robert Brothers, 1880.

———. *The Journals of Louisa May Alcott.* Ed. Joel Myerson and Daniel Shealy. Boston: Little, Brown, 1989.

———. *Little Men: The Life at Plumfield with Jo's Boys.* Boston, 1871.

———. *Little Women; or, Meg, Jo, Beth and Amy.* 1868. New York: Penguin, 1989.

———. "My Boys." *Aunt Jo's Scrap-Bag.* Boston: Robert Brothers, 1872. 1–34.

———. *An Old-Fashioned Girl.* Boston, 1870.

———. *The Selected Letters of Louisa May Alcott.* Ed. Joel Myerson and Daniel Shealy. Boston: Little, Brown, 1987.
———. *Under the Lilacs.* Boston, 1870.
Alcott, William. *The Boy's Guide to Usefulness.* Boston, 1844.
Aldrich, Thomas Bailey. *The Story of a Bad Boy.* Boston, 1870.
Alger, Horatio, Jr. *Ragged Dick; or, Street Life in New York with the Boot-Blacks.* 1868. New York: Penguin, 1986.
Aliaga-Buchenau, Ana-Isabel. *The "Dangerous" Potential of Reading: Readers and the Negotiation of Power in Nineteenth-Century Narratives.* New York: Routledge, 2004.
Ammons, Elizabeth. "Stowe's Dream of the Mother-Savior: *Uncle Tom's Cabin* and American Women Writers before the 1920s." *New Essays on Uncle Tom's Cabin.* Ed. Eric J. Sundquist. New York: Cambridge University Press, 1986. 155–95.
"The Arabian Nights." *Woodworth's Youth's Cabinet* Sept. 1850: 290.
Arac, Jonathan. *Huckleberry Finn as Idol and Target: The Functions of Criticism in Our Time.* Madison: The University of Wisconsin Press, 1997.
Arthur, T. S. *Advice to Young Men on Their Duties and Conduct in Life.* Boston, 1852.
———. *The Mother's Rule; or, The Right Way and the Wrong Way.* Philadelphia, 1856.
Auerbach, Nina. *Communities of Women: An Idea in Fiction.* Cambridge: Harvard University Press, 1978.
An Autobiography: In Three Parts. Boston, 1873.
Avery, Gillian. *Behold the Child: American Children and Their Books, 1621–1922.* London: Bodely Head, 1994.
Barlow, Thomas A. *Pestalozzi and American Education.* Boulder, CO: Este Es, 1977.
Barnard, Charles. "The Voyage of the Salt Mackerel." *Robert Merry's Museum* May 1872: 234–38.
Barnes, Elizabeth. "Affecting Relations: Pedagogy, Patriarchy, and the Politics of Sympathy." *American Literary History* 8 (1996): 597–614.
———. *States of Sympathy: Seduction and Democracy in the American Novel.* New York: Columbia University Press, 1997.
Baym, Nina. *Novels, Readers, and Reviewers: Responses to Fiction in Antebellum America.* Ithaca: Cornell University Press, 1984.
———. *Woman's Fiction: A Guide to Novels by and about Women in America, 1820–1870.* Ithaca: Cornell University Press, 1978.
Beecher, Catharine. *A Treatise on Domestic Economy.* Boston, 1842.
"Benefit of Hard Knocks." *Youth's Companion* 40 (1867): 7.
Bennett, Paula. "'The Descent of the Angel': Interrogating Domestic Ideology in American Women's Poetry, 1858–1890." *American Literary History* 7 (1995): 591–610.

Bethune, George W. "To My Mother." *Lays of Love and Faith. With Other Fugitive Poems*. Philadelphia, 1848.
Bonney, Mrs. P. P. "Going into Business for Himself." *The Youth's Companion* 31 Aug. 1865: 137.
"Booth and Bad Literature." *The Youth's Companion* May 11, 1865: 74.
Boudreau, Kristin. *Sympathy in American Literature: American Sentiments from Jefferson to the Jameses*. Gainesville: University Press of Florida, 2002.
"Boyhood and Barbarism." *The American Whig Review* 7 (1851): 278–83.
Boylan, Anne. "Growing Up Female in Young America." *American Childhood: A Research Guide and Historical Handbook*. Ed. Joseph M. Hawes and N. Ray Hiner, Westport, CT: Greenwood, 1985.
"The Bright Side." *The Mother's Rule; or, The Right Way and the Wrong Way*. Ed. T. S. Arthur. Philadelphia, 1856. 193–98.
Brod, Harry. "A Case for Men's Studies." *Changing Men: New Directions in Research on Men and Masculinity*. Ed. Michael Kimmel. London: Sage, 1987. 263–77.
Brodhead, Richard. *Cultures of Letters: Scenes of Reading and Writing in Nineteenth-Century America*. Chicago: University of Chicago Press, 1993.
———. "Sparing the Rod: Discipline and Fiction in Antebellum America." *Representations* 21 (1988). 67-96.
Brown, Gillian. "Child's Play." *Differences: A Journal of Feminist Studies* 11 (1999–2000): 76–106. Rpt. in *The American Child: A Cultural Studies Reader*. Ed. Caroline F. Levander and Carol J. Singley. New Brunswick: Rutgers University Press, 2003.
Brown, Simon. "What Books Shall I Read?" *The Mother's Assistant, and the Young Lady's Friend*. 1845: 37–39.
Burns, Sarah. "Barefoot Boys and Other Country Children: Sentiment and Ideology in Nineteenth-Century American Art."*American Art Journal* 20 (1988): 24–50.
Callios, Roger. *Man, Play, and Games*. Trans. Meyer Barash. New York: Free Press, 1961.
Carnes, Mark C., and Clyde Griffen. *Meanings for Manhood: Construcions of Masculinity in Victorian America*. Chicago: University of Chicago Press, 1990.
Cherniavsky, Eva. *That Pale Mother Rising: Sentimental Discourse and the Imitation of Motherhood in 19th-Century America*. Bloomington: Indiana University Press, 1995.
Child, Lydia Maria. *The Mother's Book*. Boston, 1831.
Clark, Beverly Lyon. *Kiddie Lit: The Cultural Construction of Children's Literature in America*. Baltimore: Johns Hopkins University Press, 2003.

———. "A Portrait of the Artist as a Little Woman." *Children's Literature* 17 (1989): 81–97.

Clark, Rufus W. *Lectures on the Formation of Character, Temptations and Mission of Young Men*. Boston, 1853.

Cobb, Lyman. *The Evil Tendencies of Corporal Punishment as a Means of Moral Discipline in Families and Schools, Examined and Discussed*. New York, 1847.

Cogan, Frances. *All-American Girl: The Ideal of Real Womanhood in Mid-Nineteenth-Century America*. Athens: University of Georgia Press, 1989.

Cohoon, Lorinda. *Serialized Citizenships: Periodicals, Books, and American Boys, 1840–1911*. Lanham, MD: Scarecrow, 2006.

"The Comforts of Playing 'Hookie.'" *The Mother's Magazine for Daughters and Mothers* 25 (1856): 91–92.

"Confessions of a Schoolmaster, No. VII." *American Annals of Education and Instruction* 8 (1838): 86–91.

"Confessions of a Schoolmaster, No. IX." *American Annals of Education and Instruction* 8 (1838): 154–58.

"Corporal Punishment." *American Annals of Education and Instruction* 6 (1836): 337.

Cott, Nancy F. *Bonds of Womanhood: "Woman's Sphere" in New England, 1780–1835*. 2nd ed. New Haven: Yale University Press, 1997.

———. "Notes toward an Interpretation of Antebellum Childrearing." *Psychohistory Review* 6 (1978): 4–20.

Cox, James M. *Mark Twain: The Fate of Humor*. Princeton: Princeton University Press, 1966.

Crane, Stephen. *Whilomville Stories*. New York, 1900.

Crain, Caleb. *American Sympathy: Men, Friendship, and Literature in the New Nation*. New Haven: Yale University Press, 2001.

Crowley, John W. "*Little Women* and the Boy-Book." *New England Quarterly* 58 (1985): 384–99.

Dalhstrand, Frederick C. *Amos Bronson Alcott: An Intellectual Biography*. Rutherford [N.J.]: Fairleigh Dickinson University Press, 1982.

Dalke, Anne. "'The House-Band': The Education of Men in *Little Women*." *College English* (47) 1985: 571–78.

Dana, Richard Henry. *Two Years before the Mast*. New York, 1840.

Darling, Richard L. *The Rise of Children's Book Reviewing in America, 1865–1881*. New York: R. R. Bowker, 1968.

Davidson, Cathy N., and Jessamyn Hatcher, eds. *No More Separate Spheres! A Next Wave American Studies Reader*. Durham: Duke University Press, 2002.

Davis, Glenn. *Childhood and History in America*. New York: Psychohistory Press, 1976.

Davis, Rebecca Harding. "Men's Rights." *A Rebecca Harding Davis Reader*. Ed. Jean Pfaelzer. Pittsburgh: University of Pittsburgh Press, 1995. 343–61.

Dawson, Melanie. "The Miniaturizing of Girlhood: Nineteenth-Century Playtime and Gendered Theories of Development." *The American Child: A Cultural Studies Reader*. Ed. Caroline F. Levander and Carol J. Singley. New Brunswick: Rutgers University Press, 2003. 63–84.

Degler, Carl N. *At Odds: Women and the Family in America from the Revolution to the Present*. New York: Oxford University Press, 1980.

Dobson, Joanne. "The Hidden Hand: Subversion of Cultural Ideology in Three Mid-Nineteenth Century American Women's Novels." *American Quarterly* 38 (1986): 223–42.

———. Introduction. *The Hidden Hand*. By E.D.E.N. Southworth. 1888. New Brunswick: Rutgers University Press, 1988. xi–xli.

———. "Reclaiming Sentimental Literature." *American Literature* 69 (1997): 263–88.

Donovan, Ellen Butler. "Reading for Profit *and* Pleasure: *Little Women* and *The Story of a Bad Boy*." *The Lion and the Unicorn: A Critical Journal of Children's Literature* 18 (1994): 143–53.

Driscoll, Catherine. *Girls: Feminine Adolescence in Popular Culture and Cultural Theory*. New York: Columbia University Press, 2002.

Dubbert, Joe L. *A Man's Place: Masculinity in Transition*. Englewood Cliffs: Prentice Hall, 1979.

Duck, Lloyd. *Understanding American Education: Its Past, Practices, and Promise*. Burke, VA: Chateline, 1996.

Eddy, Daniel C. *The Young Man's Friend*. Boston, 1855.

———. *The Young Man's Friend*. New York, 2nd ed. 1865.

Elbert, Monika. *Separate Spheres No More: Gender Convergence in American Literature, 1830–1930*. Tuscaloosa: University of Alabama Press, 2000.

Ellis, Mrs. "The Mother's Love." *Godey's Lady's Book* 44 (1852): 163–64.

"Errors in Discipline; or Reminiscences of a Schoolmaster." *American Annals of Education and Instruction* 5 (1835): 27–30.

Everts, W. W. *Manhood: Its Duties and Responsibilities*. New York, 1854.

Felski, Rita. *Beyond Feminist Aesthetics: Feminist Literature and Social Change*. Cambridge: Harvard University Press, 1989.

———. "The 'Doxa of Difference': Working Through Sexual Difference." *Signs* 23 (1997): 1–21.

Fetterley, Judith. "*Little Women*: Alcott's Civil War." *Feminist Studies* 5 (1979): 369–83.

———. "Nineteenth-Century American Women Writers and the Politics of Recovery." *American Literary History* (Fall 1994): 600–611.

———. *The Resisting Reader: A Feminist Approach to American Fiction.* Bloomington: Indiana University Press, 1978.

Fiedler, Leslie. *Love and Death in the American Novel.* New York: Criterion Books, 1960.

Finkelstein, Barbara. "Casting Networks of Good Influence: The Reconstruction of Childhood in the United States, 1790–1870." *American Childhood: A Research Guide and Historical Handbook.* Ed. Joseph M. Hawes and N. Ray Hiner. Westport, CT: Greenwood, 1985. 11–152.

Fitts, Deborah. "Una and the Lion: The Feminization of District School-Teaching and Its Effect on the Roles of Students and Teachers in Nineteenth-Century Massachusetts." *Regulated Children / Liberated Children: Education in Psychohistorical Perspective.* Ed. Barbara Finklestein. New York: Psychohistory, 1979.140–57.

Flint, Kate. *The Woman Reader, 1837–1914.* New York: Oxford University Press, 1994.

Florin, Christina, and Ulla Johansson. "Discipline in Grammar Schools, Private Girls' Schools, and Elementary Schools in Sweden, 1850–1900." *Discipline, Moral Regulation, and Schooling: A Social History.* Ed. Kate Rousmaniere, Kari Dehli, and Ning de Conick-Smith. New York: Garland, 1997. 43–72.

Forrester, Francis [Daniel Wise]. *Dick Duncan: The Story of a Boy Who Loved Mischief, and How He Was Cured of His Evil Habit.* New York, 1860.

Foucault, Michel. *The History of Sexuality.* New York: Pantheon Books, 1978.

———. *Discipline and Punish.* New York: Vintage, 1995.

Gaard, Greta. "'Self-Denial Was All the Fashion': Repressing Anger in *Little Women*." *Papers on Language and Literature* 27 (1991): 3–19.

Gallaudet, T. H. "The Mother's Face." *The Mother's Magazine* 6 (1838): 16–20.

Gardiner, Judith Kegan. "Theorizing Age and Gender: Bly's Boys, Femininity, and Maturity Masculinity." *Masculinity Studies & Feminist Theory: New Directions.* New York: Columbia University Press, 2002. 90–118.

Geller, Evelyn. "Tom Sawyer, Tom Bailey, and the Bad-Boy Genre." *Wilson Library Bulletin* (1976): 245–50.

Giffen, Allison. "Dutiful Daughters and Needy Fathers: Lydia Sigourney and Nineteenth-Century Popular Literature." *Women's Studies* 32 (April–May 2003): 255–80.

Gilligan, Carol. Prologue. *Making Connections: The Relational Worlds of Adolescent Girls at Emma Willard School.* Ed. Gilligan, Nona P. Lyons, and Trudy J. Hanmer. Boston: Harvard University Press, 1990. 6–29.

Gilmore, Paul. *The Genuine Article: Race, Mass Culture, and American Literary Manhood.* Durham: Duke University Press, 2001.

Gleason, Gene. "Whatever Happened to Oliver Optic?" *Wilson Library Bulletin* 49 (1975): 647–50.

Glenn, Myra. *Campaigns Against Corporal Punishment: Prisoners, Sailors, Women, and Children in Ante-bellum America.* Albany: State University of New York Press, 1984.

Golden, Catherine. *Images of the Women Reader in Victorian British and American Fiction.* Gainesville: University Press of Florida, 2003.

Grant, Julia. *Raising Baby by the Book: The Education of American Mothers.* New Haven: Yale University Press, 1998.

Grauerholz, Elizabeth, and Bernice A. Pescosolido. "Gender Representation in Children's Literature: 1900–1984." *Gender and Society* 3 (1989): 113–25.

Graves, H. A. *The Family Circle: Its Affections and Pleasures.* Boston, 1844.

Graves, Mrs. A. J. *Girlhood and Womanhood.* Boston, 1844.

Griffin, Christine. "Good Girls, Bad Girls: Anglo-Centrism and Diversity in the Constitution of Contemporary Girlhood." *All About the Girl: Culture, Power, and Identity.* New York: Routledge, 2004.

Griswold, Jerry. *Audacious Kids: Coming of Age in America's Classic Children's Books.* New York: Oxford University Press, 1992.

Gurian, Michael. *The Wonder of Boys: What Parents, Mentors, and Educators Can Do to Shape Boys into Exceptional Men.* New York: Putman, 1994.

Haefner, George E. *A Critical Estimate of the Educational Theories and Practices of A. Bronson Alcott.* New York: Haddon, 1937.

Haight, Gordon. *Mrs. Sigourney: The Sweet Singer of Hartford.* New Haven: Yale University Press, 1930.

Hall, Georgiana. *Hallowed Memories: A Mother's Tribute to Her Boy.* New York, 1877.

Hall, G. Stanley. *Adolescence.* Boston, 1904.

Hall, John. *Familiar Talks to Boys.* New York, 1876.

Hall, Samuel R. *Lectures on School-Keeping.* Boston, 1829.

Hamill, Samuel E. "Discipline; School Government." *The American Journal of Education* 1 (1855): 123–33.

Harris, Susan K. *19th-Century American Women's Novels: Interpretive Strategies.* New York: Cambridge University Press, 1990.

Hawes, Joel. *Lectures to Young Men on the Formation of Character.* Hartford, 1851.

Hays, Sharon. *The Cultural Contradictions of Motherhood*. New Haven: Yale University Press, 1995.
Hendler, Glenn. "The Limits of Sympathy: Louisa May Alcott and the Sentimental Novel." *American Literary History* 3 (1991): 685–706.
———. *Public Sentiments: Structures of Feeling in Nineteenth-Century American Literature*. Chapel Hill: University of North Carolina Press, 2001.
Hendler, Glenn, and Mary Chapman. *Sentimental Men: Masculinity and the Politics of Affect in American Culture*. Berkeley: University of California Press, 1999.
Higginson, Thomas W. "Address of T. W. Higginson." *The Library Journal* 4 (1879): 357–59.
Hilkey, Judy. *Character Is Capital: Success Manuals and Manhood in Gilded Age America*. Chapel Hill: University of North Carolina Press, 1997.
Hinz, John. "Huck and Pluck: 'Bad' Boys in American Fiction." *South Atlantic Quarterly* 51 (January 1952) 51: 120–29.
Hogan, David. "Modes of Discipline: Affective Individualism and Pedagogical Reform in New England, 1820–1850." *American Journal of Education* 99 (1990): 1–56.
Hope, A. R. *A Book about Boys*. Boston: Robert Brothers, 1869.
Hovet, Grace Ann. "Lydia Sigourney." *Nineteenth-Century American Women Writers*. Ed. Denise D. Knight. Westport, CT: Greenwood, 1997. 361–67.
Howard, June. "What Is Sentimentality?" *American Literary History* 11 (1999): 63–81.
Howells, William Dean. *A Boy's Town*. New York, 1890.
———. Rev. of *The Adventures of Tom Sawyer*, by Mark Twain. *Atlantic Monthly* 37 (1876): 621–22.
Huizinga, Johan. *Homo Ludens: A Study of the Play Element in Culture*. Boston: Beacon, 1950.
Hunter, Jim. "Mark Twain and the Boy-Book in 19th-Century America." *College English* 24 (1963): 430–38.
Humphrey, Heman. *Domestic Education*. Amherst, 1840.
Irving, Washington. "The Love of a Mother." *The Prose Writers of America*. Ed. Rufus Griswold. Philadelphia, 1847.
———. *The Sketchbook of Geoffrey Crayon, Gent*. 1820. New York: Penguin, 1988.
Jacobson, Marcia. *Being a Boy Again: Autobiography and the American Boy Book*. Tuscaloosa: University of Alabama Press, 1994.
Jordan, Alice. *From Rollo to Tom Sawyer, and Other Papers*. Boston: Horn Book, 1948.

Kaplan, Amy. "Manifest Domesticity." *No More Separate Spheres! A Next Wave American Studies Reader.* Ed. Cathy N. Davidson and Jessamyn Hatcher. Durham: Duke University Press, 2002. 183–207.

Kett, Joseph F. *Rites of Passage: Adolescence in America, 1790 to the Present.* New York: Basic Books, 1977.

Keyser, Elizabeth. *Little Women: A Family Romance.* New York: Twayne, 1999.

———. *Whispers in the Dark: The Fiction of Louisa May Alcott.* Knoxville: University of Tennessee Press, 1993.

Kidd, Kenneth. "Boyology in the Twentieth Century." *Children's Literature* 28 (2000): 44–72.

———. *Making American Boys: Boyology and the Feral Tale.* Minneapolis: University of Minnesota Press, 2004.

Kilcrup, Karen. "Lydia Sigourney." *Writers of the American Renaissance.* Ed. Denise D. Knight. Westport, CT: Greenwood, 2003. 324–27.

Kimmel, Michael S. *Changing Men: New Directions in Research on Men and Masculinity.* London: Sage, 1987.

———. *Manhood in America: A Cultural History.* New York: Free Press, 1996.

Kirk, E. N. "Useful Monarchs Educated by Mothers." *The Mother's Magazine and Family Library* 11 (1843): 167.

Kortenhaus, Carole M., and Jack Demarest. "Gender Role Stereotyping in Children's Literature: An Update." *Sex Roles* 28 (1993): 219–32.

Larcom, Lucy. *A New England Girlhood.* New York, 1889.

Lehr, Susan. "The Hidden Curriculum." *Beauty, Brains, and Brawn: The Construction of Gender in Children's Literature.* Portsmouth, NH: Heinmann, 2001. 1–20.

Lehuu, Isabelle. *Carnival on the Page: Popular Print Media in Antebellum America.* Chapel Hill: University of North Carolina Press, 2000.

Leverenz, David. *Manhood and the American Renaissance.* Ithaca: Cornell University Press, 1989.

Lewis, Jan. "Mother's Love: The Construction of an Emotion in Nineteenth-Century America." *Mothers and Motherhood: Readings in American History.* Ed. Rima D. Apple and Janet Golden. Columbus: Ohio State University Press, 1997. 52–71.

"Look at the Results." *The Mother's Magazine* 11 (1843): 54–59.

Machor, James L. "Historical Hermeneutics and Antebellum Fiction: Gender, Response Theory, and Interpretive Contexts." *Readers in History: Nineteenth-Century American Literature and the*

Contexts of Response. Baltimore: Johns Hopkins University Press, 1993. 54–84.

MacLeod, Anne Scott. *American Childhood: Essays on Children's Literature of the Nineteenth and Twentieth Centuries.* Athens: University of Georgia Press, 1994.

———. *A Moral Tale: Children's Fiction and American Culture, 1820–1860.* Hamden, CT: Archon Books, 1975.

Mailloux, Stephen. "The Rhetorical Use and Abuse of Fiction: Eating Books in Late Nineteenth-Century America." *Boundary* 2 (Spring 1990): 133–57.

Mann, Horace. "Lecture on School Punishments." *Lectures on Education.* Boston, 1855.

———. *Sixth Annual Report of the Board of Education, Together with the Sixth Annual Report of the Secretary of the Board.* Boston, 1843.

Manning, John. "Discipline in the Good Old Days." *Corporal Punishment in American Education: Readings in History, Practices, and Alternatives.* Ed. Irwin A. Hyman and James A. Wise. Philadelphia: Temple University Press, 1979. 50–61.

Marshall, David. *The Surprising Effects of Sympathy: Marivaux, Diderot, Rousseau, and Mary Shelley.* Chicago: University of Chicago Press, 1988.

Martino, Wayne, and Bob Meyenn, eds. *What About the Boys? Issues of Masculinity in Schools.* Philadelphia: Open University Press, 2001.

Marvel, Ik. *Dream Life: A Fable of the Seasons.* New York, 1851.

"Maternal Influence." *Godey's Lady's Book* 11 (1835): 73.

McCall, Laura, and Donald Yacovone. *A Shared Experience: Men, Women, and the History of Gender.* New York: New York University Press, 1998.

McCuskey, Dorothy. *Bronson Alcott, Teacher.* New York: Macmillan, 1940.

Meigs, Cornelia. *A Critical History of Children's Literature; A Survey of Children's Books in English from Earliest Times to the Present.* New York: Macmillan, 1953.

Messent, Peter. "Discipline and Punishment in *The Adventures of Tom Sawyer.*" *Journal of American Studies* 32 (1998): 219–35.

Minadeo, Christy. "Little Women in the 21st Century." *Images of the Child.* Ed. Harry Eiss. Bowling Green: Bowling Green State University Popular Press, 1994. 199–214.

Mintz, Steven. *Huck's Raft: A History of American Childhood.* Cambridge: Harvard University Press, 2004.

Moon, Michael. "Nineteenth-Century Discourses on Childhood Gender Training: The Case of Louisa May Alcott's *Little Men* and *Jo's Boys.*" *Queer Representations: Reading Lives, Reading Cultures.* Ed. Martin Duberman. New York: New York University Press, 1997. 209–15.

"Moral Discipline of Children." *The Mother's Magazine and Family Circle* 10 (1858): 275–81.

"The Mother of Washington." *Ladies' Magazine and Literary Gazette* 4 (1831): 385–94.

"Mothers, Do You Sympathize With Your Children?" *The Mother's Rule; or, The Right Way and the Wrong Way.* Ed. T. S. Arthur. Philadelphia, 1856. 126–31.

"The Mother's Love." *The Mother's Magazine* 13 (1845): 115–17.

Mott, Frank. *Golden Multitudes; The Story of Best Sellers in the United States.* New York Macmillan, 1947.

Murphy, Ann. "The Borders of Ethical, Erotic, and Artistic Possibilities in *Little Women.*" *Signs* 15 (1990): 562–85.

Murray, Gail Schmunk. *American Children's Literature and the Construction of Childhood.* New York: Twayne, 1998.

"My School-Boy Days in New York City Forty Years Ago." *The New York Teacher, and American Educational Monthly* 6 (1869): 89–100.

Nelson, Claudia, and Lynne Vallone. Introduction. *The Girl's Own: Cultural Histories of the Anglo-American Girl, 1830–1915.* Ed. Nelson and Vallone. Athens: University of Georgia Press, 1994.

Nelson, Dana D. *National Manhood: Capitalist Citizenship and the Imagined Fraternity of White Men.* Durham: Duke University Press, 1998.

Newcomb, Harvey. *How to Be a Man: A Book for Boys.* Boston, 1846.

Newkirk, Thomas. Foreword. *Reading Don't Fix No Chevys: Literacy in the Lives of Young Men.* Ed. Michael W. Smith and Jeffrey D. Wilhelm. Portsmouth, NH: Heinemann, 2002.

Nord, David Paul. *Faith in Reading: Publishing and the Birth of Mass Media in America.* New York: Oxford University Press, 2004.

Northend, Charles. *The Teacher's Assistant, or, Hints and Methods in School Discipline.* New York, 1859.

"Novels and Romances." *The Guardian; or Youth's Religious Instructor,* 1820: 369–71.

"Now Be a Man." *The Rhode Island Schoolmaster* 2 (1857): 253.

O'Keefe, Deborah. *Good Girl Messages: How Young Women Were Misled by Their Favorite Books.* New York: Continuum, 2000.

Old Harlo. *The Village Boys,; or, How to Teach Boys Not to Quarrel.* Boston, 1836.

"On the Preparation of Young Men for the Perils of Our Cities." *The Mother's Magazine* 9 (1841): 8–12.

"The Only Son." Review. Quoted in *The Boy's Book; Consisting of Original Articles in Prose and Poetry.* New York, 1843.

Onuf, Peter. Introduction. *The Life of Washington.* By Mason Weem. 1800. Armonk, NY: M. E. Sharpe, 1996.

Optic, Oliver [William T. Adams]. *Little by Little; or, The Cruise of the Flyaway.* Boston, 1888.

———. *The Sailor Boy; or, Jack Somers in the Navy.* Boston, 1863.

———. *Work and Win; or, Noddy Newman on a Cruise.* Boston, 1866.

Oriard, Michael. "From *Tom Sawyer* to *Huckleberry Finn:* Toward Godly Play." *Studies in American Fiction* 8 (1980): 183–202.

Osgood, Frances S. "Hours of Yore." *The Snow-Drop; A New Year's Gift for Children.* Providence, 1842.

———. "My Mother's Sigh." *The Ladies Wreath; A Selection of Female Poetic Writers of England and America.* Ed. Sarah Hale. Boston, 1837. 354.

Page, David. "The Schoolmaster." *The Schoolmaster in Literature.* New York, 1892. 232–41.

———. *The Theory and Practice of Teaching.* New York, 1847.

Parille, Ken. "Alfred Whitman." *The Louisa May Alcott Encyclopedia.* Ed. Gregory Eiselein and Anne K. Phillips. Westport, CT: Greenwood, 2001. 345–46.

———. "Boyhood." *The Louisa May Alcott Encyclopedia.* Ed. Gregory Eiselein and Anne K. Phillips. Westport, CT: Greenwood, 2001. 40–41.

Parris, Brandy. "Difficult Sympathy in the Reconstruction-Era Animal Stories of *Our Young Folks.*" *Children's Literature* 31 (2003): 25–49.

Pattee, Fred. *A History of American Literature since 1870.* New York: Cooper Square, 1915.

"The Pawtucket Free Public Library and the Dime Novel." *The Library Journal* 10 (1885): 105.

Peabody, Elizabeth. *Record of a School: Exemplifying the General Principles of Spiritual Culture.* Boston, 1835.

Peirson, Lydia J. "Life's Changes." *The Forest Minstrel.* Philadelphia, 1846. 112–16.

Pestalozzi, Johann H. *How Gertrude Teaches Her Children.* Syracuse: Bardeen, 1900.

Review of *The Pilgrim Boy, with Lessons from His History. The Mother's Magazine and Daughter's Friend* 25 (1857): 64.

Pipher, Mary. *Reviving Ophelia: Saving the Selves of Adolescent Girls.* New York: Ballantine Books, 1995.

Pollack, William. *Real Boys: Rescuing Our Sons from the Myths of Boyhood.* New York: Henry Holt, 1998.

"The Profession of Schoolmaster." *North American Review* 86 (1858): 40–59.

Quinn, Arthur Hobson. *The Literature of the American People: An Historical and Critical Survey.* New York: Appleton-Century-Crofts, 1951.

"Reading Is Not Thinking." *Youth's Magazine,* May 26, 1837: 157–58.

"The Reading of Young Ladies." *Youth's Magazine,* July 7, 1837: 236–37.

Reardon, Colleen. "Music as Leitmotif in Louisa May Alcott's *Little Women*." *Children's Literature* 24 (1996): 74–85.

Reinier, Jaqueline. *From Virtue to Character: American Childhood, 1775–1850.* New York: Twayne, 1996.

Reynolds, David S. *Walt Whitman's America: A Cultural Biography.* New York: Vintage Books, 1996.

Richards, Z. "Discipline—Moral and Mental." *The American Journal of Education* 1 (1855): 107–19.

Robbins, Sarah. *Managing Literacy, Mothering America: Women's Narratives on Reading and Writing in the Nineteenth Century.* Pittsburgh: University of Pittsburgh Press, 2004.

Roberts, Heather. "'The Public Heart': Urban Life and the Politics of Sympathy in Lydia Maria Child's *Letters from New York*." *American Literature* 76 (2004): 749–75.

Robinson, Forrest G. "Social Play and Bad Faith in *The Adventures of Tom Sawyer*." *Nineteenth-Century Literature* 39 (1984): 1–24.

Romero, Lora. *Home Fronts: Domesticity and Its Critics in the Antebellum Unites States.* Durham: Duke University Press, 1997.

Rotundo, E. Anthony. *American Manhood: Transformations in Masculinity from the Revolution to the Modern Era.* New York: Basic Books, 1993.

Rousmaniere, Kate, Kari Dehli, and Ning de Conick-Smith. Introduction. *Discipline, Moral Regulation, and Schooling: A Social History.* Ed. Rousmaniere, Dehli, and Conick-Smith. New York: Garland, 1997.

Rust, Marion. "'Into the House of an Entire Stranger': Why Sentimental Doesn't Equal Domestic in Early American Fiction." *Early American Literature* 37 (2002). 281–309.

Ryan, Mary. *Cradle of the Middle Class: The Family in Onedia County, New York, 1790–1865.* New York: Cambridge University Press, 1981.

———. *Empire of the Mother: American Writing about Domesticity, 1830–1860.* New York: Haworth, 1982.

Sanborn, F. B., and William T. Harris. *A. Bronson Alcott: His Life and Philosophy.* Boston, 1893.

Saxton, Martha. *Louisa May: A Modern Biography of Louisa May Alcott*. Boston: Houghton Mifflin, 1977.

Saxton, Ruth O. *The Girl: Constructions of the Girl in Contemporary Fiction by Women*. London: Macmillan, 1998.

Scharnhorst, Gary, and Jack Bales. *Horatio Alger, Jr.: An Annotated Bibliography of Comment and Criticism*. Metuchen, NJ: Scarecrow, 1981.

Sedgwick, Catharine Maria. *Home*. Boston, 1835.

———. *Life and Letters of Catharine Maria Sedgwick*. Ed. Mary Dewey. New York, 1871.

———. *Means and Ends; or, Self-Training*. Boston, 1840.

———. *The Power of Her Sympathy: The Autobiography and Journal of Catharine Maria Sedgwick*. Ed. Mary Kelley. Boston: Massachusetts Historical Society, 1993.

See, Fred G. "Tom Sawyer and Children's Literature." *Essays in Literature* 12 (1985): 251–71.

Segel, Elizabeth. "'As the Twig Is Bent . . .': Gender and Childhood Reading." *Gender and Reading*. Ed. Elizabeth Flynn and Patrocinio Schweickart. Baltimore: Johns Hopkins University Press, 1986. 165–86.

Scharnhorst, Gary, and Jack Bales. *Horatio Alger, Jr.: An Annotated Bibliography of Comment and Criticism*. Metuchen, N.J.: Scarecrow Press, 1981.

Shamir, Milette, and Jennifer Travis. *Boys Don't Cry? Rethinking Narratives of Masculinity and Emotion in the U.S.* New York: Columbia University Press, 2002.

Shaw, S. Bradley. "The Pliable Rhetoric of Domesticity." *The Stowe Debate: Rhetorical Strategies in Uncle Tom's Cabin*. Ed. Mason I. Lowance Jr., Ellen E. Westbrook, R. C. De Prospero. Amherst: University of Massachusetts Press, 1994. 73–98.

Shillaber, B. P. "The Old Time Apple-Bee." *Lines in Pleasant Places*. Chelsea, 1874. 244.

Showalter, Elaine. Introduction. *Little Women*. By Louisa May Alcott. 1868. New York: Penguin, 1989. vii–xxviii.

Sicherman, Barbara. "Sense and Sensibility: A Case Study of Women's Reading in Late-Victorian America." Ed. Cathy N. Davidson. *Reading in America: Literature and Social History*. Ed. Cathy N. Davidson. Baltimore: Johns Hopkins University Press, 1989. 201–25.

Sigourney, Lydia. *The Boy's Book; Consisting of Original Articles in Prose and Poetry*. New York, 1843.

———. *The Boys' Reading-Book; in Prose and Poetry, for Schools*. New York, 1839.

———. *The Child's Book; Consisting of Original Articles in Prose and Poetry*. New York, 1844.
———. "Death of a Beautiful Boy." *Poems*. New York, 1875. 104–5.
———. *The Faded Hope*. New York, 1853.
———. "The Farmer." *The Boy's Book; Consisting of Original Articles in Prose and Poetry*. New York, 1843. 151–56.
———. *The Farmer and the Soldier; A Tale*. Northampton, 1836.
———. *History of Marcus Aurelius, Emperor of Rome*. Hartford, 1836.
———. "John and James Williams." *The Boys' Reading-Book; in Prose and Poetry, for Schools*. New York, 1839. 170–78.
———. *Letters of Life*. New York, 1866.
———. *Letters to Mothers*. New York, 1838.
———. "Mother and Boy." *The Pearl; or, Affection's Gift*. Boston, 1830.
———. "Napoleon Bonaparte." *The Child's Book; Consisting of Original Articles in Prose and Poetry*. New York, 1844. 8.
Silber, Kate. *Pestalozzi: The Man and His Works*. London: Routledge, 1960.
Simms, William Gilmore. "Harbor by Moonlight." *Grouped Thoughts and Scattered Fancies*. Richmond, 1845. 61.
———. "Six Years." *Lyrical and Other Poems*. Charleston, 1827. 173–75.
Smith, Elizabeth Oakes. "Childhood's Laugh." *The Poetical Writings*. New York, 1846. 153–55.
Smith, Henry Nash. Introduction. 1958. *The Adventures of Tom Sawyer*. By Mark Twain. 1876. Ed. Susan Harris. Boston: Houghton Mifflin, 2000.
Smith-Rosenberg, Carroll. "The Female World of Love and Ritual: Relations between Women in Nineteenth-Century America." *Signs* 1 (1975): 1–29.
Sommers, Christina Hoff. *The War against Boys: How Misguided Feminism Is Harming Our Young Men*. New York: Simon and Schuster, 2000.
Spacks, Patricia. *The Female Imagination*. New York: Knopf, 1975.
Sparks, Jared. *The Life of Washington*. Auburn, MA, 1853.
Stearns, Peter. "Girls, Boys, and Emotions: Redefinitions and Historical Change." *Journal of American History* 80 (1993): 36–74.
Steele, Jeffrey A. "The Limits of Political Sympathy: Emerson, Margaret Fuller, and Woman's Rights." *The Emerson Dilemma: Essays on Emerson and Social Reform*. Ed. T. Gregory Garvey. Athens: University of Georgia Press, 2001. 115–35.
Stern, Madeleine B. *Louisa May Alcott*. Norman: University of Oklahoma Press, 1950.
Stowe, Harriet Beecher. *Uncle Tom's Cabin; or, Life among the Lowly*. 1852. New York: Penguin, 1981.

Strickland, Charles. "A Transcendentalist Father: Child-Rearing Practices of Bronson Alcott." *Perspectives in American History* 3 (1969): 5–73.

Sumner, William Graham. "What Our Boys Are Reading." *Scribner's Monthly* 15 (1878): 681–85.

Susina, Jan. "Men and *Little Women:* Notes of a Resisting (Male) Reader." *Little Women and the Feminist Imagination: Criticism, Controversy, Personal Essays.* Ed. Janice M. Alberghene and Beverly Lyon Clark. New York: Garland, 1999. 161–72.

Tebbel, John, and Mary Ellen Zuckerman. *The Magazine in America: 1741–1990.* New York: Oxford University Press, 1991.

Teed, Melissa Ladd. "A Passion for Distinction: Lydia Huntley Sigourney and the Creation of a Literary Reputation." *New England Quarterly* 77 (2004): 51–69.

Theriot, Nancy. *Mothers and Daughters in Nineteenth-Century America: The Biosocial Construction of Femininity.* Rev. ed. Lexington: University Press of Kentucky, 1996.

Thoreau, Henry David. *Walden.* New York: Penguin, 1983.

Titcomb, Timothy [Josiah Holland]. *Letters to Young People.* New York, 1863.

Todd, John. *Nuts for Boys to Crack.* New York, 1866.

Tompkins, Jane. Afterword. *The Wide, Wide World.* By Susan Warner. 1850. New York: Feminist Press, 1987. 584–608.

———. *Sensational Designs: The Cultural Work of American Fiction, 1790–1860.* New York: Oxford University Press, 1985.

"Training of Boys I." *The Mother's Journal and Family Visitant* 10 (1845): 117–19.

"Training of Boys III." *The Mother's Journal and Family Visitant* 10 (1845): 147–49.

"Training of Boys IV." *The Mother's Journal and Family Visitant* 10 (1845): 164–67.

"Training of Boys V." *The Mother's Journal and Family Visitant* 10 (1845): 181–84.

Trensky, Anne. "The Bad Boy in Nineteenth-Century American Fiction." *Georgia Review* 27 (1973): 503–17.

———. "The Saintly Child in Nineteenth-Century American Fiction." *Prospects* 1 (1975): 389–413.

Tuthill, Louisa. *The Young Lady's Home.* Philadelphia, 1848.

Twain, Mark. *Adventures of Huckleberry Finn.* 1884. New York: Oxford University Press, 1999.

———. *The Adventures of Tom Sawyer.* 1876. New York: Oxford University Press, 1993.

———. "The Story of the Good Little Boy Who Did Not Prosper." *Mark Twain's Sketches, New and Old*. Hartford, 1875. 14–20.

Useful Lads; or, Friendly Advice to Boys in Business. Philadelphia, 1847.

Vallone, Lynne. *Disciplines of Virtue: Girls' Culture in the Eighteenth and Nineteenth Centuries*. New Haven: Yale University Press, 1995.

"Vicious Novels: Cause of Their Increase." *The Mother's Magazine* December 1845: 374–79.

Wadsworth, Sarah A. "Louisa May Alcott, William T. Adams, and the Rise of Gender-Specific Series Books." *Lion and the Unicorn* 25 (2001): 17–46.

Warner, Charles Dudley. *Being a Boy*. Boston, 1877.

Watkins, Bari. "Woman's World in Nineteenth-Century America." *American Quarterly* 31 (1979): 116–27.

We Boys. Boston: Robert Brothers, 1876.

Weems, Mason. *The Life of Washington*. 1800. Armonk, NY: M. E. Sharpe, 1996.

Weitzman, L. J., et al. "Sex Role Socialization in Picture Books for Preschool Children." *American Journal of Sociology* 77 (1972): 1125–50.

Welter, Barbara. *Dimity Convictions: The American Woman in the Nineteenth Century*. Athens: Ohio University Press, 1976.

Wexler, Laura. "Tender Violence: Literary Eavesdropping, Domestic Fiction, and Educational Reform." *The Culture of Sentiment: Race, Gender, and Sentimentality in Nineteenth-Century America*. Ed. Shirley Samuels. New York: Oxford University Press, 1992. 9–38.

"What Is to Be Done with Charley?" *The Mother's Magazine and Family Circle* 28 (1860): 14–17.

Whitman, Walt. "Death in the School-Room." *United States Magazine and Democratic Review* 9 (1841): 177–81.

Williams, Edward Irwin. *Horace Mann: Educational Statesman*. New York: Macmillan, 1937.

Wilson, Sarah. "Melville and the Architecture of Antebellum Masculinity." *American Literature* 76 (2004): 59–87.

Wines, E. C. *How Shall I Govern My School?* Philadelphia, 1838.

Winnicott, D. W. *Playing and Reality*. 1971. London: Routledge, 1991.

Wise, Daniel. *Ralph Rattler; or, The Mischief-Maker*. Boston, 1853.

Wishy, Bernard. *The Child and the Republic: The Dawn of Modern American Child Nurture*. Philadelphia: University of Pennsylvania Press, 1968.

Wood, Halsey M. "Be Patient." *Babyhood* 3 (1887): 50–52.

Woodworth, Francis C. [Francis Channing]. *Uncle Frank's Boy's and Girl's Library: The Diving Bell; or, Pearls to Be Sought For.* Boston, 1851.

Wyman, Morrill. *Progress in School Discipline: Corporal Punishment in the Public Schools.* Cambridge, 1867.

Zboray, Ronald. "Antebellum Reading and the Ironies of Technological Innovation." *Reading in America: Literature and Social History.* Ed. Cathy N. Davidson. Baltimore: Johns Hopkins University Press, 1989. 180–200.

Zimet, Sara Goodman. "Little Boy Lost." *Teachers College Record* 72 (1970): 31–40.

Index

Abbott, Jacob, xii, xviii, xxvii, 5, 6, 7, 9, 11, 13, 15, 19, 21, 33, 34, 35, 39, 40, 107n9; book by, quoted, 115n23; novels of, xxiii, 8, 105n13, 106n15

Abbott, John S. C.: book by, quoted, 54

Adams, William T. *See* Optic, Oliver

"Address of T. W. Higginson": quoted, 94

Adolescence (book by G. Stanley Hall), 99

"Advantages of Discerning Peculiarities of Character in Pupils, and of Adapting Oneself to Them" (article by Jacob Abbott): quoted, 27, 108nn15–16

Adventures of Huckleberry Finn (novel by Mark Twain) 2, 13, 14, 15, 75, 77; quoted, 116n32

Adventures of Tom Sawyer, The (novel by Mark Twain), xxi, xxiv, xxvii, 2, 3, 4, 5, 6, 9, 10, 13, 15, 17, 75, 79, 92, 101, 102, 105n8, 106n16, 108n14; introduction to (by Henry Nash Smith), 14; quoted, 11, 74

Advice to Young Men on Their Duties and Conduct in Life (book by T. S. Arthur): quoted, 65, 83

"Against Boys" (essay): quoted, xix, 24, 109n19

Alcott, Bronson, xiv, xvii, 8, 19, 20, 22, 31, 35, 36, 39, 40, 107n9; quoted, 33

Alcott, Louisa May, xii, xiii, xvii, xxiii, xxv, 8, 10, 13, 15, 61, 64, 66, 69, 75, 94, 95, 100, 102, 110n29; books by, quoted, 90, 92, 93, 94; portion of letter of, quoted, 114n16

Alcott, William, 82, 92; book by, 5, quoted, 92, 93, 94, 118n17

Aldrich, Thomas Bailey, xiv, xv, xxvii, 8: book by, quoted, 74, 79

Alexander the Great, 87, 88, 89, 90

Alger, Horatio, xi, 12, 14, 89, 91; essay by, quoted, 119n24

Aliaga-Buchenau, Ana-Isabel, 80, 117n4; book by, quoted, 93

All about the Girls: Culture, Power, and Identity, 120n2

American Child, The (collection by Caroline F. Levander and Carol J. Singley), 104n3

American Children's Literature and the Construction of Childhood (book by Gail Schmunk Murray): quoted, 108n14

American Literature since 1870 (book by Fred Pattee), 13

American Manhood: Transformations in Masculinity from the Revolution to the Modern Era (book by E. Anthony Rotundo): cited, 10, 24, 49, 50; quoted, 65, 67, 70, 73

American Sympathy (study by Caleb Crain), 104n7

Amos Bronson Alcott: An Intellectual Biography (book by Frederick C. Dahlstrand), 109n23

Ancient History (book by Charles Rollin), 89, 90

Arac, Jonathan, 14; book by, quoted, 2

Arthur, T. S.: book by, quoted, 65, 83

"'As the Twig Is Bent . . .': Gender and Childhood Reading" (essay by Elizabeth Segel): cited, 117n2

At Odds: Women and the Family in America from the Revolution to the Present (book by Carl N. Degler): cited, 36

Audacious Kids: Coming of Age in America's Classic Children's Books (book by Jerry Griswold): cited, 104n6

Auerbach, Nina, 62; 112n4; book by, quoted, xix

Aunt Chloe (fictional character in Harriet Beecher Stowe's *Uncle Tom's Cabin*), 57

Aurelius, Marcus, xii, 87

Autobiography, An: In Three Parts: quoted, 24

Avery, Gillian: book by, quoted, 10

"Bad Boy in Nineteenth-Century American Fiction, The" (article by Anne Trensky): cited, 115n24

Bailey, Tom (fictional character in Thomas Bailey Aldrich's *The Story of a Bad Boy*), 74, 79

Bancroft, George, 84

Bangs, Tommy (fictional character in Louisa May Alcott's *Little Men*), 115n24

Barclay, Charles (fictional character in Catharine Maria Sedgwick's *Home*), 37, 39

Barclay, Haddy (fictional character in Catharine Maria Sedgwick's *Home*), 37, 39

Barclay, Wallace (fictional character in Catharine Maria Sedgwick's *Home*), 24, 37, 38, 39, 53

Barker, Tim (fictional character in Walt Whitman's "Death in the School-Room"), 30

Barnard, Charles: serial by, quoted, 92

Barnes, Elizabeth: book by, cited, 47; quoted, 52

Baym, Nina, xviii

"Be Patient" (article by Halsey M. Wood): quoted, 24

Beecher, Catharine: book by, quoted, 54

Behold the Child: American Children and Their Books (book by Gillian Avery): quoted, 10

Being a Boy (book by Charles Dudley Warner): quoted, xvi

Being a Boy Again (study by Marcia Jacobson): quoted, xv, 103n2

"Benefit of Hard Knocks" (article): quoted, 38, 39

Bennett, Paula: article by, quoted, 47

Bess (fictional character in Louisa May Alcott's *Jo's Boys*), 108n12

Beyond Feminist Aesthetics: Feminist Literature and Social Change (book by Rita Felski): quoted, xx

Bhaer, Mr. (fictional character in Louisa May Alcott's *Little Men*), 69, 73, 110n29

Bird, Mrs. (fictional character in Harriet Beecher Stowe's *Uncle Tom's Cabin*), 57, 58

Bird, Senator (fictional character in Harriet Beecher Stowe's *Uncle Tom's Cabin*), 56

Boat Club, The (book by Oliver Optic), 6

Bonaparte, Napoleon, 85, 86, 87, 88

Bonds of Womanhood: "Woman's Sphere" in New England, 1780-1835 (book by Nancy F. Cott): quoted, 46

Bonney, Mrs. P. P.: article by, quoted, 118n18

Book about Boys, A (by A. R. Hope): cited, 115n25

Boone, Daniel, 69, 114n14

"Borders of Ethical, Erotic, and Artistic Possibilities in *Little Women*, The"

(article by Ann Murphy), 112n4; quoted, 61, 62, 67, 77
Boudreau, Kristin, 111n14
"boy-as-savage" trope, 24, 25, 37, 48, 49, 51, 54
"boy-book" (genre of novels), xiv-xv
"boy-culture," 50
"Boyhood and Barbarism" (article): quoted, 25
"boyhood depravity," xvi, 22, 47, 94
Boylan, Anne: article by, quoted, 32 "boy-nature," 23-24, 27, 28, 45, 47, 54, 94
"boyology" (movement concerned with boyhood and national character), xv, xxvi
Boyology; or, Boy Analysis (study by Henry William Gibson), xv
"Boyology in the Twentieth Century" (article by Kenneth Kidd): cited, 49; quoted, 100
Boy's Book, The (collection by Lydia Sigourney), 83, 85
Boys in Children's Literature and Popular Culture: Masculinity, Abjection, and the Fictional Child (book by Annette Wanamaker), 101
Boys Don't Cry? (collection), xxi
Boy's Guide to Usefulness, The (book by William Alcott), 5; quoted, 92, 93, 94, 118n17
Boys' Reading-Book, The; in Prose and Poetry, for Schools (collection by Lydia Sigourney), 85
Boy's Town, A (book by William Dean Howells), 75, 106n19
"boys will be boys' (phrase found in late nineteenth-century writing), 8, 9, 15, 17, 100
"Bright Side, The" (article), 55; quoted, 48, 52
Brodhead, Richard, 19, 109n27
Bronson Alcott, Teacher (study by Dorothy McCuskey): cited, 109n23; quoted, 32

Brooke, John (fictional character in Louisa May Alcott's *Little Women*), 64
Brown, Gillian, xx, 14, 106n18; article by, quoted, 2, 4, 25, 105n6
Brown, Simon: essay by, cited, 61
Bumppo, Natty, xii

Campaigns Against Corporal Punishment: Prisoners, Sailors, Women, and Children in Ante-bellum America (book by Myra Glenn), 19; quoted, 36
Carlton, Guy (fictional character in Francis Forrester's *Dick Duncan*), 89
Carnes, Mark C.: book by, cited, xxi
Carnival on the Page: Popular Print Media in Antebellum America (book by Isabelle Lehuu): cited, 116n1
Cassy (fictional character in Harriet Beecher Stowe's *Uncle Tom's Cabin*), 111n13
"Casting Networks of Good Influence: The Reconstruction of Childhood in the United States, 1790-1870" (essay by Barbara Finkelstein): quoted, 20
Changing Men: New Directions in Research on Men and Masculinity (study by Michael S. Kimmel): cited, xxii
Chapman, Mary: book by, quoted, xxii
Character Is Capital: Success Manuals and Manhood in Gilded Age America (book by Judy Hilkey): cited, 64, 65, 86; quoted, 66, 71, 114n18
Charlotte Temple (novel by Susanna Rowson), 79, 84
Cherniavsky, Eva: book by, cited, 55, 111n13
Child, Lydia Maria, xxv, 22; book by, cited, 21, quoted, 23
Child and the Republic, The: The Dawn of Modern American Child Nurture (book by Bernard Wishy): cited, 36

Childhood and History in America (book by Glenn Davis): cited, 36
"Childhood's Laugh" (poem by Elizabeth Smith): quoted, 105n5
Child's Book, The; Consisting of Original Articles in Prose and Poetry (by Lydia Sigourney): cited, 118n12
"Child's Play" (article by Gillian Brown): quoted, 2, 4, 25, 105n6
Clark, Beverly Lyon, xx; article by, quoted, 72, 114n21
Clark, Mollie: quoted, 73
Clark, Rufus W.: book by, quoted, 83-4
Cobb, Lyman, 19, 20, 34, 35, 36, 38, 39, 40, 53, 107n3, 107n9; book by, quoted, 21
Cogan, Frances, xvii
Cohoon, Lorinda: book by, cited, 101, 116n1
"Comforts of Playing 'Hookie,' The" (essay), 45, 51-2, 53
Common Sense philosophers, 21, 22
Communities of Women: An Idea in Fiction (book by Nina Auerbach): quoted, xix
"Confessions of a Schoolmaster" (series of articles): quoted, 27, 28
Connie (character in novel by Dorothy Lyons), 97, 98
Coolidge, Susan, 90; book by, 12
Cooper, James Fenimore, xii, 67
corporal punishment, 30, 33, 40, 49; and denial of sympathy, 52; employed in Francis Forrester's *Dick Duncan*, 11; and girls, 40
"Corporal Punishment" (article): quoted, 24
Cott, Nancy F., 22, 36; book by, quoted, 46
Critical History of Children's Literature, A; A Survey of Children's Books in English from Earliest Times to the Present (book by Cornelia Meigs): quoted, 118n19
Crowley, John W., 67; book by, cited, 115n26

Dalke, Anne: article by, cited, 63, 112n4
Dan (fictional character in Louisa May Alcott's *Little Men*), 113n12
Dana, Richard Henry, 9
"Dangerous" Potential of Reading, The: Readers and the Negotiation of Power in Nineteenth-Century Narratives (book by Ana-Isabel Aliaga-Buchenau): quoted, 93
Davis, Glenn: book by, cited, 36
Dawson, Melanie: essay by, quoted, 4
"Death of a Beautiful Boy" (poem by Lydia Sigourney): quoted, 84
"Death in the School-Room" (sketch by Walt Whitman): quoted, 30
Degler, Carl N.: book by, cited, 36
depravity. *See* boyhood depravity
"'Descent of the Angel, The': Interrogating Domestic Ideology in American Women's Poetry, 1858-1890" (article by Paula Bennett): quoted, 47
Dick Duncan: The Story of a Boy Who Loved Mischief, and How He Was Cured of His Evil Habit (book by Francis Forrester), 5, 10, 17, 91, 92; illustration from, reproduced, 78; quoted, xxiv, 11, 88, 89, 89–90, 90, 91
"Difficult Sympathy in the Reconstruction-Era Animal Stories of *Our Young Folks*" (article by Brandy Parris): cited, 111n8
discipline (for boys): employed in plots of *The Sailor Boy*, 10, of *Dick Duncan*, 10, 11, 90; and sympathy, 52; types

of, suggested by domestic theorists, xii–xiii
Discipline and Punish (book by Michel Foucault): cited, 19
"Discipline—Moral and Mental" (essay): quoted, 18
Discipline, Moral Regulation, and Schooling (collection of essays), xxii
"Discipline; School Government" (essay by Samuel E. Hamill): quoted, 27, 63, 64
Disciplines of Virtue: Girls' Culture in the Eighteenth and Nineteenth Centuries (book by Lynne Vallone): quoted, 2, 4, 91
Diving Bell, The (book by Francis Woodworth), 105n13
Dobson, Joanne: article by, quoted, 45; introduction by (to E. D. E. N. Southworth's *The Hidden Hand*), cited, 112n2
Doctrine and Discipline of Human Culture, The, 31
Domestic Education (book by Heman Humphrey): quoted, 107n1
domestic utility: importance of, in boys' fiction, 5
Donovan, Ellen Butler: essay by, quoted, 118n19
"'Doxa of Difference, The': Working Through Sexual Difference" (article by Rita Felski): cited, xxiii
Driscoll, Catherine: book by, quoted, xx, 99
Dubbert, Joe L.: book by, cited, 64, 66, 86, quoted, 65
Duncan, Dick (protagonist of Francis Forrester's *Dick Duncan*), 89, 90

Eddy, Daniel C., 82, 114n19; book by, quoted, 5, 84, 117n11

Edgeworth, Maria, 70
Educational Theories and Practices of A. Bronson Alcott (study by George E. Haefner), 109n23
Eight Cousins; or, The Aunt Hill (book by Louisa May Alcott): quoted, 92-3, 93, 94
Eliza (fictional character in Harriet Beecher Stowe's *Uncle Tom's Cabin*), 56
Ellen (heroine of Susan Warner's *The Wide, Wide World*), 12
Ellis, Mrs.: essay by: quoted, 46
Emerson, Ralph Waldo, xx, 14; quoted, 31
Empire of the Mother: American Writing about Domesticity, 1830-1860 (study by Mary Ryan): quoted, 47
"Errors in Discipline; or Reminiscences of a Schoolmaster" (article): quoted, 27
"ethic of submission" (in Louisa May Alcott's *Little Women*), 62, 63
Everts, W. W.: book by, quoted, 10
Evil Tendencies of Corporal Punishment as a Means of Moral Discipline in Families and Schools, Examined and Discussed, The (treatise by Lyman Cobb), 19, 31; quoted, 21, 28, 29, 30, 109n25

Faded Hope, The (biography by Lydia Sigourney): 81, 86; quoted, xix, 82, 83, 84, 85
Faith in Reading: Publishing and the Birth of Mass Media in America (book by David Paul Nord): cited, 92
Familiar Talks to Boys (book by John Hall): cited, 106n15; quoted, 10, 11
Farmer and the Soldier, The; A Tale (book by Lydia Sigourney), 85; quoted, 85, 86

Felski, Rita: article by, cited, xxiii; book by, quoted, xx
Female Imagination, The (book by Patricia Spacks): quoted, 62
"female influence" (doctrine endorsed by Lyman Cobb), 33, 109n25
"Female World of Love and Ritual, The" (article by Carroll Smith-Rosenberg): quoted, 110n4
Fetterley, Judith, 62; article by, cited, 76, quoted, xxv, 112n5; book by, quoted, 113n13
"Filial Virtues of Washington" (essay by Lydia Sigourney): quoted, 83
Finkelstein, Barbara: essay by, quoted, 20
Finley, Martha, 90
Finn, Huckleberry, xi, xii, 1
Fitts, Deborah, 22; cited, 107n2
Flint, Timothy: quoted, 71
Florin, Christina: essay by, xxii
Forrester, Francis (pen name of Daniel Wise), xiii, xxvii, 5, 6, 10, 11, 13, 14, 17, 90–91, 91, 95; book by, quoted, xxiv, 11, 88, 89, 89–90, 90, 91
Forrester's Boys' and Girls' Magazine, and Fireside Companion (publication by Francis Forrester), 119n21
Forrester's Pictorial Miscellany for Boys and Girls (publication by Francis Forrester), 119n21
Foucault, Michel, 24; books by, cited, 19; quoted, 44
From Rollo to Tom Sawyer, and Other Papers (book by Alice Jordan): quoted, 13

Gaard, Greta: article by, quoted, 64
Gardiner, Judith Kegan: article by, cited, xxi
Gentle Measures in the Management and Training of the Young (manual by Jacob Abbott), 25
Genuine Article, The (study by Paul Gilmore), xxi
Gibson, Henry William, xv, xvi
Gilligan, Carol: quoted, 100
Girl, The: Constructions of the Girls in Contemporary Fiction by Women (book by Ruth O. Saxton): quoted, 102
girlhood: defined by relationship to boyhood, xix, xx; scholarship on, xx
girls: cultural limitations on, 62; relationships with mothers, 46; varying views on nature of, 29
Girls: Feminine Adolescence in Popular Culture and Cultural Theory (book by Catherine Driscoll): quoted, xx, 99
"Girls, Boys, and Emotions: Redefinitions and Historical Change" (article by Peter Stearns): cited, 110n2
girls' fiction, 13, 14, 97, 98
Glenn, Myra, 19; book by, quoted, 36
"Going into Business for Himself" (article by Mrs. P. P. Bonney): quoted, 118n18
"good bad boy," 74, 75
Good Girl Messages: How Young Women Were Misled by Their Favorite Books: (book by Deborah O'Keefe), 97
"Good Girls, Bad Girls: Anglo-Centrism and Diversity in the Constitution of Contemporary Girlhood" (essay by Christine Griffin): quoted, 99
Griffen, Clyde: book by, cited, xxi
Griffin, Christine: essay by, quoted, 99
"Growing Up Female in Young America" (article by Anne Boylan): quoted, 32
Gund, Francis: quoted, 72–73
Gurian, Michael, 99, 100
Gypsy Breynton (book by Elizabeth Stuart Phelps), 13

Haight, Gordon, 87
Hall, G. Stanley, 99
Hall, John: book by, cited, 106n15, quoted, 10, 11
Hall, Samuel Read: book by, quoted, 21
Halliday, Rachel (fictional character in Harriet Beecher Stowe's *Uncle Tom's Cabin*), 57, 58
Hamill, Samuel E.: article by, quoted, 27, 63, 64
"Harbor by Moonlight" (poem by William Gilmore Simms): quoted, 4
Harris, Joel Chandler: quoted, 13
Hawkes, Joel: book by, quoted, 83
Hawthorne, Nathaniel, xxi
Hemingway, Ernest, xii
Hendler, Glenn, xxii; article by, cited, 57; books by, quoted, xxii, 58–59
Hidden, Hand, The (book by E. D. E. N. Southworth): introduction to (by Joanne Dobson): cited, 112n2
Hidden Treasures (advice manual by H. A. Lewis), 70
Higginson, Thomas Wentworth: address of, quoted, 94
Hilkey, Judy, 63; book by, cited, 64, 65, quoted, 66, 71, 114n18
History of Marcus Aurelius, Emperor of Rome (book by Lydia Sigourney), 86; quoted, 87, 117n6
History of Sexuality, The (book by Michel Foucault): cited, 19; quoted, 44
Hogan, David: article by, cited 20, quoted, 108n15
Holland, Josiah: quoted, 69. *See also* Titcomb, Timothy
Home (book by Catharine Maria Sedgwick), 20, 36; quoted, 25, 36, 37, 38, 39, 53
Hope Leslie (novel by Catharine Maria Sedgwick), 36, 49
Hope, A. R.: book by, cited, 115n25

"Hours of Yore" (poem by Frances Osgood): quoted, 4
"'House Band, The': The Education of Men in *Little Women*" (article by Anne Dalke): cited, 63, 112n4
How Gertrude Teaches Her Children (book by Johann H. Pestalozzi), 32
How Shall I Govern My School? (book by E. C. Wines): cited, 21
How to be Happy (advice manual by Lydia Sigourney), 119n21
How To Be a Lady: A Book for Girls (book by Harvey Newcomb), xxiii
How To Be a Man: A Book for Boys (book by Harvey Newcomb), xxiii; quoted, xviii
Howard, June: article by, quoted, 111n15
Howells, William Dean, xv, xvi, xxv, 8, 65; review of *Adventures of Tom Sawyer* by, quoted, 13
Huck's Raft: A History of American Childhood (book by Steven Mintz), 13; cited, xiv
Huckleberry Finn as Idol and Target: The Functions of Criticism in Our Time (book by Jonathan Arac): quoted, 2
humor (in girls' and boys' texts), 105n13
Humphrey, Heman: book by, quoted, 107n1
Hutcheson, Francis, 21

"infant depravity," 22

Jack and Jill (novel by Louisa May Alcott), 89
Jacobson, Marcia: study by, quoted, xv
Johansson, Ulla: essay by, xxii
"John and James Williams" (story by Lydia Sigourney), 86; quoted, 85
Jonas (fictional boy character in Jacob Abbott's *Rollo at Work*), 8

Jordan, Alice: book by, quoted, 13
Jo's Boys (novel by Louisa May Alcott): quoted, 113n12
Journals of Louisa May Alcott, The (book edited by Joel Myerson and Daniel Shealy): quoted, 64, 67

Kaplan, Amy, xii
Kett, Joseph F., 22; book by, quoted, 114n19
Keyser, Elizabeth: book by, quoted, 63
Kidd, Kenneth: article by, cited, 49, quoted, 100; study by, xv, 101, quoted, 25
Kimmel, Michael S., xxii, 63, 66; book by, quoted, 72; cited, 64
Kirk, E. N.: article by, quoted, 54

Lancewood, Lawrence (pen name of Daniel Wise), 88
Laurie (fictional boy character in Louisa May Alcott's *Little Women*), xviii, xxv, 62, 63, 64, 65, 66, 67, 68-9, 70, 71, 72, 73, 74, 75, 76, 77, 82, 90, 112n2, 113n7, 116n32, 117n10
"Lazy Lawrence" (story by Maria Edgeworth), 70, 71, 72, 76
Leatherstocking tales (by James Fenimore Cooper), 67
"Lecture on School Punishments" (by Horace Mann): quoted, 18
Lectures on the Formation of Character, Temptations and Mission of Young Men (book by Rufus W. Clark): quoted, 83-84
Lectures on School-Keeping (book by Samuel Read Hall): quoted, 21
Lectures to Young Men on the Formation of Character (book by Joel Hawkes): quoted, 83
Legree, Simon (fictional character in Harriet Beecher Stowe's *Uncle Tom's Cabin*), 55, 56

Lehuu, Isabelle: book by, cited, 116n1
Letters of Life (autobiography by Lydia Sigourney): quoted, 85, 87
Letters to Mothers (book by Lydia Sigourney), 44; quoted, 50, 51
Lewis, H. A., 70
Life of George Washington, The (book by Jared Sparks), 83; 117n7
Life of Washington, The (book by Mason Weems), 83; introduction to (by Peter Onuf), quoted, 83; quoted, 117n11
"Life's Changes" (poem by Lydia J. Peirson): quoted, 4
"Limits of Sympathy, The: Louisa May Alcott and the Sentimental Novel" (article by Glenn Hendler): cited, 57
Little by Little (book by Oliver Optic): quoted, 9
Little Men (novel by Louisa May Alcott), 110n29; quoted, 113n7, 113n12, 115n23, 115n24
Little Women (novel by Louisa May Alcott), xiii, xxiii, xxiv, xxv, 5, 12, 13, 61, 62, 66, 82, 90, 106n16, 117n10, 118n19; illustration from, reproduced, 60; introduction to (by Elaine Showalter), quoted, 69; quoted, xviii, 9, 63, 64, 65, 68, 69, 71, 72, 74, 75, 76, 77, 90
"*Little Women*: Alcott's Civil War" (article by Judith Fetterley): cited, 76; quoted, 112n5
"*Little Women* and the Boy-Book" (article by John W. Crowley): cited, 115n26; quoted, 68
"Little Women Series" (children's novels by Louisa May Alcott), xvii
"Little Women in the 21st Century" (essay by Christy Minadeo): quoted, 76
Littleton, Captain (fictional character in Oliver Optic's *Little by Little*), 9
Locke, John, 22, 45
Longfellow, Henry Wadsworth, 40
"Look at the Results" (article): quoted, 50

146   Index

"Louisa May Alcott, William T. Adams, and the Rise of Gender-Specific Series Books" (essay by Sarah A. Wadsworth): quoted, xxiv
Lowell, James Russell, 40
Lyons, Dorothy, 97

McCuskey, Dorothy: study by, cited, 109n23, quoted, 32
MacLeod, Anne, 36; book by, quoted, xxiv, 13, 22, 23
Mailloux, Stephen, 93, 94; essay by, cited, 119n25
Making American Boys: Boyology and the Feral Tale (study by Kenneth Kidd), xv, 101; quoted, 25
Man's Place, A: Masculinity in Transition (study by Joe Dubbert), xxi; cited, 64, 86; quoted, 65
Managing Literacy, Mothering America: Women's Narratives on Reading and Writing in the Nineteenth Century (book by Sarah Robbins): quoted, 81
Manhood in America: A Cultural History (study by Michael S. Kimmel), xxi; cited, 64; quoted, 72
Manhood and the American Renaissance (study by David Leverenz), xxi
Manhood: Its Duties and Responsibilities (book by W. W. Everts): quoted, 10
"Manifest Domesticity" (essay by Amy Kaplan), xii
Mann, Horace, xii, 8, 23, 34, 36, 40, 107n3, 107n9; defends corporal punishment for boys, opposes it for girls, 18; lecture by, quoted, 18, 114n17
March, Amy (fictional character in Louisa May Alcott's *Little Women*), 63, 69, 70, 71, 72, 73, 76
March, Jo (protagonist of Louisa May Alcott's *Little Women*), 12, 13, 62, 63, 64, 67, 68, 69, 70, 73, 74, 75, 76, 113n12, 116n32

March girls (fictional characters in Louisa May Alcott's *Little Women*), 62, 64
Marshall, David: book by, quoted, 47
Martino, Wayne: collection edited by, 101, quoted, 100, 120n2
Masculinity: recent writings on, xxi, xxii
Masculinity Studies Reader, The (book by Rachel Adams and David Savran), xxi
"Maternal Influence" (article): quoted, 111n11
maternal sympathy, 43, 44, 45, 46, 52, 53, 54, 59; as treated in *Uncle Tom's Cabin*, 55, 58
Meanings for Manhood: Constructions of Masculinity in Victorian America (study by Mark C. Carnes and Clyde Griffen): cited, xxi
Meigs, Cornelia: book by, quoted, 118n19
"Melville and the Architecture of Antebellum Masculinity" (article by Sarah Wilson): quoted, xxi
Melville, Herman, xx, 14
"Men and *Little Women*: Notes of a Resisting (Male) Reader" (article by Jan Susina): quoted, 63, 115n26
Merry's Museum (children's magazine): poem from, quoted, 4
Messent, Peter: cited, 107n4
Meyenn, Bob: collection edited by, 101, quoted, 100, 120n2
Minadeo, Christy: essay by, quoted, 76
"Miniaturizing of Girlhood, The: Nineteenth-Century Playtime and Gendered Theories of Development" (essay by Melanie Dawson): quoted, 4
Mintz, Steven, 13; book by, cited, xiv
Moby-Dick (novel by Herman Melville), 14, 67, 77
"Modes of Discipline: Affective Individualism and Pedagogical Reform in New England, 1820-1850" (article by David Hogan): cited, 20

Index **147**

Moon, Michael: article by, quoted, 38
"Moral Discipline of Children" (article): quoted, 24
moral suasion, 21, 29, 38, 40, 43
Mother at Home, The; Or, The Principles of Maternal Duty Familiarly Illustrated (book by John S. C. Abbott): quoted, 54
Mother's Book, The (by Lydia Maria Child): cited, 21; quoted, 23
Mothers and Daughters in Nineteenth-Century America: The Biosocial Construction of Femininity (book by Nancy Theriot): quoted, 46, 47
"Mothers, Do You Sympathize with Your Children?" (article), 45; quoted, 47-8
"Mother's Love, A" (article): quoted, 46, 54
"Mother's Love, The" (essay by Mrs. Ellis): quoted, 46
Mrs. Sigourney: The Sweet Singer of Hartford (biography by Gordon Haight), 87
Murphy, Ann, xx, 112n4; article by, quoted, 61, 62, 67, 77
Murray, Gail Schmunk: book by, quoted, 108n14
"My Mother's Sigh" (poem by Frances Osgood): quoted, 4
My Own Annual: A Gift Book For Boys and Girls (publication by Francis Forrester), 119n21

Nailer, Mr. (fictional character in Francis Forrester's *Dick Duncan*), 11
"Napoleon Bonaparte" (essay by Lydia Sigourney): quoted, 86
National Manhood (study by Dana Nelson), xxi
Native Americans, 49, 113n12
Nelson, Claudia, xx
"New England pedagogy," 20

Newcomb, Harvey, xviii; book by, quoted, xxiii
Newkirk, Thomas, 120n3
Newman, Noddy (fictional character in Oliver Optic's *Work and Win*), 2, 12
Newman, Ogden (fictional character in Oliver Optic's *Work and Win*), 12
"Nineteenth-Century American Women Writers and the Politics of Recovery" (article by Judith Fetterley): quoted, xxv
"Nineteenth-Century Discourses on Childhood Gender Training: The Case of Louisa May Alcott's *Little Men* and *Jo's Boys*" (article by Michael Moon): quoted, 38
No More Separate Spheres! (collection by Cathy Davidson and Jessamyn Hatcher), 3
Nord, David Paul: book by, cited, 92
Northend, Charles: book by, quoted, 17
Norton Anthology of Children's Literature, 15
"Notes toward an Interpretation of Antebellum Childrearing" (article by Nancy F. Cott), 22
Nuts for Boys to Crack (book by Rev. John Todd): quoted, xviii

Observations on the Principles and Methods of Infant Instruction, 31
O'Keefe, Deborah, 97, 101; book by, cited, 98
Oliver Optic's Magazine for Boys and Girls, 104n9
"On the Preparation of Young Men for the Perils of Our Cities" (article): quoted, 54
"Only Son, The" (story by Lydia Sigourney): quoted, 118n15
Onuf, Peter: introduction by, to Mason Weems's *Life of Washington*: quoted, 83

Optic, Oliver (pen name of William T. Adams), xxvii, 5, 6, 8, 11, 12, 13, 15, 89, 91, 93, 106n15, 118n18; book by, quoted, 73; boys' stories of, xxiv, 9, 10, 14, 67, 102; quoted, xxiv

Osgood, Frances: poems by, quoted, 4

Owen, William: book by, quoted, 65, 71

Page, David: manual by, 20

Parley, Peter, 6

Parris, Brandy: article by, cited, 111n8

Pattee, Fred: book by, cited, 13

Paul (fictional character in Oliver Optic's *Little by Little*), 9

Peabody, Elizabeth, 22; book by, quoted, 34

Peirson, Lydia J.: poem by, quoted, 4

Pestalozzi, Johann H., 22, 32

Phelps, Elizabeth Stuart: book by, 13

Pilgrim Boy, The: review of, quoted, 24

Pipher, Mary: book by, quoted, 99

"Pliable Rhetoric of Domesticity, The" (essay by S. Bradley Shaw): cited, 111n12

Pollack, William, 99, 100

"Portrait of the Artist as a Little Woman" (article by Beverly Lyon Clark): quoted, 72, 114n21

"pragmatic" discourses, 45, 46, 47, 48, 55, 57

Prescott, William H., 84

"Profession of Schoolmaster, The" (article): quoted, 24, 25, 26

Progress in School Discipline: Corporal Punishment in the Public Schools (book by Morrill Wyman): quoted, 21, 39, 40

Public Sentiments: Structures of Feeling in Nineteenth-Century American Literature (book by Glenn Hendler): quoted, 58–59

Ragged Dick; or, Street Life in New York with the Boot-Blacks, xi, 11, 12, 75, 91, 101, 105n7, 118n13, 119n21; quoted, 12, 112n6

Ralph Rattler; or, The Mischief-Maker (book), 108n14; quoted, 33

Reading Don't Fix No Chevys: Literacy in the Lives of Young Men: foreword to, cited, 120n3

"Reading for Profit and Pleasure: *Little Women* and *The Story of a Bad Boy*" (essay by Ellen Butler Donovan): quoted, 118n19

"Reading of Young Ladies, The" (essay): cited, 116n1

Real Boys: Rescuing Our Sons from the Myths of Boyhood (book by William Pollack), 99

"Reclaiming Sentimental Literature" (article by Joanne Dobson): quoted, 45

Record (text that discusses gender and punishment), 31, 32; quoted, 32, 33, 34, 35

Record of a School: Exemplifying the General Principles of Spiritual Culture (book by Elizabeth Peabody), xiv; cited, 19; quoted, 31, 34

Redwood (novel by Catharine Maria Sedgwick), 36

Reinier, Jacqueline, 104n10

"Report on Corporal Punishment in Schools" (by Roxbury Massachusetts School Committee): quoted, 23

Resisting Reader, The: A Feminist Approach to American Fiction (book by Judith Fetterley): quoted, 113n13

Reviving Ophelia: Saving the Selves of Adolescent Girls (book by Mary Pipher): quoted, 99

Reynolds, David S.: book by, quoted, 18

"Rhetorical Use and Abuse of Fiction, The: Eating Books in Late

"Rhetorical Use" (cont.)
  Nineteenth-Century America" (essay by Stephen Mailloux): cited, 119n25
Rites of Passage: Adolescence in America, 1790 to the Present (book by Joseph F. Kett): quoted, 114n19
Robbins, Sarah: book by, quoted, 81
Robinson Crusoe, 92, 106n14
Rockwell, James (fictional character in Horatio Alger's *Ragged Dick*), 12
Rodolphus (book by Jacob Abbott), 108n14
Rollo (fictional boy character in works of Jacob Abbott), xviii, 8, 14, 22, 63, 89, 90, 108n14
Rollo at Home (book by Jacob Abbott): illustration from, reproduced, frontispiece
Rollo at Play (book by Jacob Abbott), 5, 6, 102, 108n14; illustration from, reproduced, quoted, 7
Rollo at Work (book by Jacob Abbott), 5, 6, 102, 108n14; illustrations from, reproduced, xxviii, 16; quoted, 6, 7, 8, 115n23
Rollo books (by Jacob Abbott), 5, 6, 14, 15
Rollo's Philosophy: Water (book by Jacob Abbott): illustration from, reproduced, 42
Rotundo, E. Anthony, xv, 22, 63; book by, cited, 10, 49, 50, quoted, xx–xxi, 24, 65, 67, 70, 73
Rousseau, Jean Jacques, 22
Rowson, Susanna, 79
Ryan, Mary: book by, quoted, 47

Sailor Boy, The (novel by Oliver Optic), 9; quoted, 10
"Saintly Child in Nineteenth-Century American Fiction, The" (article by Anne Trensky): quoted, 30
Sawyer, Tom, xi, xii, xxi, 1, 2, 14, 74, 92, 105n13

Saxton, Martha, 13
Saxton, Ruth O.: book by, quoted, 102
Sedgwick, Catharine Maria, xxv, xxvii, 20, 36, 39, 40, 52, 53
See, Fred G.: essay by, quoted, 2
Segel, Elizabeth, 92; essay by, cited, 104n2, 117n2
"'Self-Denial Was All the Fashion': Repressing Anger in *Little Women*" (article by Greta Gaard): quoted, 64, 113n7
Sensational Designs: The Cultural Work of American Fiction, 1790-1860 (book by Jane Tompkins): quoted, 58, 62
"sentimental" discourses, 45, 46, 47, 55, 56, 57
Sentimental Men: Masculinity and the Politics of Affect in American Culture (collection by Glenn Hendler and Mary Chapman), xxi; quoted, xxii
sentimentality, 46; and sympathy, 45
Separate Spheres No More (study by Monika Elbert), xxii
Serialized Citizenships: Periodicals, Books, and American Boys, 1840-1911 (book by Lorinda Cohoon): cited, 101, 116n1
Shared Experience, A (study by Laura McCall and Donald Yacovone), xxii
Shaw, S. Bradley: essay by, cited, 111n12
Shelby, George (fictional character in Harriet Beecher Stowe's *Uncle Tom's Cabin*), 57
Shelby, Mrs. (fictional character in Harriet Beecher Stowe's *Uncle Tom's Cabin*), 57
Showalter, Elaine, xx; introduction to *Little Women* by, quoted, 69
Sigourney, Andrew, 81, 82, 83, 84, 85, 86, 89, 92, 94, 98
Sigourney, Lydia, xii, xiii, xxv, xxvii, 8, 15, 47, 54, 80, 92, 93, 95, 98, 102, 119n21; works by, quoted, 50, 51, 53, 82, 83, 84, 85, 86, 87, 89, 91, 94, 100, 118n12

Simms, William Gilmore: poems by, quoted, 4
"Six Years" (poem by William Gilmore Simms): quoted, 4
slavery, 56, 57
Smith, Elizabeth: poem by, quoted, 105n5
Smith, Henry Nash: essay by, quoted, 14
Smith-Rosenberg, Carroll: quoted, 46
Somers, Jack (hero of Oliver Optic's *The Sailor Boy*), 9, 10, 14
Sommers, Christina Hoff, 99, 100
Spacks, Patricia: book by, quoted, 62
"'Sparing the Rod': Discipline and Fiction in Antebellum America" (essay by Richard Brodhead), 19
Sparks, Jared, 83, 84
St. Clare, Alfred (fictional character in Harriet Beecher Stowe's *Uncle Tom's Cabin*), 56
St. Clare, Augustine (fictional character in Harriet Beecher Stowe's *Uncle Tom's Cabin*), 55, 56, 58
States of Sympathy: Seduction and Democracy in the American Novel (book by Elizabeth Barnes): cited, 47
Stern, Madeleine, 13
Story of a Bad Boy, The (novel by Thomas Bailey Aldrich), xiv, 13, 75, 115n30; 118n19; quoted, 74, 79
"Story of the Bad Little Boy, The" (by Mark Twain), 108n14
"Story of the Good Little Boy Who Did Not Prosper, The" (by Mark Twain), 95, 108n14
Stowe, Harriet Beecher, xxv, xxvii, 49, 55, 56, 57, 58
Strickland, Charles, 32
Student and Schoolmate (periodical published by Francis Forrester), 119n21
Success in Life, and How to Secure It: or Elements of Manhood and Their Culture (manual by William Owen): quoted, 65, 71
Sumner, William Graham: article by, quoted, 92, 94
Surprising Effects of Sympathy, The: Marivaux, Diderot, Rousseau, and Mary Shelley (book by David Marshall): quoted, 47
Susina, Jan: article by, quoted, 63, 115n26
sympathy, 43, 44, 47, 49, 51, 52, 54, 59; and sentimentality, 45

Taylor, Dr. Samuel: quoted, 25
Teacher, The (manual by Bronson Abbott), 20
Teacher, The. Moral Influences Employed in the Instruction and Government of the Young (manual by Jacob Abbott): quoted, 25–26, 26
Teacher's Assistant, The, or, Hints and Methods in School Discipline (manual by Charles Northend): quoted, 17
"Tender Violence: Literary Eavesdropping, Domestic Fiction, and Educational Reform" (essay by Laura Wexler): quoted, 48
That Pale Mother Rising: Sentimental Discourse and the Imitation of Motherhood in 19th-Century America (book by Eva Cherniavsky): cited, 55, 111n13
"Theorizing Age and Gender: Bly's Boys, Femininity, and Maturity Masculinity" (article by Judith Kegan Gardiner): cited, xxi
Theory and Practice of Teaching, The (manual by David Page), 20
Theriot, Nancy: quoted, 46, 47
Thoreau, Henry David, xx, 14
"thrashing," 115n29
Titcomb, Timothy (pen name of Josiah Holland), 106n15
"Tom Sawyer and Children's Literature" (essay by Fred G. See): quoted, 2

Tompkins, Jane, xviii; afterword by (in Susan Warner's *The Wide, Wide World*), cited, 90, quoted, 12; book by, quoted, 58, 62
"Training of Boys" (series of articles), 45; quoted, 49, 51, 113n9
"Training of Boys III" (article): quoted, 51, 58
"Training of Boys IV" (article): quoted, 51, 54
"Training of Boys V" (article): quoted, 24, 53
Treasure Island (novel by Robert Louis Stevenson), 92, 104n2
Treatise on Domestic Economy, A (book by Catharine Beecher): quoted, 54
"tremendous law!" 32, 34
Trensky, Anne: article by, cited, 115n24, quoted, 30
Twain, Mark, xi, xv, xx, xxv, xxvii, 1, 5, 6, 8, 11, 13, 14, 17, 92, 95
"Two Ways of Being Manly": quoted, 8
Two Wheelbarrows, The, 105n12
Two Years before the Mast (novel by Richard Henry Dana), 9

Uncle Frank's Boy's and Girl's Library (series of books by Francis Woodworth), 105n13
Uncle Morris (fictional character in Francis Forrester's *Dick Duncan*), 90
Uncle Tom's Cabin (novel by Harriet Beecher Stowe), 44, 49, 55, 59; quoted, 55, 56, 57, 58
Understanding American Education: Its Past, Practices, and Promise (book by Lloyd Duck), 109n23
Useful Lads; or, Friendly Advice to Boys in Business: quoted, 5, 11, 105n13
"Useful Monarchs Educated by Mothers" (article by E. N. Kirk): quoted, 54

Vallone, Lynne, xx; book by, quoted, 2, 4, 91
Village Boys, The; or, How to Teach Boys Not to Quarrel (book), 108n14
violence (between males), 75
"Voyage of the Salt Mackerel, The" (serial by Charles Barnard): quoted, 92

Wadsworth, Sarah A.: essay by, quoted, xxiv
Walden (book by Henry David Thoreau), 14; quoted, 68
Walt Whitman's America: A Cultural Biography (book by David S. Reynolds): quoted, 18
Wanamaker, Annette, 101
War Against Boys, The: How Misguided Feminism Is Harming Our Young Men (book by Christina Hoff Sommers), 99, 100; quoted, 100
Ware, Henry, Jr.: quoted, 36
Warner, Charles Dudley, xv, xvi; book by, quoted, xvi
Warner, Susan, xxvii; book by, 12, 90
Washington, George, 83
We Boys (novel): quoted, 66
Weems, Mason, 83, 84, 117n11
Wexler, Laura: essay by, quoted, 48
What about the Boys? Issues of Masculinity in Schools (collection edited by Wayne Martino and Bob Meyenn), 101; introduction to, quoted, 101; quoted, 100, 120n2
"What Books Shall I Read?" (essay by Simon Brown): cited, 116n1
"What Is Sentimentality?" (article): quoted, 112n15
"What Is to Be Done with Charley?" (article), 45; cited, 54; quoted, 50, 55
What Katy Did (novel by Susan Coolidge), 12, 89

"What Our Boys Are Reading" (article by William Graham Sumner): quoted, 92, 94
Whispers in the Dark: The Fiction of Louisa May Alcott (book by Elizabeth Keyser): quoted, 63
Whitman, Alfred, 112n1
Whitman, Walt, xx, 28; sketch by, quoted, 30
Whitney, Frank (fictional character in Horatio Alger's *Ragged Dick*), 112n6
Wide, Wide World, The (book by Susan Warner), 12, 90
Williams, James (fictional character in Lydia Sigourney's "John and James Williams"), 85, 86, 89
Williams, John (fictional character in Lydia Sigourney's "John and James Williams"), 86
Wilson, Frank (fictional character in Lydia Sigourney's "The Only Son"), 118n15
Wilson, Sarah: article by, quoted, xxi
Wines, E. C.: book by, cited, 21
Wise, Daniel, 6, 88. *See also* Forrester, Francis
Wishy, Bernard: book by, cited, 36
women's fiction, 13, 14
Wonder of Boys, The: What Parents, Mentors and Educators Can Do to Shape Boys into Exceptional Men (book by Michael Gurian), 99
Wood, Halsey M.: article by, quoted, 24
Work and Win (book by Oliver Optic), 5; quoted, 2, 12, 73
"Writing Stories for Boys" (essay by Horatio Alger): quoted, 119n24
Wyman, Morrill: book by, quoted, 21, 39, 40

Young Man's Friend, The (book by Daniel C. Eddy): cited, 82; quoted, 5, 84, 117n11

Boys at Home was designed and typeset on a Macintosh OS X, version 10.4.11 computer system, using CS3 InDesign software. The body text and titling is set in 10/14 ITC Galliard Standard Roman. This book was designed and typeset by Barbara Karwhite.

www.ingramcontent.com/pod-product-compliance
Lightning Source LLC
Chambersburg PA
CBHW020414080526
44584CB00014B/1326